Entrepreneur MAGAZINE'S

SUCCESS FOR LESS

100

LOW-COST

Businesses You Can Start Today

BY
ROB & TERRY ADAMS

2000

Current titles from Entrepreneur Media Inc.:
Business Plans Made Easy: It's Not as Hard as You Think
Knock-Out Marketing: Powerful Strategies to Punch Up Your Sales
Start Your Own Business: The Only Start-up Book You'll Ever Need
303 Marketing Tips Guaranteed to Boost Your Business
Young Millionaires: Inspiring Stories to
Ignite Your Entrepreneurial Dreams
Where's the Money? Sure-Fire Financial Solutions
for Your Small Business

Forthcoming titles from Entrepreneur Media Inc.:
Gen E: Generation Entrepreneur is Rewriting the Rules of
Entrepreneurship—and You Can, Too
Get Smart: 365 Tips to Boost Your Entrepreneurial IQ
Financial Fitness in 45 Days: The Complete Guide to Shaping Up
Your Personal Finances

Entrepreneur MAGAZINE'S

SUCCESS FOR LESS

100 LOW-COST Businesses You Can Start Today

BY
ROB & TERRY ADAMS

Entrepreneur Media Inc.
2392 Morse Ave., Irvine, CA 92614

Managing Editor: Marla Markman
Copy Editor: Karen Spaeder
Interior Book Design: Sylvia H. Lee
Proofreader: Lynn Beresford
Production Company: Coghill Composition Co.
Cover Design: Mark A. Kozak
Illustrations: John McKinley
Indexer: Alta Indexing

This publication is designed to provide accurate and authoritative information in regard to the subject matter covered. It is sold with the understanding that the publisher is not engaged in rendering legal, accounting or other professional services. If legal advice or other expert assistance is required, the services of a competent professional person should be sought.

Library of Congress Cataloging-in-Publication Data

Adams, Terry, 1952–
    Success for less : 100 low-cost businesses you can start today / by Terry & Robert Adams.
    p. cm.
  Includes index.
  ISBN 1-891984-06-3
  1. New business enterprises—United States—Case studies.
2. Small business—United States—Case studies. I. Adams, Rob (Robert D.), 1950– II. Title.
  HD62.5 .A34B 1999
  658'.041—dc21   99-35029
                                               CIP

Printed in Canada

09 08 07 06 05 04 03 02 01 00   10 9 8 7 6 5 4 3 2 1

For Gordon,
who taught us all the right stuff
about being entrepreneurs,
and about life. We miss you.

Acknowledgments

We could not have produced this book without the generous assistance of the 25 star entrepreneurs who shared their stories and then patiently answered lots of "just one more" questions. You're all terrific. Thank you! We also received lots and lots of wonderful assistance from folks all over the country—other outstanding entrepreneurs as well as staffers at professional associations and organizations who shared their insights into their industries. Thank you, too. And super-thanks to Marla Markman, the best book editor/adventurer ever.

TABLE OF CONTENTS

Success For Less

INTRODUCTION

Congratulations! You've taken the first step toward owning your own business. You've picked up this book. Perhaps you're skimming through it in the bookstore and deciding whether to buy it. Or maybe you've already purchased it and you're sitting on your living room sofa or at your kitchen table—probably with a cup of coffee close at hand—and you're hoping this book holds the key to your dreams of self-employment success.

This is the perfect time to start your own business. Not so many years ago, entrepreneurs were generally considered to be unemployable crackpots who were working for themselves because nobody else would have them. Today, being an entrepreneur is a hallmark of success, a badge of honor that tells the world you've made it—and to paraphrase the old Frank Sinatra song, you've made it your way.

Start Me Up

The entrepreneurial spirit may have gotten a swift kick-start from the baby boomers who first dropped out of the capitalistic rat race and then decided to drop back in—on their own terms. Thousands of boomers have rethought success, put a twist on the traditional ways of doing business and established themselves as entrepreneurial achievers. But boomers are not the only ones starting and running their own businesses. Generation Xers make fabulously creative and savvy entrepreneurs, and Golden Agers, those with the time and wisdom to devote to new enterprises, are also terrific self-employers.

Today, 23 million small businesses swell the ranks of American enterprise, with about one million start-ups each year. We wrote this book to give you the tools to join them. Being an entrepreneur is fun, exciting and rewarding. And, as our book title says, it can be inexpensive: Most of the businesses we present can be started for well under $5,000.

The majority of these businesses can easily be homebased. (In fact, we recommend you start out that way. It's less expensive and more rewarding—so much so that a SOHO, a *small office/home office*, is one of the hottest trends in small business today.) Many of these businesses can be started part time and, with the proper nurturing, grown into full-time operations. Within the parameters of the business you choose, you can set your own hours, your own rules and your own earnings. You can build a better world by sharing your happiness and success with your family and your community. (Grumpy, unfulfilled people don't make good neighbors.)

It's All You

Which brings us back to you, thumbing through this book and hoping it holds the key to your success.

It does. But not by itself—because the real key to success is you. Being an entrepreneur means mega-doses of creativity, persistence, drive and plain old hard work. It also means having a heck of a lot of fun, being your own person and being your own boss. It's one of the most exhilarating things you can do for yourself and your family.

It's also one of the scariest. Suddenly there's no kind employer taking care of you with benefits like health insurance and paid vacations. There's not even unemployment compensation. You can't call in sick (especially when you're the only employee), you can't let somebody else worry about making enough to cover payroll and expenses, and you can't defer that cranky client or intimidating IRS letter to a higher authority. You're it.

So how do you know if you've got the right stuff? Through brainstorming, soul searching, and discussions with family and friends.

First, think about why you want to start your own business. Decide which one of these is your primary motivation:

- Financial security
- A less stressful lifestyle with fewer rush-hour miles
- The possibility of making a living at something you enjoy, like a craft or hobby
- The need to earn an income while staying home with the kids or an elderly parent
- You see a need in your community and a way to fill it.

● You're just not the work-for-somebody-else type.

All of these are valid reasons for starting your own business, and they're all situations where you can have your cake and eat it, too—achieve both your financial and your lifestyle goals, and smile indulgently at your friends still in the rat race.

Get The Facts

Next, consider exactly what starting your own business entails. Unless you develop a way to spin straw into gold, you're not going to get rich overnight. There will be times when you'll burn the 3 a.m. oil and times when you'll wish you could clone yourself. If you're going into business for yourself as a get-rich-quick scheme, make a U-turn. It's not going to work. And if you don't like responsibility, take that same U-turn. But if you view starting your own business as a series of goals to be met, challenges to overcome, and fun to be had, then you're on your way to success.

We've designed this book to help you make the most of your business start-up. We start off with "Business Basics," which tells you everything you need to know to get up and running, from penning a winning business plan to romancing the bank for financing to blowing your own public relations horn.

Talent Show

Don't know what kind of business to start? Don't worry. We'll also explore 100 terrific businesses you can start for less than $25,000. We've arranged them in "Interest Categories" so that if you know the kinds of things you like doing, you can go right to that section. With 20 different categories, there's plenty to choose from. If you're a kid at heart and you love working with children, for instance, check out "Kids' Stuff." If your garden is the envy of everybody in the neighborhood, look into "Green Thumb." If you're a die-hard briefcase person who loves the thrill of corporate life but doesn't want to live it 9-to-5, check out "How To Succeed In Business." And if you've always wanted to be a private eye, delve into "Super Sleuths."

But don't confine yourself to the categories that jump out at you. Read, or at least skim, through them all. Some businesses can cross boundaries—for instance, we've got "Collection Agency" in "Paying

The Piper" because it deals with bill-paying. But it could also fit in with "Super Sleuths" because a collection agent has to be something of a Sherlock Holmes, performing skip traces to track down errant debtors. And you never know when reading about one business can spark an idea for a totally new company.

The Inside Scoop

For each business, we give you everything you'll need to know to decide whether it's the one for you. You'll get:

- **The Inside Scoop:** What this business is all about, how it works, its advantages and disadvantages, and industry facts and figures at your fingertips
- **Essentials:** Any skills, special knowledge or background you'll need to make this business a success
- **Tools of the Trade:** The equipment, licenses or permits you'll need to get the business on track
- **Money Talk:** Start-up costs, potential earnings, and how much you can charge
- **Pounding the Pavement:** Who your customers will be and how and where to find them
- **What's Next:** Beginning steps toward starting this business, including organizations, books and other places to go for assistance, plus franchises and business opportunities

Weekend Warriors

But that's not all! To help you get the most from this book, and to show you that it really is possible to get out there and be successful, we're giving you more. We've added 25 "Weekend Warrior" boxes that will give you ideas for inexpensive businesses you can start and run on a part-time basis, on weekends, in the evenings, or whenever you've got a few free hours to have fun and earn extra income. You can start most of them for under $500. And we've included another 25 boxes called "A Star Is Born"—success stories of entrepreneurs who have trod the same path you're setting out on and flourished.

Still standing in the bookstore? Take this book to the register and get it home. If you're already home, take a sip of that coffee and get reading. Next up: "Business Basics"!

Chapter one

BUSINESS BASICS

O K, you've decided to go into business for yourself, or you're at least strongly considering it—that's why you're reading this book. Terrific! Now let's get to work. Starting your own business is like learning to drive a car. Both involve an exhilarating sense of freedom along with some scary moments. Both carry heavy responsibilities. And both require a lot of preparation and learning before you're ready to take the wheel.

Bait And Beauty Products

This is where most people stop—they think there's too much work involved and they get overwhelmed before they've begun. They're afraid of the unknown or afraid of success. (Yes, some people actually program themselves for failure.) Some people think that they have to start from ground zero, that if they don't have a concept for something completely new and radical—maybe a combination bait and beauty products shop—they can't succeed. Not! On all of the above counts.

If you think there's a lot of work involved, you're right—but doing it for yourself and your family puts a different spin on the word. Being an entrepreneur is tough—but fun. Working for yourself, setting your own goals, then meeting and even exceeding them is far more exciting than any 9-to-5er can imagine.

As for those fears: A little fear of the unknown is healthy—it keeps you on your toes. But fear to the point that you give up before you've begun is unfounded. Once you've taken the steps we outline in this chapter, you'll know enough to make informed choices about your business and your future. You won't have a crystal ball that will absolutely, positively, 100 percent predict your financial prospects, but let's face it: Life isn't like that. And a large part of the entrepreneurial spirit is being willing to take a chance after receiving the proper education and preparing yourself.

Now for that misconception that you have to come up with a brand-new idea. You don't. All you have to do is take a look at what's already out there and decide how you can tweak it a little, make it better or tailor it to a specific community's needs. Remember the bait and beauty products shop? Don't laugh. A very successful one's been operating in a small beach community in Florida for years. And while this concept undoubtedly wouldn't fly in a lot of places (downtown Los Angeles or uptown Chicago to name two), its owners looked at what they knew about their own town and at their own interests and desires and those of their neighbors, and put together a package that works, and works well.

If you don't feel this daring, you can go with a franchise or business opportunity—businesses that have been pre-tested and come complete with guidelines for success. And for most of the businesses in this book, we list professional organizations that are in existence just to help you, if you choose to join.

Test-Driving Ideas

In this book, we've simplified the process of coming up with a business idea by presenting 100 terrific options for entrepreneurs. But as we explained in the introduction (you did read it, didn't you?), any one of these concepts can lead you to another one—or to something entirely different. So while you're reading, keep your eyes open, your inner ears tuned and your mind honed toward how these businesses can work for you, your family, your lifestyle and your community.

One of the entrepreneurs we interviewed for this book had a dog-training business, and as he looked around, he discovered that many so-called trainers didn't know what they were doing. Thus his training academy for dog trainers was born. Another entrepreneur who owns a consignment clothing boutique realized that Internet shopping could play a major role in her Silicon Valley-based business, because just about everybody in town is into computers. Her computer-whiz husband designed and implemented an e-commerce plan integrated with the store's inventory, and it's been a runaway success.

The point? While neither dog-training nor consignment clothing are new, both of these entrepreneurs devised ways to tailor them to the needs they saw around them.

How can you do the same thing? Talk—to everybody you know. Test-drive that idea with family, friends, co-workers and colleagues. Don't be afraid someone's going to steal your plans—it's highly unlikely. Most people are either too busy working on their own ideas or just don't have the entrepreneurial spirit to run with yours (or anybody else's).

The Umbrella Of Self-Confidence

Starting a business takes a lot of work and a lot of energy, but it's not as complicated or scary as some people believe. It's a step-by-step common-sense procedure. So take it one step at a time. First, read this book, ponder the ideas you get from it, and decide which business is the one for you. Then ask everybody in your circle what they think. Would they buy the product or service? How much would they pay? How often would they buy or use it?

You'll get a lot of interesting feedback. And not all of it will be positive. Some people hate to see others succeed. They may actively discourage you or subtly attempt to plant seeds of doubt. These are the ones who will "have your best interests at heart" or will "hate to see you throw away your family's future" or try to dump some other damper on your parade. Put up that umbrella of self-confidence and don't let them get to you.

One of the most popular warnings will be about the risk of starting your own business. Well, heck, that's true—but what is there in life that doesn't involve at least some element of risk? And there's a big difference between a foolish risk and a calculated one. If you carefully consider every step along the way, get help when you need it, and never stop asking questions and analyzing the answers, you can mitigate the risk.

Now, commit yourself to a business. You can't succeed on any level until you've decided to give entrepreneurship your all. Once you have, pat yourself on the back. You deserve it.

But you've still got plenty to do—lots of research, lots of homework, and lots of decisions to make. And lots of fun to have. So sit back, fasten your seatbelt, and let's get going!

Franchise Yeas

One of your first decisions will be whether to start your own business from scratch or to purchase one in the form of a franchise or business opportunity. What are the differences? In a franchise, you, as the franchisee, pay an initial fee and ongoing royalties to the franchisor in exchange for the use of the trademark, ongoing support and the right to use the franchisor's system of doing business as well as sell its products or services.

There are obvious advantages to this method. If you buy a McDonald's, for instance, your customers know what to expect in terms of food and service, so you're assured a certain amount of loyalty. Customers feel confident marching into a McDonald's, so a Mickey D's in a new location has an advantage over a company nobody has heard of, say a Humbug Burger.

Besides the brand name, you get more when you buy a franchise. For starters, there's a proven system of operation and training in how to use that system—something you wouldn't get as an independent newbie. New franchisees can avoid a lot of mistakes common to start-up entrepreneurs because the franchisor, through its own trial and error, has already perfected daily operations.

Reputable franchisors do a lot of market research before they sell a new location, so you can feel more confident that there's a demand for the product or service in that area. The franchisor also provides you with a clear picture of the competition as well as ways to differentiate yourself from it.

Finally, franchisees get the benefit of strength in numbers. You'll get far greater advertising as a McDonald's burger joint than as a Humbug Burger. You'll get bulk-buying opportunities for materials, supplies and services, and in negotiating for locations and lease terms. By contrast, the independent entrepreneur can't always command the same negotiating strength, and some suppliers won't deal with new businesses that haven't yet proved themselves.

Franchise Nays

OK, you're saying, sounds good. But surely there must be some drawbacks to franchising. There are. For one thing, a franchise can be expensive. In this book, we've recommended franchises as well as business opportunities that have appeared within the pages of *Entrepreneur* magazine (most in *Entrepreneur*'s Franchise 500). And we've chosen only those that can be purchased for less than $25,000. But bear in mind that you'll have other fees besides the franchise fee: Most franchisors require you to prove that you have a certain amount of capital behind you to see you through start-up.

If you go solo, however, you can start for far less money, on as much of a shoestring as you can wisely manage. The start-up costs we've quoted in these pages for our 100 businesses are for solo starters; if you plan to go the franchise or business opportunity route, be prepared to tack on a fair amount of funds. Consider this example: A maid-service franchise typically goes for at least $12,000. The cost to start your own business? As little as $150.

A lot of people don't like franchises because they feel shoehorned into a tight fit. Most franchisors impose strict rules on franchisees, specifying everything from how you should greet customers to how to prepare the product or service. While this can be helpful—and many franchisors welcome input from their franchisees—if you're a lone-wolf type, you may chafe at franchise limitations to creativity.

Business Opportunity Bonuses

Now, if a franchise sounds too restrictive but the idea of coming up with your own business idea, systems and procedures is too intimidating, you can go for the middle ground: the business opportunity.

Simply put, a business opportunity is a sort of "business in a box," a packaged investment that gives you all the tools to start your operation but with none of the brand advertising, loyalty or support of the franchise. For instance, if you purchased a Humbug Burger business opportunity, you'd likely receive an operating manual, a video describing the best way to start and run a hamburger joint, and another manual with marketing and advertising tips. You might also enjoy other perks: Some include phone support and several days or weeks of hands-on training. Still others offer none of the above.

In most cases, you don't pay royalties for business opportunities and you don't get trademark rights. You can call your burger joint anything you like and run it however you wish—there are generally no ties to the seller after the initial purchase is made.

Business Opportunity Boos

So what's the downside to the business opportunity? The same thing that's the chief upside: no family ties. Because there's no continuous relationship, the world of biz ops has its share of con artists who promise instant success, then take your money and run. Increased regulation has considerably lessened the risk of rip-offs, but it's still important to carefully investigate before laying your money on the line.

As a rule, business opportunities are far less expensive than franchises, but you'll still pay more than you would if you wing it on your own. And keep in mind that while some offer ongoing support, you're usually on your own after you purchase the materials.

Show Time

Now that you know everything there is to know about franchises and business opportunities, it's time to put that knowledge to work. If you can, attend a franchise and biz op trade show. If not, start researching on your own by calling the companies that interest you, requesting information, and meeting with the folks behind the glossy brochures.

READING COMPREHENSION

After the franchise and biz op show (or after you've collected materials by mail):

- *Organize everything into file folders.* You can't make a sound business decision if your materials are disorganized.

- *Read all franchise information carefully.* The Uniform Franchise Offering Circular (UFOC) can seem daunting, but take it in stages: Review some of the key topics: the franchisor's management experience, litigation and bankruptcy history; territorial rights granted to franchisees; initial investment figures; and the franchisor's financial statements. If the franchisor makes earnings information available—and only about 15 percent to 20 percent do—you'll find it in Item 19. If earnings information isn't included, ask why it isn't. It might be that the sales statistics don't paint an attractive picture.

- *Scrutinize all business opportunity information.* Business opportunities don't have UFOCs, but they do have offering documents and promotional materials. If it sounds too good to be true, it probably is.

- *Explore the market for the product or service on your own.* Even if the program is beautifully put together, it won't fly if there's no market for it.

- *Call the Better Business Bureau and government agencies that regulate consumer-protection and small-business activities in your state.* Find out if there are complaints on file or active investigations against the franchisor or business opportunity. If franchises are required to register with your state, find out if the franchisor has done so, and if not, why not.

- *Get professional advice.* You're making a substantial investment and dealing with complicated legal documents. The money you spend for your accountant or attorney to review the program is well worth it.

- *Ask lots of questions!* This is the hardest part for most people, yet it's vitally important. Request a complete list of franchisees or biz op purchasers in your area and visit at least five of them. Don't let the company pick the contacts for you. Do it yourself so you have a fair cross section to interview. And don't forget the dropouts. Their feedback will probably be negative but will give you a balanced assessment of the program.

- *Stay cool in the face of high-pressure sales tactics.* When you do act on the opportunity, don't put up all your money at once. Suggest withholding a portion until the product is delivered.

IN SEARCH OF

OK, you're ready to do market research. So what exactly do you want to find out? Absolutely as much as you can about these questions:

- Who will buy your product or service?
- Why will they buy it?
- Where will they buy it—specialty shops, department stores, mail order, directly from you?
- How often will they buy it?
- What do you need to charge to make a healthy profit?
- What products or services will be competing with yours?
- What are your competitors charging for similar products or services?
- Are you positioning your product or service correctly? (In other words, if there's a lot of competition, you'll need to develop a special market niche. For instance, if your particular area is saturated with gift basket services, can you make yours different by targeting hospital patients or corporate types?)

Before the show (or before you get started):

- **Figure out your financial resources.** What's liquid? What can you borrow from family and friends? How much do you need to live on? What are your financial goals for the business?

- **Get serious.** Dress conservatively, carry a briefcase and leave the kids at home. Bring business cards if you have them. Show the representatives you meet that you're a serious prospect.

At the show (or while you're searching):

- **Put defense shields in place.** Develop a healthy skepticism about promises of instant success and be prepared to spend time investigating. If you're in a hurry, you might end up rushing into the wrong franchise for the wrong reasons.

- **Don't waste time.** Pass up sellers who are out of your price range or don't meet your criteria. Have a short list of questions and requests ready:

1. What is the total investment?
2. Tell me about a franchisee's typical day.
3. What arrangements are made for product supply?

4. Is financing available from the franchisor?

5. Ask for a copy of the company's UFOC or *Uniform Franchise Offering Circular*, a gold mine of material that franchisors are required by law to provide to serious prospects. It contains extensive information about the company, the investment, and the rights and obligations of franchisees. It also contains a list of franchisees in your state, a list of franchisees who have been terminated in the past year, three years' worth of the franchisor's audited financial statements and a copy of the standard franchise agreement. By law, a UFOC must be provided to you either during the first personal meeting in which you have a real heart-to-heart with the franchisor about purchasing, or at least 10 business days before you sign a binding agreement or pay money for the franchise, whichever comes first.

● **Collect handout information and business cards from all the companies that interest you.** And don't forget any freebies like tote bags!

Market Research Magic

By now, you've either chosen a franchise or business opportunity or decided to go solo. Terrific! Your next step is market research. Every business needs consumers for its products or services in order to, as the Vulcans so eloquently put it, live long and prosper. So start planning or targeting your market, determining who your potential clients will be, what areas you'll draw from, and what specific merchandise or services you'll offer to attract clients.

This is a very important phase in growing your business. The proper market research can help boost your company into a true profit center, and the more research you do, the better prepared you'll be before you officially open your doors.

Up Close And Personal

Along with targeting your market—determining your niche among your competitors—you'll want to go directly to your potential customers to find out how they really feel about your potential products or services. If you offer it, will they buy? How much will they spend?

One way to do this is to get cozy with a *focus group*. This is an informal meeting between you and a medley of potential customers,

DIGGING UP DEMOGRAPHICS

You've found out all sorts of interesting things about people in your area, like what they're willing to spend and what products or services they'll want to buy. Great! But you also need to uncover demographic information, like how many people live in your area, what their income levels are and what their ages are. Try the following resources:

- *The public library:* Reference librarians can be fantastically helpful with this sort of thing. Just call and tell them that you need to know how many medical professionals, or fly fisherman, or disabled children under age 14, there are in your area. They'll look up the information and call you back with the answer. Or you can go into the library and dig through whole books of demographic statistics yourself, unearthing more facts and figures than you could use in a quadruple round of Trivial Pursuit.

- *The Internet:* A world library at your fingertips! If you're not yet Net-savvy, make becoming so a priority—you'll have access to all sorts of demographics without ever leaving your desk. For starters, consult the U.S. Census Bureau (yes, they collect all that data for a reason—here's your chance to take advantage of it) and the Department of Commerce.

- *Organizations and associations:* What better places to go for information on your specific market? If you're targeting senior citizens, for example, you could contact the American Association of Retired Persons for a count of its members; for a count of primary schoolteachers, you'd talk to people at state and regional teachers' associations.

usually about five to 12 people. If your focus group is comprised of people you know, you needn't offer payment, but if you don't know them, you'll need to offer an incentive—about $30 per person is customary.

Make sure your group consists of the audience you want to reach. If you're targeting a specific audience, say, physical fitness buffs, don't invite couch potatoes. In this instance, you could cull your group from members of your local gym or fitness center, local college athletes, or constituents of a nearby running club.

Once you have them assembled and you've distributed some sort of refreshment (always a nice touch), you've got a captive audience to address your most pressing marketing concerns. Keep your questions focused on your objectives: determining which products to choose, how to price your products, and what your company name should be.

Ask as many questions as you feel your group can comfortably handle. (Don't try keeping people captive until three in the morning.) Hand out questionnaires containing not only questions about your new business, but also about your group—their age range, income level, education and interests. Have plenty of pens and pencils on hand and encourage discussion. You'll learn more than you could imagine!

Hello, Central

Telephone surveys are another market research tool. Some folks are delighted to answer questions—after all, it's always flattering to have somebody seek your opinion. In this era of caller ID, others are wary of any unsolicited calls and reluctant to squander valuable time on telephone strangers. Unless you have thick skin, it can be difficult to cold-call people and pick their brains. But if you can home in on people in a specific audience and explain why you're calling, you'll have a much better shot at getting relaxed responses.

And remember, you can use your focus group questionnaire as the basis of your telephone survey, but keep it short and to the point.

Where do you get the phone numbers? If you belong to an association or organization and it happens to be affiliated with your target market, you've got it made. You may already have at hand a directory packed with names and phone numbers. If not, you may be able to beg, borrow or buy a directory from the organization's main office. If your specialty is something more general, like chocolates (who doesn't love chocolate?), you might still start off with the members of your club or group. Your common membership will act as the proverbial foot-in-the-door.

If you don't know anybody and you don't belong to any groups, how about a church roster or neighborhood association? Use your imagination!

Laying Your Foundation

All right, the market research is done. Check that one off. Now, to appease those picky IRS people, your business must have a structure. You can operate it as a sole proprietorship, a partnership or a

CHECKING IT TWICE

One of the best ways to put your direct-mail marketing and advertising materials directly into the hands of your target customers is through mailing lists—those Santa-sized rosters of names, addresses and phone numbers. A good list broker has hundreds of lists of qualified buyers at his command. He can pull out just about any criteria, or selects, you're looking for; for instance, people who own dogs and earn more than $50,000 per year, people who buy foods through mail order, or businesses in a particular city that have a certain number of employees.

How do you find a list broker? Look in your local Yellow Pages or go to the library and check into any issue of magazines like *Catalog Age* or *Target Marketing*—advertisements for list brokers, managers and owners abound.

Most lists rent for about $50 for 1,000 names, and most brokers will insist that you rent a minimum of 3,000 to 5,000 names. We say "rent" instead of "buy" because you only get to use the name one time per rental, but once a person or company on the list responds, you can add it to your own list, which you can use over and over again.

If you don't want to go the list broker route, you can make up your own list from sources you may already have available, like church groups, professional organizations, neighborhood associations, client lists, school groups, alumni associations, sororities and fraternities, scouting groups, or your company's employee directory.

corporation, with variations therein. Many business newbies go with the simplest version, the sole proprietorship. If you'll be starting out on your own, you may choose the same option—it's the least complicated and the least expensive. You can always switch to another format later if and when you take on partners and/or employees.

It's always wise to consult your attorney and your accountant before you embark on any one of these journeys. They can point out things about your particular business that you may not have considered. And it's always nice to know they're waiting in the wings should questions or problems arise later.

And while you're going the professional-consult route, don't forget your insurance agent. Just because you're homebased doesn't mean your homeowners insurance will cover any catastrophe that might occur—chances are it won't. Be sure to check into special policies for your business equipment, yourself and any employees you may hire. You should also check into liability insurance and bonding, especially for any businesses where you work in people's homes or offices.

Planning Ahead

OK, now that you've checked off business structure, you'll need to prepare a business plan. Yes, it's another version of the term paper or thesis come back to haunt you, but it's extremely important. Preparing a business plan helps you spot both the pitfalls and potentials of your new venture. And a business plan is a necessity when approaching any source of start-up capital.

So what is a business plan? It describes in detail your company goals, the strategies you'll use to meet them, potential problems and how you'll solve them, the organizational structure of your business, and the amount of capital you'll need to finance it.

And like all legendary greats—the Seven Dwarfs, the Seven Wonders of the World and the Seven Brides for Seven Brothers—a great business plan has seven basic elements:

1. **Executive summary:** Although it's the last part you write, the executive summary is the first thing the reader sees. Make sure it delivers a punch by clearly stating the nature of your business and—if you're seeking capital—the type of financing you're seeking.

   The summary describes your business—its legal structure, the amount and purpose of the requested loan, repayment schedule, the borrower's equity share, and the debt-to-equity ratio after the loan, security or collateral is offered. You'll also list market value and estimated value or price quotes for any equipment you plan to purchase with the loan proceeds. The summary should be short and businesslike—a half-page to a page.

2. **Business description:** This section gives the reader a more detailed description of your business concept. Specify your industry. Is it wholesale or retail, food service, manufacturing, or service-oriented? Describe your product or service, emphasizing any unique features that set it apart. Explain your target market, how the product or service will be distributed and your support systems—advertising, promotions and customer service strategies.

   If you're seeking financing, explain why the money will make your business more profitable. Will you use it to expand, to create a new product or to buy new equipment?

3. **Marketing strategies:** Define your market's size, structure, growth prospects, trends and sales potential. Document how and from what sources you compiled your information. Then present the strategies you'll use to fulfill your sales objectives.

4. **Competitive analysis:** Detail your competitors' strengths and weaknesses, the strategies that give you an advantage, and any particular weakness in your competition that you can exploit.

5. **Design and development plans:** If your product is already developed, you can skip this section entirely. But if all you have so far is an idea or if you plan to improve a product or service, this section is essential. The design portion describes your product's design and materials and also provides diagrams. The development portion generally covers three areas: product, market and organizational development. If you plan to offer a service, you'll cover only these last two items and not worry at all about the design or product.

6. **Operations and management plans:** Here you explain how your business will function on a daily basis. You describe the responsibilities of the management team, the tasks assigned to each department (if this is applicable) and the capital required. You go over key management and their qualifications and explain what support personnel will be needed.

7. **Financial factors:** You knew it was coming—this is the math part, where you present your financial statements, including the following:

   ● An *income statement* detailing your business's cash-generation capabilities. It projects things like revenue, expenses, capital (in the form of depreciation) and cost of goods. Develop a monthly income statement for the business's first year, quarterly statements for the second year, and annual statements for each year thereafter for the term indicated in your business plan.

   ● A *cash flow statement* detailing the amount of money going into and coming out of your business—monthly for the first year and quarterly for each year thereafter specified in the plan. The result is a profit or loss at the end of each period. Both profits and losses carry over to the next column to show a cumulative amount. If your cash flow statement shows you consistently operating at a loss, you probably need additional cash to meet expenses.

- A *balance sheet* showing the business's assets, liabilities and equity over the period specified.

And that's it. Not so hard, eh? You can also find a host of books and software titles to help write that terrific business plan. For starters, check out *Entrepreneur's Business Plans Made Easy: It's Not as Hard as You Think!* from Entrepreneur Media Inc., available at all major bookstores and online from www.amazon.com and www.barnesandnoble.com.

Bringing Home The Bacon

Now it's time to go for the bacon, the money that will get your new business up and oinking, er, running. While you might think there are only two options available, the bank and the Small Business Administration (SBA), there are actually several.

- **Pig power:** Taking from your own piggy bank is the safest and most satisfying borrowing technique for the business newbie. You can use your savings, pension money, early retirement pay-out, or equity in your own investments (real estate, stocks and bonds, collectibles). Plan ahead sufficiently and you just might be able to finance yourself. (While we've quoted start-up costs for the businesses themselves in this book, keep in mind that unless you start part time, you'll also need a certain amount of funds to pay your living expenses until your fledgling company starts generating profits.)

- **Going friendly:** Your first line of credit is usually your family and friends—more small businesses than you might imagine start off this way. But while this method appears the simplest, it's also potentially dangerous. If you don't manage to pay back the money as promised, you lose not only funds, but also friends and family. Treat personal investments as serious business transactions. Put everything in writing and factor in some profit for the lenders.

- **Chaarrge it!** Some entrepreneurs finance their new ventures with that little plastic rectangle called a credit card. This, too, while often a simple method, can cause a slew of problems if you max out all your cards and then can't pay them back. If you use them, use them wisely.

- **Romance the bank:** This is the most traditional but generally the most difficult way to raise capital. Bankers are often reluctant to lend the small amounts entrepreneurs need because it isn't as profitable as making bigger loans. If they do decide to lend to you, they'll look for the four C's—character, capacity, capital and collateral. Your reputation and track record (character) are the most important, and capacity is your ability to repay.

● **The SBA way:** The federal government has a vested interest in the growth of small businesses. As a result, some Small Business Administration loans have less stringent requirements for owners' equity and collateral than do commercial loans, which makes the SBA an excellent financing source for start-ups. And the SBA will make more loans for smaller sums than will most banks.

Nothing's Free

Of course, this doesn't mean the SBA is giving away money. In fact, the SBA doesn't even make direct loans; instead it provides loan guarantees to entrepreneurs, promising the bank to pay back a certain percentage of your loan if you don't.

Banks participate in the SBA program as regular, certified or preferred lenders. The SBA can help you prepare your loan package, which you then submit to banks. If the bank approves your loan, it submits your loan package to the SBA. Applications submitted by regular lenders are reviewed by the SBA in about two weeks; certified lender applications are reviewed in three days; and approval through preferred lenders is even faster, what you might think of as the express lane.

What does the SBA look for in a loan applicant? The most basic requirement is the ability to repay the loan from cash flow, but personal credit history, industry experience or other evidence of management ability, collateral, and owner's equity contributions are also considerations. If you own 20 percent or more equity in the business, the SBA asks that you personally guarantee the loan. After all, you can't ask the government to back you if you're not willing to back yourself.

Lookin' Good

So you've decided what business you'll start, written that brilliant business plan and obtained your financing. Now what? It's time to develop that polished image. Just because you're a new company doesn't mean you have to look like one. With the right identity, your company can appear highly professional and give the impression of having been in business for years.

Here's a step-by-step guide to creating the perfect image with your logo, business cards and letterhead.

Logo-Motion

Your logo is a very important design element—it's the basis for all your other materials. Through color and graphics, it will give clients, suppliers, vendors and everybody else you come in contact with their initial—and probably lasting—impression of your firm.

Let's say your company specializes in makeup sessions. If your logo is plain and simple, on earth-toned paper with hunter green print, people will realize you're a back-to-basics, organic company that uses environmentally friendly cosmetics and makes its clients look as natural as possible. Take the same company, make the typeface high-tech wacky and the colors screamingly neon, and you're conveying a different impression entirely—here's the place to go for the latest in green nail polish, purple lipstick, and nouveau fashion.

Creating a logo on your own may seem like the best way to avoid the high cost of a professional design firm, which may charge $4,000 to $15,000. But even if you have an eye for color and a sense of what you want, you should still consult a professional designer. She'll know whether your logo concept will transfer easily into print or onto a sign, while you might come up with a design that's stunning but can't be transferred or would cost the same as a trip to Mars to print and would take as long.

Not to panic, however. Hiring a designer doesn't have to drain your start-up funds. If you're on a tight budget, shop around for independent graphic designers—their rates can be surprisingly low. Or hire an art student who can take on your job as a class project or to add credentials to his or her resume.

Card Yourself

Once you have a logo, apply it to the marketing items you'll use most, starting with your business cards. Don't expect your cards to tell the entire story of your business—they can't. What they can do is present a professional image people will remember in a positive way.

The color, wording and texture of your card have a lot to do with its appeal and its ability to convey your company image, so use your common sense. If your business is children's party planning, you might try a card with bright primary colors and the words written in a child's hand. But if you run a tax preparation service, the last thing your clients want to see is childishness, so you'd stick to traditional black print on a gray, beige or white background.

Moving Stationery

Every letter you send to a prospective or existing client leaves an impression—so make it a good one. Again, the paper you choose, along with the colors and graphics on it, plays an important part in your company image. That neon-pink stock might be perfect for a hip makeup artist but not for a corporate consulting service.

Don't get so caught up in the design elements that you forget the obvious. Stationery needs to include the same basics you have on your business card: your company name and logo, your address, phone and fax numbers, and your e-mail and Web site addresses.

There is much to consider when creating a professional image. If you're on a tight budget, start with the items the public will see right

CARD TRICKS

I f you can't afford to hire a professional to design your business cards, keep these tips in mind:

- Make your logo the focus of your card. It should be the largest element.
- Don't make the card an unusual shape—it's usually perceived as weird instead of clever.
- Keep it simple. Don't cram too much information on the card—this will only make it hard to read and cluttered-looking.
- Be sure to include the essentials: your name, title, company name, address, phone and fax numbers, and e-mail and Web site addresses.
- Make sure the typeface is easily readable.
- Stick to just one or two colors.

off the bat. If you expect to get most of your customers through direct mail, concentrate on stationery instead of business cards. If you'll get most of your business through networking, make cards your prime directive. But make sure you do something. With a strong professional image, you'll stand a stronger chance of impressing potential customers—and achieving success.

Permit Me

When you're involved in the excitement of starting a new business, it's easy to ignore licenses and permits. "Oh, that's just bureaucratic mumbo-jumbo," you think. "I'll take care of those little details later, when things settle down."

Sure, getting those business licenses and permits is about as much fun as that perennial trip to the Department of Motor Vehicles to renew your drivers' license, but failing to obtain them—right from the beginning—is one of the most common mistakes new entrepreneurs make.

What if your business becomes a success beyond your wildest dreams—and then, a few years from now, gets shut down by the county when they discover you don't have the proper license or permits? Short of a shutdown, lack of a license could lead to hefty fines, restrictions on your operations, lawsuits from suppliers or employees, or problems with the IRS. In short, an Excedrin headache size 90-plus.

This is one situation where an ounce of prevention really pays off. So—for your express edification—we hereby present some of the most common licenses and permits for small businesses and where to go for more information.

Making It Up

You'll need to go for a fictitious business name, a k a a dba, to register your business name (for instance, Dorothy Dane doing business as Donut Doodles). The procedure for doing this varies according to where you're located. In many states all you have to do is go to the county offices and pay a registration fee to the county clerk. In others, you also have to place a fictitious name ad in a local newspaper for a specified period of time. Your bank may require a dba before they'll let you open a business account. If so, they can tell you where to go to register. Filing costs range from $10 to $100—and in some states the newspaper will do the filing for you for a small fee.

In most states, corporations don't have to file fictitious business names unless they're doing business under names other than their own. Incorporation documents have the same effect for corporate businesses as do dba filings for sole proprietorships and partnerships.

Beeswax License

Contact your city's business license department to find out about getting a business license, which essentially grants you the right (after you pay a fee, of course) to operate within the city limits. When you file your application, the city planning or zoning department will check to make sure your area is zoned for the type of business you're proposing and that there are enough parking spaces to meet codes. If you're opening your firm in a building that previously housed a similar business, you probably won't run into problems.

If your area isn't zoned for the kind of business you plan to operate, you'll have to apply for a variance or a conditional use permit, which usually involves presenting your case before the planning commission in a sort of mini-courtroom drama. Variances can be easy to obtain as long as you can demonstrate that your business won't disrupt the character of the neighborhood in which you'll operate.

Investigate zoning ordinances very carefully if you plan to be homebased, as most of the businesses in this book are. Residential neighborhoods often have strict zoning regulations prohibiting business use of the home. Not to worry—it's entirely possible to get a variance or conditional use permit, and in many areas, people are becoming more supportive of homebased businesses.

That's Taxing

Before you open your doors, be sure to register to collect sales tax by applying for a sales license or permit. Sales taxes vary by state and are imposed at the retail level. It's important to know the rules because if you're a retailer, you must collect state and/or local taxes on every sale you make. While many states and localities exempt service businesses from these rules, some have recently changed their rules and now require taxes on services, too. If you'll have a service business, the best course of action is to contact your state revenue and/or local revenue offices for information.

And don't think you can slip away without a permit. You may get away with it for a while, but the final outcome won't be pleasant. In some states it's a criminal offense to undertake sales without a license, and you can be held liable for any uncollected sales taxes if and when they catch you.

If you ship retail goods out of state, as in mail order, be careful. In the past, many retailers, unaware of the laws, haven't collected sales taxes on these goods, but the law never considers ignorance an excuse. Check with your accountant before you carry out your plans.

As a saving grace, some of this works to your advantage. When you apply for a resale license, you don't have to pay tax on materials, merchandise or supplies you purchase wholesale to resell to your customers. Check it out!

To Your Health

If you plan to sell food—either directly to customers as in a restaurant or as a wholesaler to other retailers—you'll need a county health department permit. This costs about $25 and varies depending on the size of the business and the amount and type of equipment you'll have. The health department will want to inspect your facilities before issuing the permit, so make sure everything gleams.

I'll Drink To That

In most states, you need one type of license to sell wine and beer and another for hard liquor. (The latter is harder to obtain.) Your telephone white pages will have the number for the nearest beverage control agency, which can tell you everything you'll need to know about both types of licenses.

County Matters

County governments often require essentially the same types of permits and licenses as cities. If your business is outside any city or town jurisdiction, then these county permits apply to you. The good news? County regulations are frequently not as strict as city ones.

Publicity Power

Now let's get to something that's a little more fun than applying for business permits. Publicity—it's not just for movie stars. It's a terrific form of free advertising, and for homebased business owners, there's never been a better time to get publicity. With the new move toward cocooning—focusing on home and family life—millions of Americans are interested in homebased businesses. You can capitalize on this fascination by getting your company written up in magazines and newspapers and spotlighted on radio and television.

To use publicity effectively, however, you have to understand the road rules. And these can best be explained with the good old-fashioned Five W's Plus an H—who, what, when, where, why, and how.

The Price Is Right

Why should a homebased business seek publicity? For a variety of reasons. One, of course, is the price. As compared to advertising, publicity is absolutely free—your only costs are for materials preparation, mailing and phone calls. Another is that people tend to believe that if you've been covered by the media, you must be for real and really great. (And of course, you are.) So you've got built-in credibility. And when you cite the fact that you've been written up in *USA Everyday* or seen on "Good Morning Muskogee" to potential clients, it gives added oomph to your sales presentation.

Then there's audience coverage. If the national media picks up your story—and this can happen more readily than you might imagine—or if you land your piece in a national publication, you've got a far wider sweep than you could ever achieve with an ad in your local paper.

SIGN LANGUAGE

If your business will be homebased, as most of the businesses in this book can be, you probably won't need to worry about sign ordinances, but you should know that most cities and 'burbs have rules that restrict the size, location, and sometimes even the lighting and type of sign allowed. If you plan to have a sign, and especially if you will have a commercial storefront, be sure to check regulations and get the written approval of your landlord (who may have his own rules) before having your sign designed and installed.

As with signs, the homebased businessperson doesn't usually need to worry about fire and environmental protection regulations, but if you plan to go the storefront route or will be using potential ecological hazards, you may want to check in with your local fire department and/or environmental protection agency.

Where should you publicize your business? Target the media that will reach your potential customers. What magazines and newspapers do they read? What radio stations do they listen to? What TV programs do they watch? How do you know all this stuff? Mail out questionnaires, interview customers and listen carefully to the kinds of things they talk about.

Who should you contact? You'll need to know which reporters cover your type of business. Check media reference books at your local library to get a listing of sources, including addresses and phone numbers.

What questions should you ask? When you contact programmers and editors, you have two options—you can offer to write an article or participate in a radio interview about your area of expertise, or you can ask that a reporter cover your business as part of a planned article or TV show.

When should you make contact? As soon as you've come up with a hot angle. To garner media attention, you've got to have a pertinent, interesting and either topical or unique subject. The Dick-and-Jane book report format won't make a dent. Do your homework before approaching media types and come up with a concept to convince them your business will appeal to their audience.

How do you submit materials? Ask your media contact what he prefers. Some take phone calls, others want a press release package, still others want photos or product samples (if they apply). Be sure to find out the time frame involved. Most media—particularly magazines—work several months ahead of the cover date, so if you want your story in the December issue, you may need to submit it in June or even earlier.

All-Star Sales

Once you've achieved that terrific publicity, you'll need to sign up the potential customers who flock to you as a result. A lot of entrepreneurs run into difficulties when it comes to sales, but you can be an all-star. These six simple steps can take you from a bang-up beginning all the way to that cracker-jack close.

1. **Establish rapport.** This means a relaxed, pleasant attitude and a smile, even over the phone. (People can hear a smile.) Use your customer's name, maintain eye contact if you're meeting in person, and if you're on the phone, try talking for a minute about personal issues.

2. **Get customers to tell you what they want.** Maybe it's nerves, but many people plunge into lengthy spiels before learning what the customer wants to buy. It's a tactic doomed to failure. Even if you have exactly what the customer wants, he may be so afraid to make a decision that he resorts to no decision at all—which means no sale. Find out what he's looking for before telling him you've got it.

3. **Get the customer to commit to a purchase if you can provide what he or she needs.** It seems simple, but countless salespeople miss the big picture—they don't get the customer to commit. They work away toward a potential sale, but at the moment when the customer should be buying, he or she wriggles away with a muttered need to get someone else's approval, like a partner, spouse or boss. So how do you get a commitment? Ask for it—tactfully. Don't patronize your customer, but do ask "Are you the one to talk to, or will someone else be making the buying decision?"

4. **Find the customer's hot button.** Customers can rattle off a long list of needs, but there's usually one hot button that will grab their attention—and it's up to you to find it. For instance, if you're a personal trainer seeking to sign up clients, some prospects may be interested in reducing their risk of heart attacks while others might

be more taken with the idea of shedding a few pounds before summer swimsuit season. You won't always find that hot button right off the bat, but keep asking, listening and observing, and you'll figure out what it is.

5. **Eliminate the customer's objections.** Some buyers march in or call knowing exactly what they need, but most want to be wooed. These are the ones who throw out objections like petals from a flower girl's basket. ("Well, I'd like to buy it, but it's just too expensive.") Don't let them distract you. Figure out the standard objections; then figure out what to say to overcome them.

6. **Close that sale.** You can find all sorts of books and tapes on slick closing techniques, but you don't need them. If you've followed the previous five steps, all you usually have to do to close the sale is ask for the customer's order.

Now, don't expect to become an overnight selling whiz. Selling is a skill, and, like bike-riding, roller-skating or cooking, it takes practice. In this case, it means practicing on friends and family. If they or you notice rough spots, concentrate on how you can improve them. Assess your performance after real-life sales experiences and you'll soon be a sales all-star.

Feeling Rejected

Part of being an all-star is dealing with rejection. "No" is one of the most dreaded words in the English language because—unless it's in answer to a question like "Does this $100 bill belong to anyone?"—it means being rejected. For the entrepreneur, "no" can mean being turned down by a potential client, distributor or financier.

But the successful entrepreneur doesn't waste time on temper tantrums, make a beeline for the nearest bar or throw herself out the window. (Although chocolate can be an acceptable emergency restorative.) Instead, the savvy entrepreneur looks at rejection objectively, analyzes it and—most important—learns from it.

The key to overcoming rejection is persistence. So what if that prospective client doesn't see the need for your service? Pick yourself up, dust yourself off, and go on to the next one. Every smart salesperson knows that it takes about 12 cold calls to even get through to an executive with decision-making power, and nine out of 10 of them will turn you down flat. But if you don't keep steaming ahead through those nine "nos", you'll never get to that all-important 10th "yes."

JUST ASK WHY

There's one method to combat rejection that's so simple most entrepreneurs never even think of it. Just ask why. If you ask for an explanation, often rejection becomes a positive tool and helps you open the next door. Try something diplomatic like "Could you tell me why you're not interested in my service? If I understood why, maybe we could find a comfortable middle ground. I'd like to be able to work with you."

You'll be delighted to learn that customers are more flexible than you think. They like to be asked for help and they love to give advice—which helps build rapport and sets the foundation for a long-term relationship. And it's the long-term that counts. Be patient. Just because somebody says no now doesn't mean they'll feel the same way six months down the road.

Businesses aren't built overnight. It takes time, a tremendous amount of work, and yes, plenty of rejection. But as successful entrepreneurs who've weathered difficult storms can tell you, the rewards are worth the struggle. And remember, as your mother always counseled—although you may be sobbing now, someday you'll look back on the "bad" stuff and laugh. Really!

Netting Contacts

Many people are put off by the idea of networking—they think of it as a sort of phony glad-handing that oozes insincerity. But networking is one of the most important skills you can have as an entrepreneur. It's the perfect way to meet the clients and contacts you'll need to grow your business.

Take an objective look at your own interactive abilities. Are you shy and think of networking groups as an exercise in terror? Or are you a natural blab who does all the talking in any given conversation? Do you give other people referrals and ideas even if there seems to be no personal gain? (There is. When you help others, they remember—and they'll help you.) Can people count on your word?

The networking tips that follow may seem basic, but you'd be aghast at how rarely people practice them. When it comes to business functions, most folks—especially those new to networking—stick too close to their own comfort zone.

Typically, network nerds attend several groups but visit with the same friends every time. This defeats the entire purpose. If you stick to familiar faces, you never meet anyone new. And since most people stay within their own circle, newcomers view the organization as a series of cliques. This is one reason people fear going to new groups by themselves—they're afraid no one will notice them.

The trick with networking is to go proactive. This means taking control of the situation instead of reacting to it. Networking requires going beyond your comfort zone and challenging yourself. Try these tips:

The Beeline

- **Set a goal to meet five (or more) new people at each event.** Whenever you attend a group—a party, mixer or industry luncheon—make a beeline for the people you don't know. Greet newcomers. They'll love you for it!

- **Try one or two new groups a month.** You can be a self-invited guest at almost any organization's meetings a few times before you have to join. Try new ones and decide how you like them. At the same time, you'll be making new sets of contacts.

- **Carry your business cards with you at all times.** This is a biggie that a lot of people miss. You never know when you might meet a key contact, and if you don't have your cards with you, you not only miss out but look disorganized and amateurish. Take your cards everywhere you go—to church, the gym, parties, the supermarket, even on walks with the dog.

- **Don't head for your seat too soon.** Often you'll see people at networking groups sitting at the dinner table staring into space—and usually looking miserable, which is not conducive to impressing people—half an hour before the meal is served. Don't let this be you. Use every minute of networking time.

- **Don't sit with people you know.** Mealtime is prime time for meeting new people. You may be in that seat for several hours, so don't limit your opportunities by sitting with your buddies.

- **Get active.** Join a committee or become a board member. If you don't have the time for that, volunteer to help with hospitality at the door or with checking in guests. This gives you terrific visibility and a reason to talk to others, and it gets you involved in the inner workings of the group.

- **Be friendly and approachable.** Make people feel welcome. Find out what brought them there and see if there's a way you can help them. Introduce them to others, make business suggestions or give a referral. Not only will you make a friend, but you'll also put others at ease, thus eliminating your own self-consciousness.

- **Set a goal for each meeting.** Your goals can vary with each event. Try these: learning from the speaker's topic, looking for new prospects, discovering industry trends or connecting with peers. If you're homebased, you may find your purpose is simply to get out and talk with people face-to-face.

Generation Next

You can start nearly every business in this book all on your own. You don't need employees, so you're freed up to get started for less money and less paperwork, and to learn all the tricks of your new trade before you need to pass them on to somebody else. But as your business grows, you'll probably reach a stage where you'll need to take on an extra set of hands.

Once you've followed the steps in "Hire Power" on page 29, write your ad—carefully—and place it in the newspaper. You could answer the phone all day, screening nonstarter hopefuls, so make sure your ad that spells out exactly what you want and requires applicants to mail in a resume. You'll eliminate a lot of people who lack follow-through by the simple fact that they won't bother to send anything in, and you can eliminate a lot more who would like the position but are unqualified.

Interview Smarts

After you've weeded out the ones that won't work, call in the potentials for an interview. To start the process, briefly describe your company and the position available and establish a rapport before moving on to the nitty-gritty stuff.

Focus your questions by asking about several general areas: work-related experience, training, lifestyle (hobbies and related interests), then education and unrelated jobs. Move into each area with an open-ended statement like "Tell me about your last job." Don't be specific—you want to know what the applicant considers important.

When you have information on which to base further questions,

HIRE POWER

Taking on an employee can seem like scary stuff. How do you choose somebody who can be a back-up you, who can nurture your business baby and your clients the way you do, who'll be an asset instead of a hindrance? Not to panic. You can find that perfect person by following four simple steps:

- Write a job description. Start with a paragraph or two describing the tasks to be performed and the skills needed.
- Identify the personality traits for the job. Does it take a methodical, detail-oriented type, or a go-getter who can change direction in midstride?
- Consider your own personality. If you're perky, cheerful and talkative, you'll have a rough go with an employee who never says a word. And if you need lots of quiet time and not a lot of distractions, you'll go nuts if your employee is a chatterbox.
- List the 10 or 12 skills or qualities you desire most in your employees, rank them, and circle the essential three or four.

By following these steps, you'll have a clear picture of your ideal employee, which will simplify writing your ad and conducting interviews. You can't choose the perfect person if you don't know what you want!

you can ask what the applicant liked or disliked about a specific aspect of a job she's described. When you ask what sort of problems arose and how your hopeful handled them, she'll begin revealing whether the hard stuff was approached with initiative, perseverance, or by asking for help.

Each time you hear a description of a personality trait, make a written note, but don't assume that because you hear one example of initiative, this is the go-getter you're dreaming of. The benefit of taking each general area in sequence and asking the same types of exploratory questions about each is that as you hear how several problems were (or were not) solved, and you can note which characteristics are repeated.

Other probing questions include: What was most challenging about . . . ? What were your major accomplishments in . . . and why? Is there anything you regret about . . . ? What did you learn from . . . that might help you in this position?

Be alert for areas people seem unwilling to discuss. If you probe without sounding judgmental, you can usually uncover information that will help in evaluating the applicant.

Remember to avoid discriminatory questions. While you can ask if applicants are between 40 and 70, if they're citizens, what languages they speak or read fluently, if they've ever been convicted of a crime, or if they hold a valid driver's license, you can't ask about ancestry or origin, marital status, political beliefs, religion, or arrests.

Pace your interview to leave time to discuss the position in detail and let your hopeful ask questions; these—or the lack thereof—can also be extremely revealing.

Finally, if it's applicable, give a test or two. If you're hiring an interior design salesperson, for instance, let her take a window measurement and see how she does. If you're desperately seeking administrative help, sit him at the computer with, for example, a scenario for a courtesy response letter to a request for a sales package and see what he comes up with.

Choose Wisely

When you find what seems to be Mr. or Ms. Right, you can call their references and verify that they're all they've claimed to be. Then make your selection. If you've done everything we've suggested, this shouldn't be difficult, but take your time. This person is going to be your right hand and possibly your right brain, so make sure you'll be happy with the choice. If it's a case of "best of a bad batch," don't choose any of them. Go to an employment or temporary help agency, or just carry on by yourself until you can rethink your plan of attack.

As soon as you hire somebody, call the people who didn't qualify and tell them you'll keep their applications on file in case another position opens. This is a) common courtesy, b) gives you a backup in case your first choice doesn't pan out, and c) gives you a head start on the whole process if business suddenly doubles thanks to your new hire.

Be sure to let your new employee know that he's on probation for a short time while you evaluate his performance.

Fortune From Failure

What's the key to business success? Adequate capital, a winning business plan, a savvy sales technique? All these factors are important, but so is something else you might never imagine. Many prosperous entrepreneurs say previous business failures—more than any-thing else—helped fuel their current successes.

The old adage about learning from your mistakes may be a cliché, but thousands of successful business owners have done exact-ly that. Instead of letting failure frustrate them, these entrepreneurs profited from the experience, garnering valuable lessons they couldn't have learned any other way.

Failure hurts—a lot—but it also challenges, motivates and hum-bles, cutting through the illusion that success is easy and giving you the determination to dust yourself off and try it again.

To develop "intelligent failure," the kind that forms the building blocks of success, the first step is to get over the fear of failure. We all deal with failures of one kind or another on a daily basis. If one thing doesn't work, you try something else—both in your personal life and in your business.

Another fact—and this is a biggie—of business (and personal) life is that you have to disassociate failure from self-esteem. Look for what went right in any failure and pat yourself on the back for that part. Then you can examine what went wrong and see what you can do better next time.

Put your creativity to work and keep your sense of humor. You may not be able to laugh yourself silly over what seems like a catas-trophe, but if you can cling to those wisps of perspective, you'll be able to more easily handle what seems like a desperate situation. When you apply that creative mind, sometimes what seems awful is actually the door to a far better opportunity.

And remember, there's a big difference between failing and being a failure. The true failure simply gives up. The savvy entrepreneur tries again and ultimately succeeds.

COUNTDOWN TO TAKE-OFF

Use this handy checklist to make sure you've done your homework properly. Have you accomplished everything you need to do to ensure your business is an entrepreneurial success?

Franchise/Business Opportunity

- ○ Have you carefully investigated all the businesses that sound promising?
- ○ Have you read the UFOC or business opportunity informational materials?
- ○ Have you interviewed at least five franchisees or business purchasers?

Market Research

Have you determined these factors:
- ○ Is there a need for your product or service?
- ○ Who are your competitors?
- ○ Who are your customers?
- ○ How much should you charge?

Business Structure

- ○ Have you decided which route to go?

Business Plan

- ○ Yes, you need one—so get writing.

Money

- ○ Do you have adequate start-up capital?
- ○ Do you have enough money to live on?

Business Licenses

- ○ Have you checked with all the proper authorities and applied for the licenses that apply to your business?

Professional Help

- ○ Have you checked with an attorney and accountant?
- ○ Have you checked into insurance?

Networking

- ○ Have you joined a trade association and your local chamber of commerce?

If you've checked yes to all these items . . . Congratulations! You're in business!

Chapter two

BEFORE YOU GET STARTED

O K, you've read our "Intro-duction" and our "Business Basics" (or you will, right?). You're ready to roll. But here's one more thing to peruse before you get going on choosing the perfect business for you.

We've selected businesses that are hot today and have plenty of potential for tomorrow. We've carefully chosen those that can be started for as little money as possible. And we've thought those costs through for you. Here's how:

- Almost all our suggested businesses are homebased. If we don't specifically say that you need a storefront, you don't. So you immediately eliminate the costs of leases, office utilities, and things like signage and office furniture. While it's important that you have a comfortable, quiet, well-lit and well-ventilated work space, you don't need to rush out and buy special furnishings. Those can wait until your business starts bringing in income.

- Every business, no matter how small, should have a computer. The resources available on the Internet for no more than an average $25 per month service provider fee are astonishing—you really owe it to yourself and your business to take advantage of them. With a computer and a printer, you can send out letters and sales materials and keep your books far more easily than you would if you didn't have one.

  Although more people today than ever already have a computer at home, we haven't factored in computer costs unless you must have one as an essential part of the business. (Don't worry—we tell you which ones require computers.) If you choose a business that doesn't require a computer, you don't have one and you can't afford it yet, that's OK. But put it on your list of future purchases.

  One more thing about computers—we're taking for granted that your computer is Internet-ready—in other words, it already has a modem.

- We're figuring that you already have some sort of transportation. For some businesses (like child-care providers and newsletter publishers), you don't need to leave home, so you won't need a vehicle. For other businesses, you can take public transportation. But for most, you'll need wheels to get you from your homebased business to your clients' homes or offices.

- We list professional organizations for each business whenever possible. It's in your best interest to join them—or at least check them out. Many organizations offer special training and certification, which is helpful not only for providing better service but as terrific credentials to offer potential clients. Most organizations have monthly newsletters or journals with helpful tips and industry insights. And lots of professional associations provide referrals—if you're a member, they'll send potential clients in your area to you.

- We also list franchises and business opportunities for each business whenever possible, but since they're a matter of choice rather than a necessity, we don't count the fees you'll pay for these as part of our start-up costs.

- A few of our businesses require you to have state licensing or certification. If you don't already have it, your absolute best source for more information is the professional organization. Since you may already be licensed—and since costs vary around the country and with different types of training—we don't count licensing or training fees as part of our start-up costs.

As a final heads up, we believe one of the best things you can do as a new entrepreneur is to read everything you can get your hands on about business in general and your business specialty in particular. To help you get a running start, we've chosen a starter selection of books and publications for each business. To go with them, we recommend *Entrepreneur Magazine's Start Your Own Business*, a stellar guide to small-business success. Unless we give other information, you can find all of these books and publications (where else?) online—we used Amazon.com at www.amazon.com, but there are current titles readily available at other online or walk-in bookstores.

And that's it! Turn the page, get reading, and get ready to start your new business. Welcome to the world of the entrepreneur!

Chapter three

THE ART SCENE

If you're one of those artistic types with paint splotches on all your play clothes, glitter glinting on your chin and dabs of dried hot glue on your linoleum, then this is the category for you. And if you're in your element surrounded by papers, ribbons and rhymes, creating and designing gift wrappings or greeting cards, then this is your category, too.

You might think it's only a lucky few who can earn a living at arts and crafts. Not! You'll have to learn to mix good business skills with all that creativity, but you can be successful.

CRAFTS BUSINESS

The Inside Scoop

Americans are experiencing a resurgence of interest in the simpler, sweeter things in life—things like handmade birdhouses, glowing hand-dipped candles and handcrafted arts of all kinds. So much so that the crafts industry is booming, with close to $10 billion in annual sales, reports the Association of Crafts and Creative Industries.

If you're skilled at a particular craft, you can satisfy others as well as yourself with a crafts business. The trick is to sell your crafts for enough money to justify your time and materials. Think about where you'll sell. Going to art fairs and crafts shows is fun but doesn't usually net much profit unless you can come up with a low-cost, quick-turnaround product. People who attend these events tend to be looky-loos who will only buy if your craft is very inexpensive. A good way to solve this problem is by selling your wares to wholesalers or sales representatives who will turn around and market them to retailers. You can also sell to the retailers themselves, place your crafts on consignment in retail shops, or sell them yourself via mail order.

The advantages to this business are that you get to earn a living doing what you truly enjoy, start-up costs are low, special licenses and certifications are nil, and you can start part time if you like and work up to full-time earnings.

The disadvantages are that having to produce on schedule can turn a beloved, relaxing hobby into a stressful chore. And sooner or later every successful crafter/businessperson discovers that demand is outstripping supply. In other words, you reach a point where you can't do it all yourself and you have to hire others to help you turn out what you consider to be a one-of-a-kind item.

Success For Less

Essentials

While you don't need a master's degree in fine arts to be an artisan or crafter, you'll need a genuine love for your specialty and the talent and skills to turn out items other people will want to buy. It also helps to have mastered your techniques. If you've already successfully turned out candles, birdhouses, pottery or whatever your specialty is, then you have a pretty good idea of how long each project takes, what materials you'll need and how much they cost—all of which are essential to pricing your wares.

Tools Of The Trade

Your equipment will depend on what crafts you'll be turning out. A woodworker who makes whimsical birdhouses will need entirely different tools than a potter. If you're already crafting, chances are you have the necessary equipment. But take a good look at what you've got and decide if there are other pieces of equipment you could use to make your work life faster and easier—remember, the more pieces you turn out, the higher your income will be.

Money Talk

Your start-up costs will be relatively low, but again this depends on what crafts you'll be making, what tools and equipment you already have, and what your materials costs will be. A crafter working with recycled bottles will have far lower overhead than one making sterling silver trinkets. Your annual gross revenues can run from $10,000 to $250,000, based on the price and desirability of your particular craft, how aggressively you market your wares and how hard you choose to work. The amount of money you charge your customers will also vary with your particular specialty—shop your competition to find out what similar products go for in your area.

Pounding The Pavement

Your customers can be friends and neighbors, people from your community who attend shows where you display your crafts, or the world at large reached through wholesalers and sales reps. Some artisans have had success selling their products through Tupperwarelike home parties. If you plan to go the wholesale route, hook up with reps at gift shows, which you can locate by calling local and regional chambers of commerce and convention centers, reading gift-industry publications or contacting the organizations listed below.

What's Next

If you're an arts and crafts newbie, take classes (offered by most crafts stores, community centers and local colleges), read books and magazines, watch crafts-oriented TV programs, and practice, practice, practice. Whether you're a novice or an old pro at turning out crafts, you'll want to learn the business end of the industry. Talk to crafters who are already out there selling and get their advice. Because arts and crafts tend to be trendy—with cherubs replacing the

A STAR IS BORN

Artistic Ends

Four years ago, Corinne Kopf was a talented artist with a mission—to figure out how to earn an income from her art. She had numerous awards to her credit and an impressive array of paintings, but it was difficult to get people in her T-shirt-and-seashell-oriented tourist town to pay $400 and up for one of her works. Kopf, 50, now makes $800 to $1,150 per month selling hand-painted objects: lamps, glass ornaments and recycled bottles.

The trick, Kopf says, lies in determining what customers will pay for a piece and then creating artworks in that price range that pay in terms of labor and materials. The Panama City Beach, Florida, resident sells her pieces on consignment in local hotels and at crafts shops as well as from a tent at art shows and festivals. As a bonus, Kopf also sells her paintings at these events and often receives commissions to paint not only custom ornaments, but also portraits of people, pets, boats and even buildings.

Kopf's advice for those starting out in the business? It takes time, she says, to build a strong base of clients who will come back again and again to purchase your wares. Be prepared for those initial slow times and don't get discouraged.

country cows who replaced those crocheted toilet tissue-cover dollies—attend craft and gift shows, read crafts magazines, and watch crafting TV programs to get new ideas and to make sure your present ones aren't outdated.

Organizations

- *Association of Crafts and Creative Industries*, 1100-H Brandywine Blvd., P.O. Box 3388, Zanesville, OH 43702-3388, (740) 452-4541
- *National Craft Association*, 1945 E. Ridge Rd., #5178, Rochester, NY 14622-2467, (800) 715-9594, www.craftassoc.com

Books

- *The Basic Guide to Selling Arts and Crafts*, by James Dillehay, Warm Snow Publishers
- *The Business of Crafts: The Complete Directory of Resources for Artisans*, by The Crafts Center, Watson-Guptill Publications
- *Craft Market Place: Where and How to Sell Your Crafts*, by Argie Manolis (editor), Betterway Publications
- *Entrepreneur's Business Start-Up Guide #1304, Crafts Business*, Entrepreneur Media Inc., 2392 Morse Ave., Irvine, CA 92614, (800) 421-2300, www.smallbizbooks.com

Publications

- *Arts & Crafts Marketing Business Builder Kit*, National Craft Association, 1945 E. Ridge Rd., #5178, Rochester, NY 14622-2467, (800) 715-9594, www.craftassoc.com
- *The Crafts Report*, 300 Water St., Box 1992, Wilmington, DE 19899-1992, (800) 777-7098, www.craftsreport.com
- *General Arts & Crafts Business Builder Start-Up*, National Craft Association, 1945 E. Ridge Rd., #5178, Rochester, NY 14622-2467, (800) 715-9594, www.craftassoc.com

Franchises

- *Color Me Mine*, Versent Corp., 14721 Califa St., Van Nuys, CA 91411, (888) COLOR-MINE, www.colormemine.com
- *Deck the Walls*, P.O. Box 1187, Houston, TX 77210-1187, (800) 543-3325, www.deckthewalls.com
- *Stained Glass Overlay*, 1827 N. Case St., Orange, CA 92685, (800) 944-4746, www.sgoinc.com

GIFT BASKETS

The Inside Scoop

If you're the type who goes nuts at holidays and birthdays, choosing oh-so-special gifts and then dressing them up in creative packages, you'll get all wrapped up in a gift basket business. You can give gifts all year long and get paid for doing it! This is one of the hottest businesses going, with recent annual sales of $800 million. In fact, it's become so hot that the competition is getting downright fiery. But if you set your creativity on high and develop your own special niche, you can be very successful.

Gift basket entrepreneurs buy gifts and tuck them into baskets, decorative tins, boxes or bags for their customers to give to that certain someone. Each basket of goodies is designed around a theme, which can be anything from romance to travel to new baby to new home to just about anything you can dream up. There are even divorce baskets!

The gift basket business's advantages are that you can start part time, your start-up costs are relatively low, and if you're a creative person who likes conjuring up unique themes and packaging and putting them all together, it's a whole lot of fun. Plus, the business is gratifying—everybody's delighted to receive a fancy basket full of gifts.

The main drawback is that the business tends to be seasonal. You can work your fingers off during the winter holidays, wrapping everybody's gifts but your own, and have time on your hands during the summer. However, you can overcome the lag-time through creative marketing. Go after business clients who'll use your services year-round.

Essentials

A gift basket can be elegant, whimsical or sporty, but make sure it looks smart—you can't just toss in a hodgepodge of objects and stick on a bow. You'll need a flair for the creative and the design ability to pull it all together into an attractive package. You'll also need to be a savvy marketer who can sell those unique baskets to a variety of clients and customers.

Tools Of The Trade

In most states, you'll need a liquor license to add that swanky bottle of champagne or fine wine, and you'll want a resale license so you can buy gifts and supplies at wholesale prices. You'll also want a shrink-wrap machine (or use a heavy-duty hair dryer or paint peeler); that indispensable crafter's tool, the hot glue gun; and a work space large enough for you to spread out your materials and assemble your baskets. (Keep in mind that a business client may order 100 or more baskets at a time.)

Money Talk

Start-up costs, including your initial gift and supplies inventory, can run as low as $3,000. Annual sales for gift basket designers range from $20,000 for someone working part time to over $200,000 for an entrepreneur with a strong corporate clientele. Gift baskets sell for anywhere from $15 to $1,000 each—depending, of course, on what's inside, with an average price being $35.

Pounding The Pavement

The quintessential consumer gift-basket customer is the middle- to upper-income female baby boomer, but you can sell to just about anybody. Be sure to tie up business accounts. These will keep your cash flow going during slower retail seasons and can be a terrific source of repeat sales. Wrap up travel and real estate agents, innkeepers, apartment complexes, car and boat salespeople, public relations firms, or any other corporate clients who'll want to thank, wow or woo their own customers. And don't forget clubs and organizations—they're always throwing dinners, teas, parties and assorted awards banquets for which gifts are a necessary ingredient.

You can attract these clients and customers with creative marketing. Send brochures to businesses and organizations, then follow up by setting appointments to show your baskets or a professional portfolio of your designs. To reap retail customers, place ads in local newspapers, host home parties à la Tupperware and exhibit at crafts fairs. Send press releases to local and national publications, offer yourself as a guest on a local radio chat show, and donate a few baskets to other businesses' grand openings or for fund-raisers in return for free publicity.

What's Next

Launch your business the way you'd start any gift experience—go shopping! Shop your competition. Check out what sorts of baskets they sell, what their prices are and, if possible, what types of customers they sell to. Shop for gifts and supplies at craft, gift and novelty trade shows and through wholesalers you can find in the Yellow Pages or online.

Organizations

● *Gift Association of America*, 612 W. Broad St., Bethlehem, PA 18018, (610) 861-9445

● *The National Specialty Gift Association*, P.O. Box 843, Norman, OK 73070, (405) 329-7847

Weekend Warrior

PICTURE FRAMER

Get in the frame with a picture framing service. You can work with gallery owners, artists, portrait photographers and individuals who've purchased a print, painting or fine photo. If you aren't already a framing expert, read up, take classes at a local college or community center, then assemble your tools—including clamps, saws, miter boxes, glue, and a pneumatic or hand stapler. Establish relationships with local artists groups, galleries, photographers and print shops that can give you their business or refer their customers to you. **Start-up costs:** $1,500. **Expected annual gross revenues:** Up to $20,000.

Books

- *The Business of Gift Baskets: How to Make a Profit Working from Home*, by Camille J. Anderson and Don L. Price, Camille Anderson (publisher)
- *Entrepreneur's Business Start-Up Guide #1306, Gift Basket Service*, Entrepreneur Media Inc., 2392 Morse Ave., Irvine, CA 92614, (800) 421-2300, www.smallbizbooks.com
- *How to Start a Home-Based Gift Basket Business*, by Shirley George Frasier, Globe Pequot Press
- *The Official Resource Directory for the Gift Basket Industry*, Gift Basket Headquarters, 2990 Red Hill, Costa Mesa, CA 92626, (800) 833-4083

Publications

- *Gift Basket Review*, Festivities Publications Inc., 815 Haines St., Jacksonville, FL 32206, (800) 729-6338
- *Giftware Business*, 1 Penn Plaza, New York, NY 10019, (800) 255-2824 (for subscriptions)

Business Opportunities

- *Le Gourmet Gift Basket Inc.*, 516 W. Eighth Ave., Denver, CO 80204, (800) 93-GIFT-6
- *The Gift Basket Connection*, 3 Juniper Ct., Schenectady, NY 12309, (800) 437-3237

GRAPHIC DESIGNER

The Inside Scoop

If you've always pictured yourself as a commercial artist but your drawing style is closer to stick figures than Cézannes, then graphic design might be just the business for you. With the great software available today, you can conjure up logos, letterheads, brochures, product packaging and mail order catalogs—just about anything that needs a distinctive graphic ambience for the business client.

Graphic designers work on a freelance basis, creating materials for corporate clients, advertising agencies, public relations firms and publishers. But they do more than merely sketch designs—they often provide visual solutions to specific problems like company identity crises or image changes.

The advantages to this business are that, provided you have a strong design and color sense, you don't need to be able to draw, you can work full time or part time and you can do it at home. Hours are flexible—so long as you meet clients at reasonable times and meet your deadlines, you can work 'til dawn and sleep 'til noon if you want to.

The main disadvantage is that you'll often work on a deadline, which means that those flexible hours can get used up working on caffeine-powered hyper-drive. Creative types may also chafe at having to modify terrific ideas to suit seemingly dull-witted clients, but that's part of the game.

Essentials

Even if your sketching ability is mired at kindergarten level, you must have a flair for design and color. You should also have a good working knowledge of your design software—it's no fun trying to please clients and meet deadlines when you're still grappling with which function keys do what. A degree in graphic design or fine arts is a plus but not necessary; ditto for on-the-job experience working in an ad agency or for graphic designers. In addition to all that creativity, you'll need to have good listening skills so you can understand what your clients want, plus a good sense of marketing to help them sell themselves through the projects they bring to you.

Tools Of The Trade

You'll need a high-end computer (most graphic designers use Macs) with a Zip or Jaz drive, a top-quality color printer, a scanner, a fax machine and the software itself. Talk to graphic designers to find out what programs they use, then haunt computer superstores to see what's comparable and what's the newest on the market.

Money Talk

You can expect start-up costs of $2,700 to $6,900, depending on how much computer equipment and software you already have, what you buy and how fancy you get. Once you become established, you can expect to earn $20,000 to $100,000 and up per year. Charge your clients $40 to $100 per hour or bid by the job.

Pounding The Pavement

Your clients will be other businesses—ad agencies, publishing companies, small magazines, product manufacturers and others, from start-ups to old standbys who need a smart image to start with or a snappy redesign of their aged chestnut. Find these firms by placing ads in trade publications like those read by ad agencies, mail order companies and the giftware industry. Send direct-mail pieces to these same companies—let them see your work firsthand. Network in your community and keep your ear to the ground for hints of new businesses. When you hear of an opportunity, make an appointment to present your portfolio and discuss how you can be of service.

What's Next

Assemble your virtual artist's tools, your computer system and software. If you're not already experienced at using them, practice, practice, practice. Design your own letterhead, business cards and brochure. Make up a portfolio of projects—you can do some for nonprofit organizations—from churches to theater groups to museums to charitable groups—at no charge in exchange for advertising in their publications.

Organizations

● *Graphic Artists Guild*, 90 John St., #403, New York, NY 10038-3202, (212) 791-3400, www.gag.org

● *Association of Graphic Communications*, 330 Seventh Ave., New York, NY 10001-5010, (212) 279-2100, www.agcomm.org

Books

● *The Business of Graphic Design: A Sensible Approach to Marketing and Managing a Graphic Design Firm*, by Ed Gold, Watson-Guptill Publications

● *The Business Side of Creativity: The Complete Guide for Running a Graphic Design or Communications Business*, by Cameron S. Foote, W.W. Norton & Company

Publications

● *Creative Business*, 275 Newbury St., Boston, MA 02116, (617) 424-1368, www.creativebusiness.com (When you subscribe to this newsletter, you also get unlimited telephone advice and counseling—you're encouraged to call any time.)

JEWELRY & ACCESSORIES DESIGN

The Inside Scoop

If you love the art of making jewelry—you've got rings on your fingers, bells on your toes, and dazzling dangles everyplace else on your person—then you'll have a ball as a professional jewelry and accessories designer. Jewelry and accessories are always popular, especially today when all those '60s-style beads are back in style in a big way.

You can work with beads, with traditional elements like gold and silver, with glass, fabrics, feathers, clays—whatever suits your talents and fancies. And you can specialize in earrings, rings, pins or pendants, or in handcrafted handbags or hats.

The advantages to this business are that you get to be creative as a career, you meet lots of interesting people while selling your art, and you can start part time if you like.

The disadvantages are that having to produce on schedule can turn a delightful pastime into real work if you're not careful to keep your creativity on high, and you can't be all artisan—to make a living, you've got to make sure your muse has a healthy dollop of business skills.

Essentials

You'll need the talent and skills to design and turn out jewelry or accessories others will want to be seen in. And in addition to all that artistic sensibility, you'll need plenty of marketing creativity and drive—you'll need to sell your products as well as make them.

Tools Of The Trade

Your equipment will depend on what jewelry and accessories you'll design. Goldsmithing requires a different set of tools than beadwork, and leatherworking is not the same as quilting. If you're already working with your chosen medium, you probably have your tools at hand. But now that you'll be designing professionally, take an equipment inventory and decide if newer or additional tools or equipment could make your work faster and easier—remember, the more pieces you turn out, the higher your income will be.

Money Talk

Your start-up costs will be relatively low, but this depends on what jewelry or accessories you'll be making, what tools and equipment you already have, and what your materials costs will be. You can expect annual gross revenues of $10,000 to $250,000, based on how aggressively you market, how hard you choose to work, and the desirability of your product line. How you price your wares will also vary—a necklace of glass beads will go for a different price than one made of rubies.

Pounding The Pavement

You can host home parties à la Mary Kay or sell directly to local merchants, at flea markets, arts and crafts fairs, and through whole-

Weekend Warrior

GIFT WRAPPER

Wrap up tidy profits—plus a lot of fun—as a specialty gift wrapper. Most people these days don't have the time to give gifts a classy or custom look, and lots more just don't know how. Your services will be most in demand at Christmastime, but you can offer "packages" for every holiday on the calendar and birthdays, too. Customers can drop wrapables at your home, you can offer pickup and delivery, or you can arrange with a retail store or mall to offer on-site wrapping. Start off by distributing fliers in your neighborhood and at local shops that can refer customers to you. **Start-up costs:** $150. **Expected annual gross revenues:** Up to $10,000.

salers and sales reps. If you plan to go the wholesale route, hook up with reps at gift shows, which you can locate by calling local and regional chambers of commerce and convention centers, by reading gift industry publications or through the organizations listed below.

What's Next

If you're a jewelry and accessories newbie, take classes (offered by most crafts stores, community centers and local colleges), read books and magazines, watch crafts-oriented TV programs, and practice, practice, practice. Whether you're a novice or an old pro at turning out merchandise, you'll want to learn the business end of the industry. Haunt art and gift shows and talk to designers who are already out there selling and get their advice.

Organizations

● *National Craft Association*, 1945 E. Ridge Rd., #5178, Rochester, NY 14622-2467, (800) 715-9594, www.craftassoc.com

Books

● *The Art and Craft of Jewelry*, by Janet Fitch, Chronicle Books

● *The Book of Beads: A Practical and Inspirational Guide to Beads and Jewelry Making*, by Janet Coles, Simon & Schuster

● *The Encyclopedia of Jewelry Making Techniques: A Comprehensive Visual Guide to Traditional and Contemporary Techniques*, by Jinks McGrath, Running Press

Cyber Assistance

● *The Bead Fairies Page* (www.mcs.net/~simone/beadfairies.html): Everything for the bead-worker—tips, retail and wholesale catalogs, loom patterns, books, newsletters, bead societies and more. Plus how to be a Bead Fairy! What more could you want?

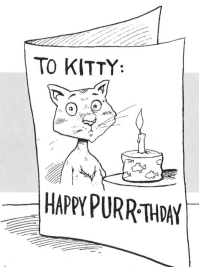

The Inside Scoop

If you're the type who can spend hours happily poring through every greeting card in the store, you love sending just the right card for every occasion, and you can never quite bring yourself to throw out a card you've been given, then niche greeting cards is the business for you. And if you're a whiz at designing that perfect card yourself, then this is the business for you, too.

You can help businesses develop and maintain a rapport with their clientele by sending customized cards for occasions from birthdays to winter holidays to National Pickle Week. You can also send cards announcing clients' special events and even embellish cards with your customers' signatures and logos. You'll purchase blank cards at wholesale prices and, depending on the size of each project, imprint the message on your own printer, have them imprinted commercially, or design and print each card on your own computer system.

Or you can go the retail route and design cards for the regular consumer market—everything from traditional Christmas and Valentine missives to "congratulations on surviving a stress-o-mania week" to "condolences on your bad hair day."

This is a field with room for growth: According to the Greeting Card Association, Americans purchased 7 billion cards in 1998. And while the big players like Hallmark do tend to dominate the market, most of the country's more than 1,800 greeting card companies are small ones. But it's not as easy as scribbling "Happy Birthday" on a picture of a cake—you must have a terrific design sense, a flair for the written word, and a real feel for what will appeal to the mass market.

The advantages to this business are that you can start part time, it's fun and creative, and it's a warm, fuzzy, feel-good business—even though you don't see the recipients of your cards, you know they're enjoying them.

The only disadvantages are that—if you choose the custom corporate version—you've got to go by the calendar 365 days a year. If you promise clients you'll send their customers birthday cards and then plan to go on vacation for two weeks, you'll have to make sure those cards get sent anyway. (Send them a few days early or make them up ahead of time and have a trusted "card sitter" send them for you.)

If you decide to design and market cards for retail, you'll face tough competition. Don't expect to be an overnight success—in this version of this business it can take time to build a following.

Essentials

For this business, you'll need a sense of fun, creativity and—the flip side of the coin—good organizational and time-management skills. When you send out cards for business clients, you need to stay on top of things—a Happy Chanukah card mailed in January won't work. But you'll need to stay far ahead of the calendar with a retail design business, too. Winter holiday cards hit the stores soon after Halloween, and Mother's Day missives appear soon after St. Patty's Day—which means that you'll have to have yours designed, printed and ready to ship even earlier.

Tools Of The Trade

You'll need a computer, a high-quality color printer, a scanner, greeting card or desktop publishing software, and—if you'll be taking the custom corporate route—database software for maintaining mailing lists and a resale license for buying cards at wholesale prices.

Money Talk

Figure your start-up costs at $2,200 to $15,000 and up, depending on whether you go the corporate or retail route. You'll need a line of at least 25 different designs to interest retailers or their distributors, so make sure you price your materials and printing costs very carefully before you embark on your journey, or you'll likely run into immediate difficulties. You can expect annual gross revenues of $20,000 to $60,000 and up, depending on how many clients you sign and how many customers they have or what your retail sales are. For custom corporate cards, you'll charge your clients $2 to $3 per card, plus an annual mailing list update fee of 50 cents per name.

When you sell your designs to retailers, you'll look at a different set of figures. Most cards sell to consumers for $1.95 to $2.50. But you'll sell that $1.95 card wholesale for $1, and of that, your costs (including the envelope) will be 40 cents to 60 cents. As a rule of thumb, you can mark up your costs twice to arrive at your price to retailers.

Pounding The Pavement

For custom corporate cards, your clients will, of course, be other businesses. You can target just about any type, but your best bets will be those who need to stay firmly established in their customers' minds, like doctors, dentists, insurance agents, real estate brokers, apartment managers, car salespeople, hair stylists and shopkeepers. And don't forget those corporate types with customers, vendors and suppliers all over the country.

Sign up these clients by—how else?—sending them greeting cards. Design a catchy card that explains your business, then follow up by phoning for an appointment to show your card portfolio. Send a one-time mailing of your cards for a charitable organization free of charge—make sure the cards mention your company and what you do. Use this same mailing to get write-ups in local publications. Snoop friendly. While out and about town, ask business owners if they're planning a sale or promotion, then offer your services to send out card announcements.

If you choose the retail road, you'll sell to retailers or distributors. You can start out small by selling your wares to local specialty shops and boutiques or shoot for sales reps and distributors by displaying your products at trade shows like the National Stationery Show held each May in New York City. (Call George Little Management at 914-421-3200 or go to www.glmshows.com for more information.)

What's Next

Shop around for the best database and card-design programs, then get familiar with them—you can't send out cards in a timely fashion if you're stuck on figuring out how to pry the card out of the computer into the printer. Print up sample cards of various types and put them into a portfolio. Design and print brochures to leave with prospective clients. Network in your community. Shop around for the best prices on card stock, envelopes, and printing services.

Organizations

- *Greeting Card Association*, 1030 15th St. NW, #870, Washington, DC 20005, (202) 393-1778, www.greetingcard.org. (Check out the Web site for lots of terrific publications you can order, but keep in mind that you can only join the association once you're up and running as a greeting card publisher.)

Books

- *How to Make Money Publishing from Home: Everything You Need to Know to Successfully Publish: Books, Newsletters, Greeting Cards, Zines, and Software*, by Lisa Shaw, Prima Publishing

Publications

- *Giftware Business*, 1 Penn Plaza, New York, NY 10019, (800) 255-2824 (for subscriptions)
- *Giftware News Magazine*, 20 N. Wacker, #1865, Chicago, IL 60606, (800) 229-1967, www.giftwarenews.net
- *Greetings Etc.*, 10 Hanover Ave., #107, Randolph, NJ 07869, (800) 948-6189

Business Opportunities

- *CardSenders*, Boverie Investments Inc., 1201 Eubank Blvd. NE, #6, Albuquerque, NM 87112, (800) 843-6055, www.cardsenders.com
- *Babies 'N' Bells*, 2110 Springwood, Carrollton, TX 75006, (888) 418-BABY (2229), ext. 0, (972) 416-BABY (2229), www.babiesnbells.com (This company is a variation on the niche greeting cards theme—it specializes in custom birth announcements and invitations.)

ChaPter four

BITS & BYTES

So you're a computer wizard—the one everybody calls when the hard drive crashes, the printer won't print or they lose that letter to Aunt Nell in the depths of WordPerfect. If you can coax magic out of a keyboard, find anything online, and you proudly wear the badge of geek, then this is the category for you. Even if you're not a techno-nerd, but you've got advertising, marketing and graphic design talents coupled with Web knowledge, you can dive into the Internet surf and take advantage of the booming computer industry.

COMPUTER REPAIR & MAINTENANCE

The Inside Scoop

Everybody with a computer knows that moment of panic when the hard drive crashes—and for businesspeople, it usually happens when they're staring into the eye of a deadline. They can't pop the hood and tinker with the innards like they'd do with a car, and they can't have it towed to the local fix-it shop—and if they could, all the information on that ailing hard drive would sit in the shop, too. Panic turns to terror.

But if you're a computer physician capable of diagnosing virtual ills and then repairing them, you can take on the appearance of an angel of mercy as a computer repair specialist.

You'll drive out to clients' homes or offices with your black bag (or briefcase) of tools and equipment and heal those sickly computers and printers. You can also earn tidy revenues with preventive medicine—er, maintenance—dusting or vacuuming innards and cleaning disk drives on a quarterly or semiannual basis.

The advantages to this business are that it's recession-proof—businesses need computers to operate, and home-computer buffs can't live without their virtual pals, either. And since the computer industry is one of exponential growth, peripheral industries like computer maintenance and repair are here to stay. As a final plus, this business is satisfying—people are always appreciative when you bring an acutely ill hard drive or printer back to health.

The disadvantages are that panicky people can tend to be cranky. Also, in some states, you must have a license and a storefront to practice computer repair. (In this case you can specialize in maintenance and farm out repair work, perhaps to a shop that will share its fee with you for bringing in business.)

Essentials

You'll need to have the knowledge and skills of a good computer physician, including how to change motherboards, repair and replace hard drives, and add memory chips. And you should have a good computer-side manner so you can soothe panicky owners and tactfully instill the benefits of good preventive maintenance.

Tools Of The Trade

You'll need a computer, an inkjet or laser printer, computer tinkering tools like screwdrivers and miniature vacuums, computer cleaning supplies, diagnostic software, commonly used parts, and reference manuals. In some states, you'll need a license and a commercial shop to perform repairs; be sure to check with the business licensing department.

Money Talk

You can prescribe start-up costs of about $3,500, unless you need a license and commercial shop—in which case your costs will be dependent on what lease you negotiate or whether you can base your operation in your garage. Annual gross revenues for computer repair services range from $30,000 to $75,000. Charge your clients $20 to $50 per hour—base your rates on comparable ones in your area.

Pounding The Pavement

Your clients can be anybody with a computer, both businesses and individuals. Mail brochures, perhaps with a dentist-type appointment card to be filled in, to local businesses. Leave business cards and fliers with computer and software retailers. Place ads in the Yellow Pages and your local newspaper, and get yourself written up in the paper. Give talks on computer maintenance to professional and civic organizations and at local colleges and other adult-education centers.

What's Next

Find out if you'll need a license—if so, establish relationships with local computer repair services to whom you can contract work you get from your maintenance clients. If you feel you need experience, offer to work on the computers of friends, neighbors and relatives free of charge. They'll love the service and will act as your best advertising by spreading the word.

Books

- *The Hand-Me-Down PC: Upgrading and Repairing Personal Computers*, by Morris Rosenthal, Computing McGraw-Hill
- *PC Hardware Fat FAQs: Troubleshooting, Upgrading, Maintaining and Repairing*, by Stephen J. Bigelow, Computing McGraw-Hill
- *Upgrading and Repairing PCs*, by Scott Mueller and Craig Zacker, Que Education & Training

Cyber Assistance

- *PC Magazine Online* (www.zdnet.com/pcmag/hotlinks/index.html): Visit this site for links to lots of tech information and support.
- *Smart Computing* (www.smartcomputing.com): Besides the usual assortment of computer-oriented articles, the site contains nifty tutorials on all sorts of installation and upgrade issues.

Franchises

- *Computer Doctor Franchise Systems Inc.*, P.O. Box 487, 12 Second Ave. SW, Aberdeen, SD 57401, (888) 297-2292, www.cdfs.com
- *Support On-Site Computer Services*, 23161 Lake Center Dr., #125, Lake Forest, CA 92630, (949) 768-3398, www.support-onsite.com

COMPUTER TRAINING

The Inside Scoop

Computers and computer programs are among the most wonderful tools available—as long as you know how to use them. If you don't, you quickly learn the true meaning of frustration. And let's face it: Most programs—despite what the blurb on the back of the box may say—are not cuddly. Which leaves lots of would-be computer users, especially businesspeople, floundering instead of working successfully.

But if you're intimately familiar with one or more software packages, then you can transform the virtually flummoxed into virtual wizards (or at least computer-savvy souls) with a computer-training business. This is a hot field—according to the International Data Corporation, the worldwide market for technical computer training is nearing the $28 billion mark, with an annual average of $8,200 spent for information systems staff training and $3,000 per person spent on general staff training.

You can specialize in the software program or programs you know best like Microsoft Word, WordPerfect or Lotus applications; in a field you're familiar with like law or medicine; or, if you've got a broad base of software smarts, you can be a computer G.P., training clients in a wide variety of programs and packages. And you can work one-on-one with individual clients—from tots to seniors—or train a roomful of employees at a time for corporations.

The advantages to this business are that you're out and about, working with lots of different people; helping folks overcome computer-phobia is always rewarding; and because you have to keep up with ever-changing technology and software updates, you've got the best excuse in the world for buying new computer goodies on a regular basis.

The disadvantages are that it can be tedious to cover the basics with clients who sometimes seem dead-set on not learning, and although there's lots of room for growth in the business, it can also be competitive.

Essentials

You should know inside and out at least one software package, commonly used by the mass computer market or by a particular industry. But it's not enough to be a software egghead—you'll also need the ability to communicate your knowledge to others. Other must-haves are the patience to help clients conquer computer-phobia and the communication skills to transfer your enthusiasm and techniques to your pupils.

Tools Of The Trade

You'll need your own computer and up-to-date versions of the software you'll teach, along with a good word-processing or desktop-publishing program, and—naturally—an inkjet or laser printer, so you can spin out training materials. To go with this, you'll want a desktop projector and a laser pointer so a classroom of clients can see what you're doing.

Weekend Warrior

DATA ARCHIVER

For individuals and especially for businesses, one of the worst things that can happen is losing files in a computer crash. But most people never get around to backing up their data—it takes a lot of time, it's tedious, and there are too many other crises demanding attention. If you're a maestro at the computer keyboard, you can stave off data-loss disaster as a data archiver. You'll back up files, then neatly label and date them. Offer one-time service or sign up clients for periodic backups. Send brochures to homebased businesses and establish relationships with computer retailers and repair people who can refer you to their customers. **Start-up costs:** $500. **Expected annual gross revenues:** $10,000 to $12,000.

Money Talk

Key in costs of $3,500 to $5,500, depending on whether you'll keep your present computer or buy a new baby. You may want to add in another $500 to $1,000 for professional organizational dues. Annual revenues for a computer trainer range from $60,000 to $250,000. Charge your clients by the hour, the day, or on a per-workshop basis—an average range would be $40 to $60 per hour for private instruction or $140 to $180 per hour for a full-day group session, but you should price your services comparably with others in your area.

Pounding The Pavement

Your clients can be private individuals or corporate types who want to make their employees computer-literate. To get the business from private parties, establish relationships with computer retailers and ask them to refer customers to you. (Be sure to leave a stack of business cards for them to hand out.) Place ads in local newspapers and the Yellow Pages.

Solicit companies and corporations through direct-mail campaigns and network at professional, civic and trade organizations. Place ads in industry journals and other publications. Another excellent technique is to get certified or licensed from software manufacturers or vendors who will then refer customers to you. (Sometimes there's a fee involved for getting certified; sometimes it's a freebie.)

What's Next

Decide what programs and industries you'll specialize in. Then make sure you're up to speed with the most recent versions and all the permutations of each one.

Organizations

- *Computer Technology Industry Association*, www.comptia.org
- *ITrain—International Association of Information Technology Trainers*, 9810 Patuxent Woods Dr., Columbia, MD 21046, (410) 290-7000, www.itrain.org

Books

- *The Complete Computer Trainer*, by Paul Clothier, Computing McGraw-Hill
- *The Computer Trainer's Personal Training Guide*, by Bill Brandon (editor), Que Education & Training
- *How to Run Seminars and Workshops: Presentation Skills for Consultants, Trainers, and Teachers*, by Robert L. Jolles, John Wiley & Sons

Franchises

- *Compu-Fun*, 2 David Dr., Pelham, NH 03076, (877) COMPU-FUN
- *The Fourth R*, 1715 Market St., #103, Kirkland, WA 98033, (800) 821-8653, www.fourthr.com
- *New Horizons Computer Learning Centers*, 1231 E. Dyer Rd., #110, Santa Ana, CA 92705-5643, (714) 432-7600, www.newhorizons.com

E-ZINE PUBLISHER

The Inside Scoop

If you've always wanted to be a high-powered magazine publisher, working with writers and editors and setting trends for the nation, here's your chance. As an e-zine (online magazine) publisher, you can do all these things and more without ever paying a penny for printing or mailing. Your choices for style and content are wide open—women's and teens' issues are perennially popular, but you can devote your publication to just about any lifestyle, sport, hobby or profession that appeals to you, so long as you can find a significant readership and the advertisers to sponsor your efforts.

You'll also be at the helm of an online community because e-zines are more than magazines—they're interactive forums connecting readers to readers and readers to you. To encourage this sense of community, you'll host message boards, chat sessions and live interviews with experts in your audience's interest area.

The advantages to this business are that it's mega-creative, as challenging as any hard-copy publishing project, and far less expensive to launch than a paper magazine because you bypass the twin nemeses of printing and postage. And with a successful e-zine, you can make a significant impact on your readers' lives (and they on yours).

The disadvantages are that, like traditional paper publications, it can take up to five years to find yourself in the black, and—as with any publishing venture—you'll find yourself in a world where deadlines are a daily drama.

Essentials

As an e-zine publisher, you'll need to have your fingers on the pulse of your niche community, whether it be teenage girls, working parents or quilters. You must intimately understand what your audience wants, needs, thinks and feels—and then know how to deliver. You'll need all the skills of a traditional magazine publisher, including top-notch writing and editing abilities, the ability to guide contributors toward your particular vision, and the marketing smarts to attract advertisers and other sponsors.

In addition to all of this, you'll need to be able to build, maintain and update a Web site, or else be able to farm out these tasks. (If not, you have no e-zine.)

Tools Of The Trade

You'll need a computer with a speedy 56K modem, a high-quality scanner, a digital camera and software—start with Web site creation software like Microsoft's FrontPage or NetObjects' Fusion, a desktop publishing program and a good word-processing package. You'll want to register your domain name (the e-commerce version of trademarking your site), and you'll have to link to an Internet service provider that will get your 'zine out to all your readers.

Money Talk

While it's possible to get a small and intimate e-zine up and running for $500 to $1,000 (assuming you already have the computer), you'll need closer to $20,000 to develop one that's a major presence—the money will go toward writers, editors and other staff. This is cutting-edge publishing, so new that it's difficult to determine just what you can expect in the way of annual revenues. Of course, like any traditional paper publication, the more advertisers you attract, the higher your bottom line will be, but you can (and should) also go the budget/newbie route and develop revenues from advertising tie-ins with other Web sites. And remember that it's highly unlikely you'll see any profits for several years, so keep your day job, start with a giant capital infusion or marry rich.

Pounding The Pavement

Your market will be entirely dependent on what interest community you choose to serve. Once you decide on this, you can start direct-mail and direct e-mail campaigns to alert potential readers to your site. Establish links to complementary sites around the Web, send press releases to magazines or journals with the same target readership, and start a Net ad campaign.

You can also chat up non-Net sponsors who might be interested in developing a Web presence with your help—which will help you as well.

What's Next

Do your market research to make sure you'll have a significant readership in your area of interest. Scrutinize other e-zine communities of all types to see how they do it and how well it works. Then start devising your own style and format.

Organizations

● *Magazine Publishers of America Inc.*, 919 Third Ave., 22nd Fl., New York, NY 10022, (888) 567-3228

Books

● *How to Make Money Publishing From Home: Everything You Need to Know to Successfully Publish: Books, Newsletters, Greeting Cards, Zines, and Software*, by Lisa Shaw, Prima Publishing

● *Make A Zine: A Guide to Self-Publishing Disguised as a Book on How to Produce a Zine!*, by Bill Brent, Black Books

● *Zine Scene: The Do-It-Yourself Guide to Zines*, by Francesca Lia Block and Hilary Carlip, Girl Press

Cyber Assistance

● *Books A to Z* (www.satoz.com): This site bills itself as "your complete publishing tool box" and provides lots of links and other goodies for the Web and paper publisher.

● *WritersNet* (www.writers.net): Find writers, editors, agents and other publishers on this handy site.

INTERNET TRAINING

The Inside Scoop

Very soon, being in business without using the Internet will be like trying to conduct business without a telephone. According to a recent U.S. Department of Commerce report, more than 100 million surfers are out there hanging 10 on the Net. Even so, there are lots of folks who don't have a clue how to access the World Wide Web or where to go once they're on it.

If you're a Net whiz—you know all about Web sites, search engines and Usenets and you like nothing better than tinkering online—then you can help businesspeople learn how to navigate the information superhighway with ease as an Internet trainer.

You'll give seminars, workshops, day-long courses or one-on-one assistance to corporate executives, homebased businesspeople and individuals eager to join cyber society. And you can teach the basics or tailor your programs to the specific types of Net-surfing your clients need to know.

The advantages to this business are that—assuming you already have a computer—you can start on a shoestring, and because the industry is still in its relative infancy, there's plenty of room for growth. Plus, you get to play on the Internet every day!

The disadvantages are that going over and over the same basics can be tedious and that you may need to market your business aggressively.

Essentials

As an Internet trainer, you'll naturally need a solid background in navigating the Net, including aspects like Internet marketing and research. You'll need the patience to guide computer-phobic types through their paces, even when it seems to you that they should have picked it up a dozen mouse clicks back. And you should have the marketing skills to both land new clients and take advantage of repeat business.

Tools Of The Trade

All you really need to get started are your computer and a few online services so you can research clients' specific needs and how to solve them before you arrive on-site. You should have a laser or inkjet printer for banging out cheat sheets and guides, and if you'll be giving seminars, you'll want a desktop projector and a laser pointer so the whole group can see what you're doing.

Money Talk

Start-up costs can run as low as $2,500 to $4,500, depending on whether you go out and buy a new computer or stick with the one you already have. Annual gross revenues for an Internet trainer range from $60,000 to $250,000. Charge your clients on an hourly or daily basis or by the workshop—an average range would be $40 to $60 per hour for private instruction or $140 to $180 per hour for a full-day group session, but you should price your services comparably with others in your area.

Pounding The Pavement

Your clients can be large and small businesses—from major corporations to SOHOs to nonprofit organizations to government agencies and library systems—and individuals, from retirees to school kids. Start a direct-mail campaign aimed at businesses. Give seminars and workshops at local colleges and community centers—this identifies you as an expert and is a good way to garner business and individual clients. Establish relationships with computer stores and ask them to refer you to customers.

What's Next

Shop your competition and find out what the going prices are in your area and whether other local Internet trainers teach the basics or specialize in a particular niche. Adjust your target market accordingly and get Net surfing!

Organizations

- *Computer Technology Industry Association*, www.comptia.org
- *ITrain—International Association of Information Technology Trainers*, 9810 Patuxent Woods Dr., Columbia, MD 21046, (410) 290-7000, www.itrain.org

Books

- *The McGraw-Hill Internet Training Manual*, by Ronald Wagner and Eric Englemann, McGraw-Hill Book Co.
- *Searching Smart on the World Wide Web: Tools and Techniques for Getting Quality Results*, by Cheryl Gould, Library Solutions Press
- *A Trainer's Guide to the World Wide Web and Intranets: Using On-Line Technology to Create Powerful, Cost-Effective Learning in Your Organization*, by Wendy Webb, HRD Press

Cyber Assistance

- *Internet magazine* (www.internet-magazine.com): A British 'zine with a British flavor—but what's geography in cyberspace? Site reviews, articles, cybercafes, an expert help section and more.

Publications

- *Inside Technology Training*, 10 Presidents Landing, Medford, MA 02155, (888) 950-4302, www.ittrain.com

WEB SITE DESIGNER

The Inside Scoop

If you're in business today, a Web site is as important as an ad in the Yellow Pages. With a Web presence, you've got access to millions of potential customers around the world—it's like rolling out a major advertising supplement, marketing brochure and mail order catalog in one easily updated package. And all without printing, postage or phone costs! According to the U.S. Department of Commerce, Internet traffic is doubling every 100 days, with Web commerce expected to surpass $300 billion by 2002.

The problem is that for most people, designing a Web site is on a par with building your own TV set—a major mystery best left unexplored. But if you can unlock the secrets of HTML (hypertext markup language) and you've got a flair for graphics and copywriting, then Web site design could be the business for you.

The advantages to this business are that it's creative, you can start part time if you like on a minimum budget, and even if you don't already know HTML, it's not difficult to learn once you set your mind to it. And you can deal with clients in any geographic region without leaving your computer.

The only disadvantage is that this is one of those lone-wolf businesses, with no one around but you and your computer. So if you're a procrastinator or just not a self-starter, you can easily get bogged down, distracted or otherwise lose your edge.

Essentials

You don't need to be a computer techie, wizard or geek, but you should have a good rapport with your computer and have mastered the basic skills to get around in cyberspace. You'll also need a talent for graphics and copywriting because your goal for each client will be not only to get the Web site up and running but to design one that's easy to navigate through, visually appealing, and clearly yet cleverly worded.

Tools Of The Trade

As a Web site designer, your most important tool will be, of course, your computer; make sure yours has a sporty modem with a 56K connection speed or go for a cable connection. You'll also need a scanner (inexpensive is OK), Web page creation software, and a graphic design package. If your Web page software doesn't have the oomph to upload files to the Internet service provider, you'll want a program to carry out this task.

Money Talk

If you already have a computer that's up to the task, you can get started for less than $1,000—if you don't, pencil in another $1,500 to $2,000. You might also want to add in another $1,000 for professional organization membership fees. Annual gross revenues for Web site designers run the gamut, according to the Association of Internet Professionals, with pricing from $25 to $500 per hour, depending on whether you're doing a simple home page for a very small company or a major online catalog with shopping cart technology for a big spender (or a firm that hopes its customers will spend big).

Pounding The Pavement

Your clients will be businesses—you can target everything from SOHOs to nonprofit organizations to professional associations to government agencies. Choose a geographic or specialty area to start with—say, small businesses in your community or real estate agencies—then send direct-mail pieces explaining the values of a Web site and your services.

Put up your own Web site both to attract business and to serve as a sample of your work, and establish links with other Internet sites so potential clients can find you through as many paths as possible.

What's Next

If you don't know how to build a Web site, get learning—assuming you're already computer-literate, you should be able to grasp HTML in less than a month. Surf the Web and study all sorts of sites,

A STAR IS BORN

Web Wild

If you think a Web site is just a collection of HTML codes and pixels arranged on a virtual page, think again. "A Web site is a living, breathing organism," says Roy Fletcher of Fletcher Consulting Inc. in Pembroke Pines, Florida. To be successful, it has to change frequently, showing off new products, sprouting new information and giving customers a reason for repeat visits. That's what keeps Fletcher's Web site design and marketing company hopping.

Fletcher, 43, quietly boasts just under 50 clients, all of whom come to him first for the design process and then for all those site updates. And then, of course, there's the e-commerce stuff—affiliate programs, ad auctions and banners, to name a few. "Immerse yourself in what's going on out there," Fletcher advises would-be Web marketers. "Develop an awareness of what works and what doesn't. Marketing is not a science; it's much fuzzier than Web design."

The Internet guru admits that Web site design and Web marketing are two distinct entities, yet he's fused them into a single successful business. With a background in education, accounting, systems, and managing and marketing PCs, Fletcher realized when the World Wide Web broke onto the scene that it was right up all his alley and promptly dove in. He does the heavy-duty design and development stuff out of a home office but shares a support staff and—when it's time to meet with clients—conference space with a local CPA firm.

What's the best way to Net those clients? With the exception of his own Web site, Fletcher does no advertising. Instead, he networks—with CPA firms, general business organizations, friends and former clients. And in the early days of his business, he produced some projects for nominal fees as a way to get the word out. Although his networking takes the form of connecting with already-established contacts, Fletcher advises newbies to join professional and civic organizations.

analyzing them for what works graphically and verbally and what doesn't. Then get creative and design your own.

Organizations

- *Association of Internet Professionals*, 9200 Sunset Blvd., 6th Fl., Los Angeles, CA 90069, (800) JOIN-AIP, www.association.org. Check out the "Cool Links" section for gazillions of great resources.
- *International Webmasters Association*, 556 S. Fair Oaks Ave., #101-200, Pasadena, CA 91105, (626) 449-3709, www.iwanet.org

Books

- *Creating Killer Web Sites*, by David Siegel, Hayden Books
- *Creating Web Pages for Dummies*, by Bud E. Smith and Arthur Bebak, IDG Books Worldwide
- *Web Authoring Desk Reference*, by Aaron Weiss (editor), et al., Hayden Books

Publications

- *Web Techniques*, Miller Freeman Inc., 411 Borel Ave., #100, San Mateo, CA 94402, (650) 358-9500, www.webtechniques.com
- *Wired*, 520 Third St., 4th Fl., San Francisco, CA 94107, (800) 769-4733

Cyber Assistance

- *CommerceNet* (www.commerce.net): All sorts of materials for the e-commerce community, including the e-newsletter Buzz@ Commerce.net
- *The HTML Writer's Guild* (www.hwg.org): More resources than you can imagine! A must-surf.
- *IWA's Webmastering Resources* (www.iwanet.org/member/resources/index.html): Everything for the Web newbie—authoring, ethics, marketing, multimedia, programming, security, server technology and more
- *Webmonkey* (www.hotwired.com/webmonkey): A little weird, but fun. Bills itself as a how-to guide for Web developers—and it is.

WEB SITE MARKETING CONSULTANT

The Inside Scoop

Companies large and small are getting used to the Internet Age facts of life, one of which is that you must have a Web site. According to the U.S. Department of Commerce, some 10 million consumers in America and Canada recently purchased something via the Internet, up from 4.7 million buyers just six months earlier. But just having a Web site doesn't guarantee a company an increase in business—if those millions of potential customers don't happen to stumble on it, you're spinning your virtual wheels. What's a company to do?

If you're Net-wise and marketing-smart, you can be the solution to this dilemma as a Web site marketing consultant. You'll seek out new ways to increase a client's Web site traffic and boost sales by setting up links to other sites, developing new site content or services, creating direct-marketing programs via e-mail, and devising Web advertising campaigns.

The advantages to this business are that it's creative, challenging and has staying power—Net business is a reality and therefore Net advertising and marketing is a necessity.

The disadvantages are that, as with any cutting-edge business, you can spend what seems like an inordinate amount of time educating clients and potential clients, and, as with traditional advertising, it can be extremely competitive.

Essentials

As a Web site marketing consultant, you'll naturally need to be a whiz when it comes to the Web, with plenty of experience in links, banners, affiliate programs and all the other fine points of Net navigation and promotion. You should also have traditional advertising and marketing talents so you can invent your own unique online twists to make your clients' sites shine.

Tools Of The Trade

You'll need a computer with a high-speed modem (56K is a nice number), an inkjet or laser printer, and subscriptions to a wide variety of Internet service providers and online communities. And since you'll want to develop your own niche market—which is the best way to avoid being buried by the competition—you'll also want subscriptions to your niche's professional or trade magazines and journals.

Money Talk

Start-up costs can run as low $2,650, but you might want to key in another $1,000 for professional organization memberships. Annual gross revenues for Web site marketing consultants range from minimal to major, according to the Association of Internet Professionals. Yours will depend on how you price your services—you can go from $25 to $500 per hour, depending on the types of programs you're devising, the going rates in your area, and what your chosen client base can afford.

Pounding The Pavement

Your clients will be businesses with up-and-running but not necessarily successful Web sites. Decide on a target market, preferably one you already have experience with, then start a direct-mail campaign aimed at companies in that field. Erect your own Web site and build links to other Internet sites—this will help potential clients find you, too.

What's Next

If you're not already an Internet marketing expert, become one by reading everything you can and studying existing advertising and marketing techniques on the Net. Then get selling your services!

Organizations

- *Association of Internet Professionals*, 9200 Sunset Blvd., 6th Fl., Los Angeles, CA 90069, (800) JOIN-AIP, www.association.org

Books

- *Advertising on the Web*, by Jim Sterne, Que Education & Training
- *Guerrilla Marketing Online Weapons: 100 Low-Cost, High-Impact Weapons for Online Profits and Prosperity*, by Jay Conrad Levinson and Charles Rubin, Houghton Mifflin Co.
- *Web Advertising and Marketing by Design*, by Mary Jo Fahey, Microsoft Press

Cyber Assistance

- *CommerceNet*, (www.commerce.net): Everything for the e-commerce-inclined, including the e-newsletter Buzz@Commerce.net
- *Inside the Internet* (www.zdjournals.com/int/): An ezine featuring tips and articles for the Web-wise

Franchises

- *Connect.Ad Inc.*, 1000 W. McNab Rd., #236, Pompano Beach, FL 33069, (954) 942-5070, www.connectad.com
- *Zland Inc.*, 1221 E. Dyer Rd., #285, Santa Ana, CA 92705-5635, (714) 708-8580, www.zland.com

Cha**p**ter five

COOKIN' GOOD!

Do you love cooking— or any- thing to do with food? If you're always experimenting with new dishes, your friends adore visiting because your kitchen smells like a Keebler Elf cookie factory, and you'd rather analyze secret ingredients than the secrets of the ages, then this is the category for you.

The Inside Scoop

If you're one of those fearless people who enjoys giving elegant dinner parties, you get rave reviews from guests and your relatives beg to have holidays at your house because of your cooking, then catering might be your cup of tea.

As a caterer, you'll plan menus and elegant or playful presentations for everything from company picnics to debutante balls, then cook it all up, deliver it to the event, serve it and clean up afterward. You can specialize in affairs like weddings; specific goodies like cakes or cookies; or clients like corporations, charities or individual parties.

Essentials

While your family may clamor for mom's meatloaf and mashed potatoes, you'll need more than just the ability to whip up some spuds. You'll also need a flair for presentation—the ability to make the fruits (and other foods) of your labors look fancy—as well as a talent for the latest trends in foods and party ideas. You'll also need an abundance of organizational, time-management and record-keeping skills. Catering requires lots of hard-core planning and pacing—you have to be able to produce 12 dozen piping-hot artichoke puffs on cue while making sure the Baked Alaska doesn't scorch, the roast is nicely browned and the guests haven't run out of Washington Indiscretion on ice.

Last but not least, you need a good grounding in safe food-handling practices, product liability laws and health regulations, and good people skills—nobody wants a cranky caterer.

The advantages to this business are that it's creative and fun—you can throw a party any time you like and serve up all sorts of new dishes and new ideas—and somebody else foots the bill. It's gratifying—people always appreciate being fed, and when your presentation is elegant or intriguing, they're impressed as well. You can start part time and you can base your office at home.

The biggest disadvantage is that in most states, you can't serve food cooked in your own kitchen, so you'll have to rent a commercial facility or have your home kitchen converted into an approved commercial one. Other disadvantages are that you may need to hire servers and clean-up people (depending on the size of the function you cater); you'll generally have to work evenings and weekends, as these are favored party times; and work tends to be seasonal with the emphasis on summer weddings and winter holiday parties.

Tools Of The Trade

Other than a commercial kitchen, the only things you need to get started are a phone and a delivery vehicle. A computer and printer are always nice but not a necessity for starters. You can get around the kitchen problem by arranging to use a restaurant's facility for a small fee in its off-hours or by sharing the rental costs of a commercial kitchen and its use with other caterers.

Money Talk

According to the National Association of Catering Executives (NACE), start-up costs are next to nothing but will depend on whether you rent a kitchen and what rental arrangements you make. Annual gross revenues for off-premises caterers (meaning you're not on the staff of a hotel or restaurant) range from $50,000 to $100,000 and up. Charge your clients a 40 percent markup over what you pay for your ingredients. You can also charge extra for linens, dishes, glasses and other fineries.

Pounding The Pavement

Your clients can be people with something to celebrate—a wedding, anniversary, graduation or other milestone—or any other kind

COOKING INSTRUCTOR

Gourmet cooking has romantic and glamorous connotations—candlelit dinners, elegant table settings and sophisticated cooks. If you know the secrets to fine-food preparation, you can capitalize on all this as a cooking instructor. Host classes in your home—if your kitchen's big enough for a small crowd—or arrange with a local high school or college to use its home economics facilities. Offer a community education class through your local unified school district, advertise in your local newspaper and leave brochures with gourmet foods and culinary equipment shops, and you'll soon have students eating out of your hands, er, pots and pans. **Start-up costs:** $500. **Expected annual gross revenues:** Up to $25,000.

of bash. You can go after the corporate market, helping to make a splash at conferences, meetings, employee-morale boosters and grand openings, or you can set a course for businesses like yacht charters, sunset cruises and dinner theaters.

To snag the celebratory types, develop a referral network—introduce yourself to wedding planners, bridal boutiques, cake decorators and bakers, florists, and card and party supply shopkeepers. Hand out brochures and business cards and check in often. Bring a few choice tidbits, snazzy hors d'ouevres or sinful desserts to give as goodwill gestures. Everybody loves an unexpected treat and the person who delivers it—this is a good way to ensure that they remember you fondly and refer you to their own clients.

For corporate and other business types, send a sales letter and brochure, then follow up with a phone call requesting an appointment to discuss your services.

Cater a charity event in exchange for publicity, then get your company written up in local publications. Volunteer yourself for a local radio chat show and answer questions about throwing successful parties.

What's Next

Check with local health authorities; if you need a commercial kitchen, start shopping for one. Find out what other caterers in your area charge so you can price yourself accordingly. Do a few parties for friends in exchange for the experience and the word-of-mouth advertisement.

Organizations

- *International Association of Culinary Professionals*, 304 W. Liberty St., #301, Louisville, KY 40202, (800) 928-4227, www.iacp-online.org
- *National Association of Catering Executives*, 60 Revere Dr., #500, Northbrook, IL 60062, (847) 480-9080, www.nace.net

Books

- *Catering Like a Pro: From Planning to Profit*, by Francine Halvorsen, John Wiley & Sons
- *Catering: Start and Run a Money-Making Business*, by Judy Richards, Replica Books
- *Entrepreneur's Business Start-Up Guide #1400, Food Service Business*, Entrepreneur Media Inc., 2392 Morse Ave., Irvine, CA 92614, (800) 421-2300, www.smallbizbooks.com
- *How to Become a Caterer: Everything You Need to Know from Finding Clients to the Final Bill*, by Susan Wright, Citadel Press
- *How to Manage a Successful Catering Business*, by Manfred Ketterer, John Wiley & Sons
- *How to Run a Catering Business from Home*, by Christopher Egerton-Thomas, John Wiley & Sons

Publications

- *Food Arts: The Magazine for Professionals*, 387 Park Ave. S., New York, NY 10016, (212) 684-4224, (800) 848-7113 (for subscriptions)

Cyber Assistance

- *Foodnet* (www.foodnet.com): Bills itself as the place for food-service professionals to make their home on the Net—and it is. Food chat, food news, food links, chefs and cooks, and more.
- *The Global Gourmet* (www.globalgourmet.com): Wow! It's all here—holiday information, cookbook profiles, wines, celebrity chefs, recipes—and how can you resist the monthly feature, "I Love Chocolate"?

COOKIE ARRANGEMENTS

The Inside Scoop

Everybody loves receiving flowers, and everybody loves cookies. If you're a cookie magician—you buy every magazine at the market that features cookie recipes on the cover and then bake up a storm—you can say it with flowers of the cookie kind with a cookie gift business.

You can sell a single cookie on a "stem" or a huge bouquet of tasty morsels in one of several varieties: macadamia nut, oatmeal raisin, the ever-popular chocolate chip—whatever suits your fancy. Bouquets can be tailored to specific events: wedding or anniversary arrangements of meringue kisses, a devil's food divorce posy, or a new baby bouquet of chocolate-chip-off-the-old-block cookies.

The advantages to this business are that it's fun, creative and gratifying—you'd be hard pressed to find anyone who doesn't adore cookies.

The main disadvantage is that the business can be seasonal, with Valentine's Day being the single biggest holiday on the cookie calendar. (You can overcome this difficulty by encouraging customers to give cookies for every special occasion you can dream up, including Secretaries Day, Bosses Day, End of School, Back to School, Halloween and the Fourth of July.) You'll also need to consider that the fresher your products, the better they'll taste and smell, which means that you'll have to be on the hop to take orders, keep cooking and deliver all at the same time.

Essentials

You'll need to be a mean cookie chef—no burnt bottoms allowed—as well as possess a good working knowledge of safe food-handling practices and health regulations, sales and marketing techniques, and of course, a major dollop of creativity.

Tools Of The Trade

Since it's illegal in most states to make foods for commercial consumption in your home kitchen, you'll have to rent or arrange for commercial facilities like an after-hours school kitchen, co-op or business incubator facility, or have your own kitchen converted to comply with Health Department regulations.

Money Talk

Start-up costs, including your initial gift and supplies inventory, can run as low as $5,000, which does not include converting or renting your own kitchen. Annual gross sales for cookie bouquet designers can range from $20,000 to more than $200,000 if you've got a strong corporate clientele. Cookie bouquets sell for anywhere from $23 to $77 each, depending, of course, on what comes with it; a single long-stemmed cookie—which may smell sweeter than a rose—goes for $2 to $6.

Pounding The Pavement

Your clients can be just about anybody or any business you care to target, from the cookie-monster-on-the-street to corporate types out to impress customers. You can also sell to restaurants and gift boutiques. Hotel, inn and yacht or plane charters—any business that wants to surprise and pamper its guests—also make good cookie bouquet clients.

Have those business clients eating out of your hand by delivering bouquets, along with a brochure, to the people who'll make buying decisions. Offer bouquet-giving suggestions; for example, tell salespeople they can give potential customers a long-stemmed cookie tied up with a business card, or suggest to bed-and-breakfast owners that they place a small bouquet in their guests' rooms.

Donate a cookie bouquet to be sold at a charity auction, or a give a batch of single-stemmed cookies to attendees of a charity lunch or dinner. Get your business—and your donations—written up in local publications. Place ads in local papers.

What's Next

Develop cookie recipes that you can bake in large quantities. (You won't have any trouble finding taste-testers.) Check with local health authorities to find out if you can bake at home; if not, investigate alternatives like renting a commercial kitchen, joining a cooking co-op that shares rent on a facility, or using a restaurant or school kitchen during off-hours.

Books

- *125 Cookies to Bake, Nibble and Savor*, by Elinor Klivans, Bantam Books
- *Maida Heatter's Brand-New Book of Great Cookies*, by Maida Heatter, Random House

Franchises

- *Cookies by Design/Cookie Bouquet*, MGW Group Inc., 1865 Summit Ave., #3605, Plano, TX 75074, (800) 945-2665, www. cookiebouquet.com
- *Cookie Cadabra/Cookies in Bloom*, 5437 N. MacArthur Blvd., Irving, TX 75038, (800) 222-3104, www.cookiecadabra.com

NUTRITIONIST

The Inside Scoop

Nutrition is big in everybody's minds these days—people want to live longer, think smarter, eat healthier and weigh less doing it. As a nutritionist, you'll help your clients attain all these goals through a variety of venues—you can act as a personal diet coach or as a consultant to restaurants and food manufacturers, give classes and seminars, or work with health clubs and health-conscious companies.

If you like teaching other people about healthy lifestyles, cheering on their achievements and motivating them through plateaus, then this is the business for you.

The advantages to being a nutritionist are that you can tangibly measure your success through your clients' successes, you can make a positive difference in others' lives, and you can do it all for a small start-up cost, start on a part-time basis, and work from home.

The only real disadvantage is that you can't help people who don't want to help themselves. You'll inevitably encounter clients who refuse to take your advice, and you'll have to go over the same ground repeatedly while keeping your cool and devising new motivational techniques.

Essentials

You'll need a strong knowledge of health, nutrition and psychology, along with sales and marketing skills to snap up clients. You can get (or you may already have) a registered dietician degree (called an RD) from the American Dietetic Association. This is a definite plus but not a necessity. Since state licensing and certifications for nutritionists vary, call your state Board of Dietetics and Nutrition.

Tools Of The Trade

About all you'll need is a computer, a printer and the usual software for creating sales letters, brochures, menus and other materials for your clients.

Money Talk

Expect to spend about $2,150 on your start-up. You can expect to earn annual gross revenues of $22,500 to $45,000. Charge your clients $15 to $30 per hour, depending on the going rates in your area and your own level of expertise.

Pounding The Pavement

Your clients can be just about anybody you care to target: individuals or corporations. You can coach on a personal level in your clients' homes or offices; you can also work as a consultant for health clubs, large companies or institutions. If you choose to work with clients on a one-to-one basis as a coach, place ads in local publications. Network in your community. Offer your services to one lucky person at a charity auction or raffle in exchange for free advertising. Make up a brochure and mail it to people in the middle- to upper-income levels of your town.

Send brochures and sales letters describing your services to corporate, institutional and health-club prospects, then follow up with phone calls requesting appointments.

What's Next

Decide what type of clients you want to work with; then—if you don't have an RD—check with local authorities to make sure you can offer your services without certification. Make up a list of exactly what services you'll offer. For example, if you'll be a personal nutrition coach, will you go through clients' cupboards, eliminating evil foods? Take them on a personal supermarket tour to teach label reading? Make up menus?

Organizations

- *The American Dietetic Association*, 216 W. Jackson Blvd., #800, Chicago, IL 60606-6995, (800) 366-1655, www.eatright.org

Books

- *Building a Profitable Nutrition Practice*, by D. Katie Weidman and Dorothy J. Paige, Van Nostrand Reinhold
- *Dietetics: Practice and Future Trends*, by Esther A. Winterfeldt, Ph.D., Margaret L. Bogle, Ph.D., and Lea L. Ebro, Aspen Publishers
- *Nutrition and Diet Therapy*, by Carroll A. Lutz and Karen Rutherford Przytulski, F.A. Davis Co.

Publications

- *Journal of The American Dietetic Association*, The American Dietetic Association, P.O. Box 97215, Chicago, IL 60678-7215, (800) 366-1655

Cyber Assistance

- *Dietsite.com* (www.dietsite.com): Information on sports and alternative nutrition, diet and nutritional analysis, diet news, a chat room and more

PERSONAL CHEF

The Inside Scoop

The dream of many an American these days is to throw open the door after a long day at the office and be greeted by the homey aroma of dinner in the oven. With more and more two-income families, bread-winning single parents and hardworking young singles, however, supper is more often than not of the TV-dinner variety. But if you like cooking and the warm, fuzzy feeling of nourishing hungry bodies and weary spirits, you can save the day (or more properly, the dinner hour) with a personal chef service.

As a personal chef, you'll meet with clients to ascertain their food likes, dislikes and diet preferences, then plan meals, shop for groceries, and cook a week's worth to a month's worth of suppers to stash in the freezer in your clients' kitchens.

The advantages to this business are that it's creative, it's gratifying—there's no one so appreciative as a well-fed soul—start-up costs are low and you can start part time if you like.

The only disadvantage is that this is a labor-intensive business—you can only service so many clients. So while you'll earn a respectable living, you're unlikely to get rich.

Essentials

In addition to cooking and meal-planning skills, you'll need a solid working knowledge of nutrition and a big helping of organizational smarts. It's hard to efficiently dish up dinners when you're always running back to the market for forgotten ingredients or hunting for misplaced recipes. You'll also need to know safe food-handling practices, health regulations and product liability laws.

Tools Of The Trade

Since you're using clients' kitchens, you've got no worries, mate—you won't need to be concerned with health department regulations about commercial facilities. Although a computer and a printer are not necessities for starters, they do come in handy for keeping track of clients' food preferences, making up menus and printing out frozen-meal labels and reheating instructions. Some clients will have good, workable pots, pans and utensils; others won't. For those nightmare kitchens, you'll want to invest in a travel set of cooking utensils and pots and pans—not being able to find a measuring cup, for instance, can wreak havoc on a cooking session. And some personal chefs provide their clients with disposable microwave/oven-safe containers for reheating meals.

Money Talk

Whip up start-up costs of as little as $500—if you'll be purchasing a computer, printer and software, add in another $1,200 to $1,500. You can expect annual gross revenues of $40,000 to $50,000. Charge your clients about the same as they'd pay at a middle-of-the road restaurant, or $7 to $15 per meal, per person. Most clients will want a month of meals at a session, which means you can give them a bit of a quantity price break.

Pounding The Pavement

Your clients can be anybody who doesn't have a live-in staff—which means just about everybody. Single parents, two-income families, older people who may have difficulty getting around, young professionals who may have trouble *not* running around—you can target them all.

Since this business is still fairly new and exciting, publicity is an excellent way to go. Write up a press release and get your story in local publications. Donate two weeks' worth of meals to the lucky winner of a charity auction. Place ads in local papers. Make up a brochure and send it to a mailing list of middle- and upper-income families, retirees and young professionals.

What's Next

Don your chef's hat and develop a series of recipes you can make up in large quantities. Aim for healthy meals (don't forget desserts!) for a family of four with some recipes targeted toward low-fat and other special diet considerations.

A STAR IS BORN

Home Cookin'

If you wish you had an on-call mom to cook your dinners, then you need to talk to Patty Lewis of Kitchen Magician in Panama City, Florida. As a personal chef, Lewis not only cooks meals to your specification in your own kitchen and tidily stacks them in the freezer for reheating, but she also spends time talking at the kitchen table with clients who just need a friendly chat.

A 25-year veteran of the real estate industry, Lewis was feeling a sense of burn-out when she read about the Personal Chef program in a cooking magazine in August 1998. Since cooking is her pastime as well as her husband's, Personal Chef seemed right up her alley. She sent for the course materials and was immediately entranced. "It's a wonderful program," she says. "It really is."

Four months into her new business, Lewis counts 18 ongoing clients and a few more she's just begun cooking for. Getting those clients was easy—the Panama City native spent $295 on advertising in the local newspaper and a bit more to have brochures printed. But she didn't need them. She donated three cooking sessions to a local charity's silent auction, which netted her six long-term clients. The United States Personal Chefs Association, from whom she purchased her course materials, sent a media kit to the business editor of the local paper, who gave her a major write-up. And the rest has been word-of-mouth.

Being a personal chef is hard work, Lewis says. By the time she plans menus, prepares shopping lists, cooks, prepares meals for the freezer and writes up reheating instructions, she figures she spends abut 10 hours per client. She charges $350 for nine to 10 entrees for two, which includes groceries and disposable microwave/oven reheating containers.

Her advice for newbies? Don't overbook yourself. Four clients means more than 40 hours of work per week, and if you're working too hard, you can't give your customers your best.

Organizations

- *International Association of Culinary Professionals*, 304 W. Liberty St., #301, Louisville, KY 40202, (800) 928-4227, www.iacp-online.org
- *National Restaurant Association*, 1200 17th St. NW, Washington, DC 20036, (800) 424-5256, www.restaurant.org
- *United States Personal Chef Association*, 3615 Hwy. 528, #107, Albuquerque, NM 87114, (800) 995-2138, www.uspca.com. Terrific association offering certification, cookbooks and software, marketing tips, referrals from prospective clients to you and lots more!

Books

- *The New Professional Chef*, by the Culinary Institute of America, John Wiley & Sons
- *Personal Chef*, 3615 Hwy. 528, #107, Albuquerque, NM 87114, (800) 995-2138, www.uspca.com

Cyber Assistance

- *Fabulous Foods* (www.fabulousfoods.com): Great source for recipes, tips, an online cooking school, celebrity chefs, and can't-live-withouts like chocolate clubs

The Inside Scoop

When people go grocery shopping, they want not just a can of soup but something special. In an age when very few have the time to stay home and bake cookies, put up preserves or pickles, or spend hours over that simmering pot of soup or spaghetti sauce, most of us scan the supermarket shelves for take-home goodness. So if you're renowned among family and friends for your famous chili or killer brownies or champagne jelly, then the specialty foods business might be your piece of pie.

Specialty foods can range from salad dressing to chocolate sauce to fragrant breads. If you can make it, you can sell it—provided you know how. The specialty foods business is more about marketing than cooking, getting your product on the shelves and then off again into customers' shopping carts.

Essentials

Besides the ability to whip up a mean soufflé or sorbet, you'll need a working knowledge of safe food-handling practices, health regulations and product liability laws. A flair for food packaging is also a must—nobody's going to buy your delightful danishes if they look dumpy.

The advantages to this business are that it's creative and challenging, and if you believe in your product, it can be extremely rewarding.

The main disadvantage is that it can be difficult to get your foot in the door with market chains and distributors. (You can compensate by bypassing supermarkets and starting your sales on your own with small specialty stores and boutiques.)

Tools Of The Trade

In most states it's illegal to manufacture food products in your own kitchen, but you can rent a commercial facility or have your own cozy corner converted to a Health Department-approved site. Your best bet, however, is not to do the cooking yourself but to find a co-packer, someone who'll have your raw ingredients and all the packing materials already on-site and who will follow your recipe, leaving you free for those all-important marketing tasks. (The National Association for the Specialty Food Trade will fax you a list of co-packers if you call them at 212-482-6459.)

Money Talk

Cook up start-up costs as low as $5,000, or even less if you find a compatible co-packer who can make up a small run of a dozen cases or so with on-hand ingredients and wait until you sell them to be paid. With a willing co-packer, your biggest expense will be labels for your products. Expect annual gross sales of $30,000 to $75,000. Your product prices will depend on what you're selling and where (mail order and gourmet shops command higher prices than markets), but most specialty foods range from $3 to $25.

Pounding The Pavement

Your customers can be specialty markets like gourmet grocers, health- and natural-foods shops (if your product fits this description), department stores, restaurants, coffee bars and gift shops. You can also sell at flea markets, arts and crafts festivals, farmers' markets and through mail order. Because the competition for supermarket shelf space is fierce and because you'll be expected to pay a "slotting" fee of as much as $25,000 to get your wares on the shelves, you'll want to save marketing to major chains for the future when you know your product's a success and you can afford the fee.

The best way to start is by letting your customers sample your wares. Take your products to shopkeepers and let them savor the taste. Then ask if you can test-market a few jars or packages on their shelves. Offer to help promote your product yourself. In-store demos are terrific ways to do this. Customers sample your goodies and talk to you, which gives them a sense of connection—sort of like tasting from grandma's spoon.

Once you've landed a selection of retail accounts, you can attract food distributors, who will take your wares to the national and even international level. You'll find these people—as well as sales representatives to sell your products to other venues—through industry associations and at trade shows.

If you choose the mail order route, you'll direct-mail a brochure or catalog to lists of people who buy foods by mail. You'll also want to develop your own mailing list by having everyone who purchases your products at flea markets, festivals or other events sign a guest book with address lines. Another option is to place small magazine ads so customers can order products by mail.

What's Next

Attend a few fancy foods shows to find out what's already on the market. Develop a recipe you can make in large quantities. Then make sure your "famous food" passes the taste test beyond your own family—have as many people as possible sample it, at work, at an association or organization event, at the kids' soccer games. Design—or have a graphic designer or packaging expert design for you—product packaging that's attractive, marketable and includes the proper label for the ingredients and nutritional content. Locate a co-packer.

Organizations

● *National Association for the Specialty Food Trade*, 120 Wall St., 27th Fl., New York, NY 10005, (800) 627-3869, www.specialty-food.com

Books

● *From Kitchen to Market: Selling Your Gourmet Food Specialty*, by Stephen F. Hall, Upstart Publishing

Publications

● *Showcase*, National Association for the Specialty Food Trade, 120 Wall St., 27th Fl., New York, NY 10005, (800) 627-3869, www. specialty-food.com

Cyber Assistance

- *Epicurious* (www.epicurious.com): A compendium of cooking basics and tips, recipes, food events, a food bookstore, and more
- *National Association for the Specialty Food Trade's Fancy Food Shows* (www.fancyfoodshows.com): Everything about specialty food trade shows
- *Star Chefs* (www.starchefs.com): Like Epicurious but with more of a celebrity-chef slant

Chapter Six

DRIVING FOR DOLLARS

Some people love to drive. If you like nothing better than being out on the road, negotiating traffic and watching life unfold beyond your windshield, then this may be the Interest Category for you. And if you love the mechanics of vehicles, then this could be the category for you, too.

The businesses here, however, involve more than just driving. You'll need a good sense of logistics to send other drivers out to lots of locations while at the same time coordinating customers and vendors. If you've got the right stuff, however, this category can be fulfilling as well as lucrative.

DRY CLEANING PICKUP & DELIVERY

The Inside Scoop

Here's the problem: You've got half a dozen good suits to wear to the office. Five are lying dirty at the bottom of your laundry hamper, and you've just dribbled mustard all down the front of the sixth. If only there were time to run out to the dry cleaner and then more time to pick up the suits afterward.

The solution: a dry-cleaning pickup and delivery service. If you've got good organizational skills, you like being on the run and hope to earn good money, then this might be just the business for you.

You'll contract with dry-cleaning establishments to service your customers' clothes. Then you'll pick up the dirties from homes and offices, take them in for cleaning, pick them up after servicing and return them to their rightful owners. You can arrange regular biweekly stops, picking up fresh dirties as you drop off your last visit's load of now-clean garments, and you can have customers call for emergency pickups.

The advantages to this business are that you can work from home, and you're always on the go, so you're not sitting around waiting for activity.

The disadvantages are that since you're always running, there's little time to relax, you'll need employees and the vehicles to send them out in, and the business is time-intensive with potentially long hours. Also, you'll need a continuous and readily available cash flow because you'll pay dry cleaners for garments before you deliver them to customers and get paid yourself.

Essentials

You'll need organizational and logistical skills as well as good sales and marketing techniques to convince dry cleaners and customers to use your company.

Tools Of The Trade

A van equipped to carry hanging garments without squashing them or slinging them onto the floor is a must. You'll also need a cellular phone or pager so customers can quickly contact you. Invest in cotton, vinyl or canvas laundry bags imprinted with your logo to leave with customers—it gives them the cachet of having "their own service" and encourages them to put in garments for you to pick up.

Money Talk

Assuming you already have the van, you can clean up with startup expenses of less than $2,000, which will go toward 300 to 400 bags, your cellular phone and equipping your van. After you've been up and running for a year or two, you can expect annual gross revenues of at least $40,000, depending on how hard you want to work. You'll contract with dry cleaners to have garments cleaned at wholesale prices, then charge your customers the retail amount.

Pounding The Pavement

Your customers will be busy business and residential people who don't want to spend their time trotting to and from the cleaners. Businesses make excellent targets because, unlike residences, where people come and go and may be difficult to contact, people at work are generally on-site (or their secretaries or other employees are) and easily accessible. You might also target military bases if there are any in your area—people in the uniformed services always need clean, pressed clothes and are a good source of revenue. Be sure to check with base authorities first to make sure you'll be granted access.

Direct mail brochures to prospects in the neighborhoods you plan to service—target middle- and upper-income areas where people can afford your service. Deliver your brochures to businesses—particularly large office complexes where you can hit a lot of customers in one stop—and explain the advantages of using your company. Stop in often, even if you don't get requests for business right away. Sooner or later, people will start piling on the clothes.

What's Next

Get your delivery vehicle set up with clothes bars. Make sure the vehicle itself is clean and sparkling—a dirty van is not a good advertisement for clean clothes. If necessary, invest in a new paint job. Have your logo painted on the sides, complete with a quick description of your services and your phone number in large, legible numbers.

Organizations

● *National Association of Professional Cleaners*, P.O. Box 13182, Akron, OH 44334, (800) 997-5888, www.napcnet.com

Business Opportunities

● *Dry Cleaning to-Your-Door*, 4205 Thackery Wy., Plant City, FL 33567, (800) 318-1800

● *Pressed4Time Inc.*, 124 Boston Post Rd., Sudbury, MA 01776, (800) 423-8711, (800) 423-8711, www.pressed4time.com

● *Valet Express*, 10151 University Blvd., #224, Orlando, FL 32817, (800) 788-1107, www.valetexpress.com

FREIGHT BROKER

The Inside Scoop

We all know from those hit songs and TV shows of the '70s that Big Wheels (as in semitrucks) keep the nation's economy on the move. And if you've got experience in the industry, you probably also know that it's the freight broker who keeps those big wheels turning by arranging for delivery of consignments large and small. If you love the song of the open road but you don't want to *be* on the road, then a freight brokerage may be just the business for you.

Trucking plays a major role in the nation's economy—according to the American Trucking Association, those big wheels generated $346 billion in gross revenues in the most recently calculated year, employed more than 9.5 million people and hauled 6.5 billion tons of freight. That's a lot of stuff! And 77 percent of all American communities rely on trucks as their sole source of freight delivery.

As a freight broker, you'll work with manufacturers, wholesalers and distributors who need to get their products from point A to point B—whether those points are across town or across the country—with the help of trucking companies. You can specialize in LTL (less than a truckload) cargoes or in containerized ones.

The advantages to this business are that you can work from home and it's an industry that's unlikely to disappear—transportation will always be a necessity.

The disadvantage is that you'll spend a lot of time coordinating people and things that may not always be where you want them to be when they're supposed to be. If you're an easily stressed type, this may not be for you.

Essentials

A background in the transportation industry is important because you'll need not only hands-on experience, but also contacts in the field. If you lack this experience, work for another freight brokerage until you learn the tricks of the trade. You'll also need excellent organizational and time-management skills and the ability to get things moving quickly.

Tools Of The Trade

You'll need to be licensed by the Office of Motor Carriers (a division of the Federal Highway Administration, Department of Transportation), and you'll be required to carry a $10,000 surety bond or trust. Then you'll want a computer with the usual office software, a laser or inkjet printer, and a fax machine. The Transportation Intermediaries Association will send you a new broker kit explaining all this and more—call the association at (703) 329-1894.

Money Talk

Pencil in start-up costs of less than $3,000, which includes your bond—be sure to check with your insurance agent for exact prices. Once you get established, you can expect annual gross revenues of $50,000 to $150,000 and up. You'll charge your customers a flat fee or on a commission basis.

Pounding The Pavement

Your customers can be manufacturers, wholesalers and distributors of any types of goods and materials. You can also target companies that exhibit at trade shows or conventions and need booths and display materials moved to various sites.

Place ads in trade magazines and on import/export Internet sites. Send sales letters and brochures to mailing lists of prospective companies. Ask for referrals from satisfied customers and industry contacts.

What's Next

Design your sales letter and brochure and have them printed up. Plan your mailing list from companies you already know, or shop for one through a list broker.

Organizations

- *The American Society of Transportation & Logistics Inc.*, 320 E. Water St., Lock Haven, PA 17745-1419, (570) 748-8515, www.astl.org
- *American Trucking Association, Information Center*, 2200 Mill Rd., Alexandria, VA 22314-4677, (703) 838-1880, www.ata.org. This site is packed with helpful links, references, directories and more!
- *Transportation Intermediaries Association*, 3601 Eisenhower Ave. #110, Alexandria, VA 22304, (703) 329-1894, www.tianet.org

Books

- *Entrepreneur's Business Start-Up Guide #1328, Freight Broker*, Entrepreneur Media Inc., 2392 Morse Ave., Irvine, CA 92614, (800) 421-2300, www.smallbizbooks.com

Cyber Assistance

- *Freightworld* (www.freightworld.com): Chock-full of resources for freight transportation and logistics professionals

Weekend Warrior

HOMEBASED PRE-OWNED CAR SALES

For most people, buying a used car is like going on a blind date: Making a happy match is a matter of luck. But if you're one of those fortunate few who can tell a lemon from a honey and who can't own enough autos, this is the business for you. You'll buy one or two cars at a time, make minor repairs and polish them 'til they gleam, then sell them to private parties. In some states, you need a license to sell more than a few cars a year, so be sure to check. Advertise in the classified section of local newspapers and in "throw away" want-ad publications. **Start-up costs:** $2,500 to $10,000, which will mostly go toward your first purchases. **Expected annual gross revenues:** $10,000 to $12,000 and up, plus recouping initial investment.

- *Movin' Out* (www.movinout.com): Online magazine for truckers
- *Office of Motor Carriers* (www.fhwa.dot.gov/omc): Check this one out for regulations, news and events, and more.
- *Texas Transportation Institute* (http://tii.tamu.edu): Site of the Transportation Institute of Texas A&M University, packed with material for the transportation professional
- *Transportation Clubs International* (http://trans-clubs.org): This is a nonprofit educational organization for transportation professionals—site contains scholarship, college and university information.

MOBILE MECHANIC

The Inside Scoop

Everyone's experienced that grim sensation of rushing out to the car in the morning only to discover that it won't start, or being stuck in the supermarket parking lot or on the side of the highway. Not only have you lost your means of transportation, but you've got to deal with all the logistics of having the vehicle towed to a repair shop, then finding your way back home or to work. But if you're one of the lucky few who can deal with these problems, you know a fuel injector from a spark plug, and you like solving automotive mysteries, then you can save the day as a mobile mechanic.

You'll take your expertise and your tools directly to people's homes, workplaces or wherever the car has decided to stall. In today's hectic, hurried world, you can help your customers not only by fixing automotive ills, but also by allowing them to remain at home or the office while you work. You'll be helping a lot of folks— according to the U.S. Census Bureau, almost 100 million people used private vehicles as work transportation in a single recent year. And the average age of those beloved cars and trucks was 8.5 years, so you know there are a lot of repair situations waiting to happen out on the roads.

The advantages to the mobile mechanic business are that—unlike most auto repair businesses—you don't need employees, and if you like being an automotive physician, this can be a satisfying, stimulating career. It's also gratifying—people are appreciative when you get their baby back on the road, and doing it on their turf makes you even more of a miracle-worker.

One disadvantage is that this is a labor-intensive business. You can only be one place at a time, and you may lose a few customers who don't want to wait until you arrive. Other disadvantages are that you'll usually have to work in the elements, whether it's 110 in the shade or 10 in the sun, and that you'll occasionally have to refer customers to a specialist—unless you're equipped with the most expensive diagnostics, you can't always solve the problem on-site.

Essentials

You'll need expertise and experience in the automotive repair industry—your customers will need as quick a fix as possible, so

A STAR IS BORN

House-Call Mechanic

When Ron Trapp of Panama City Beach, Florida-based Auto Tracks pulls into your driveway on a mechanical rescue mission, you know you're in good hands. Trapp, 40, mans a 28-foot mobile auto shop, stocked with every conceivable tool and diagnostic instrument.

Trapp, an ASE-certified mechanic, has been in the vehicle repair business for 20 years and has run Auto Tracks since 1992. He developed his mobile mechanic business when, as a shop-bound specialist in the Florida Keys, he often heard people wishing for a mechanic that could come to them.

Trapp, a homebased father of two toddlers, admits that it would take around $60,000 or more to purchase and stock a truck like his but says it's entirely possible to start a mobile mechanic business on a relative shoestring. If you've got hand tools, a multimeter, a diagnostic scanner, and a serviceable van, you can get out there and get started. But, he cautions, "Know your limitations. Don't tell somebody you can repair something if you're not capable of doing it. That'll bust you in a heartbeat."

What's your best source of business? Trapp suggests leaving cards with hotel and motel managers because guests usually have vehicle predicaments that require minimal tools—things like dead batteries, flat tires, broken belts, locked doors and empty gas tanks.

Trapp, who quietly boasts a repeat customer base of well over 200, also recommends dropping cards at local businesses and introducing yourself to management—a technique, he says, that will net you far more than any print advertising.

you won't be able to spend hours tinkering under the hood, hoping to hit on the solution. A strong analytical sense is also important. Because you go to your patients, you don't have the usual mechanic's luxury of cars stacked in your "waiting room," so you must be able to do what they called triage on the old "M*A*S*H" TV show—decide who needs you first, second and then on down the line.

Tools Of The Trade

In most states, you'll have to be a certified mechanic—be sure to check with the proper business licensing authorities before you roll on the road. You'll need a set of mechanic's tools, a multimeter (ohm/voltmeter), a diagnostic scanner and of course a vehicle to carry them and you to jobs. You'll also need a cellular phone so customers can call wherever you are and a flat-rate manual and on-board calculator for determining job charges.

Money Talk

Your start-up costs can range from $500 to $24,000, depending on whether you already have tools and a vehicle and how many modifications you make. A good mobile mechanic can earn annual gross revenues of $50,000 to $200,000. Charge your customers the same as you would in a shop, according to the flat-rate manuals (sold by tool companies like Snap-On). If you take on routine maintenance tasks like oil changes or lube jobs, you can charge the going flat rate in your area. (Check the prices at drive-up oil change shops like Jiffy Lube.)

Pounding The Pavement

Your customers can be anybody with wheels. Target the average driver on the street as well as corporations and institutions that will be delighted to have you arrive on-site so their employees don't need to be away from their desks. RV parks and private campgrounds are also fertile grounds for customers—people with boats or recreational vehicles always need some sort of assistance, and people who are living in them have a hard time leaving them at the auto repair shop overnight. Hotels and motels can also be good customer sources because out-of-town guests with car woes have no idea where to turn for expert help and are usually pressed for time.

Deliver your business cards to owners or managers of all these businesses and explain the advantages of your services. A promotional item like a refrigerator magnet or pen emblazoned with your company name can also help keep you in mind when vehicle troubles arise. Place an ad in your local Yellow Pages. Get your business written up in local publications. If you live in a tourist-oriented area, introduce yourself to local visitor assistance centers and leave cards. Put your logo with a large, legible phone number and a description like "mobile mechanic" on your vehicle so potential customers can spot you on your rounds.

What's Next

Organize your tools in shelves and cabinetry so they'll stay in place while you're driving and will be easily accessible. Set up accounts with parts houses that will deliver to your job site. (You can also leave your business cards with them.) Purchase a flat-rate manual so you can figure your charges.

Organizations

● *National Automotive Technicians Education Foundation*, 13505 Dulles Technology Dr., Herndon, VA 20171-3421, (703) 713-0100, www.natef.org

● *National Institute for Automotive Service Excellence*, 13505 Dulles Technology Dr., #2, Herndon, VA 20171-3421, (703) 713-3800, www.asecert.org

Cyber Assistance

● *Car Talk @ cars.com* (www.cartalk.cars.com): Site hosted by "celebrity" mechanics, very funny hosts of a National Public Radio show—contains news, technical advice, info on car models and more fun stuff to do with cars than you can imagine

● *Fred's Garage* (www.familycar.com): Site hosted by another "celebrity" mechanic—features tips, topics and links to sites of interest to mechanics and other car-aholics

● *iATN, International Automotive Technicians Network*, (www.iatn.net): Includes professional auto tech discussion groups, Labscope Waveform files, live conferencing and more

Chapter seven

FOREIGN AFFAIRS

So you're one of those people who lives for foreign affairs—you love the excitement and intrigue of other cultures. You'd live out of a suitcase if you could, and even when things get a little weird—you end up sleeping in the train station or taking the wrong turn five times over—you're in heaven. If this is you—one of the footloose folks with wanderlust in your blood, foreign phrases on your tongue and a taste for adventure—then this is the Interest Category for you.

CRUISE-ONLY TRAVEL AGENCY

The Inside Scoop

Remember "The Love Boat," with its Brady Bunch-brained crew and all-problems-solved-in-an-hour passengers? That particular TV show may have sailed into the sunset, but the cruise industry is booming. New ships are taking to the seas daily while cruise lines fish for passengers, offering everything from three-day no-frills packages to Titanically sumptuous tours to voyages aboard authentic sailing vessels.

This is big business—the cruise industry, with sales of $8 billion per year, estimates that only 7 percent of Americans have ever cruised. Which leaves a grand 93 percent who are expected to cruise soon. In anticipation, the industry is gearing up for an immediate 55 percent increase in ships and passenger capacity.

If you love the siren song of the sea and the romance of cruising, then a cruise-only travel agency might be just the business for you. You'll work with clients to choose the ideal cruise for them, then book passage and sit back to wait for those postcards from sunny shores.

The advantages to this business are that you can work at home, start-up costs are relatively low, you get to sample lots of cruises so you'll know what to recommend, and you deal with happy, excited people.

The only disadvantage is that it can be difficult to stay on dry land in your home office while everyone around you, it seems, is off on a cruise.

Essentials

You'll need a comprehensive knowledge of cruise lines and the different packages available plus the people skills to work with a variety of clients and the organizational skills to prepare bookings.

Tools Of The Trade

All you really need to get started is a computer system, a fax machine, a phone, and an electronic data terminal for processing credit card payments, which you can get online from a number of merchant account services (otherwise known as banks). Go to your favorite search engine and key in "credit card processing"—or check with your local bank, which may offer this service.

Money Talk

Cruise into start-up costs of about $2,500—you may want to add up to another $250 for networking dues to local business groups. Once you get established, you can expect annual gross sales of $500,000 and up, which translates to net profits of about $65,000 to $90,000 and up, depending on your geographic area and how creatively and aggressively you market. Instead of charging your customers, you'll make your money through commissions paid by the cruise lines.

Pounding The Pavement

Your customers will be just about anybody who can afford a cruise—and that's more people now than ever before since many cruises are tailored to slimmer pocketbooks. You can target both individuals and corporations—which can provide you with lots of bookings for meetings, conferences or employee perks.

Send your brochure to large companies and people on mailing lists who have already purchased cruises. Place ads in local publications and in your local Yellow Pages. Get your company written up in these same publications. Donate a pair of cruise tickets to the lucky winner of a charity auction in exchange for free advertising.

And don't forget to network at local professional and civic organizations—and even the PTA.

What's Next

Set up a credit card processing account. Start cruise shopping. Have fun!

Organizations

● *Cruise & Freighter Travel Association*, 16307 Depot Rd., Flushing, NY 11358, (800) 872-8584, www.travltips.com

● *National Association of Commissioned Travel Agents*, P.O. Box 2398, Valley Center, CA 92082-2398, (760) 751-1197, www.nacta.com

Publications

● *Prow's Edge*, Many Lands, One Moon Publications Inc., Circulation Dept., 3753 W. 10th Ave., #102, Vancouver, BC V6R 2G5, CAN, www.prowsedge.com.

Cyber Assistance

● *Cruise Lines International Association* (www.cruising.org): Cruise profiles, cruise news and specials, links to cruise lines, and more

Franchises

● *Cruise Holidays International*, 9665 Chesapeake Dr., #401, San Diego, CA 92123, (800) 866-7245, www.cruiseholidays.com

● *CruiseOne Inc.*, 10 Fairway Dr., #200, Deerfield Beach, FL 33441, (800) 892-3928, (954) 428-8433, www.cruiseone.com

EXPORTING

The Inside Scoop

We are living in what is becoming more of a one-world economy with every passing day. People, languages, thoughts, ideas, currencies and products move across borders with amazing—and exciting—fluidity. If you love trying your voice at other languages, you can't be dragged away from the aisles of import stores, and you live to travel, then exporting could be the business for you.

And it's big business. In one recent year, American companies exported $349 billion in merchandise to 226 foreign countries. Everything from beverages to commodes—and a staggering list of other products you might never imagine as global merchandise—are fair game for the savvy trader and are bought, sold, represented, and distributed somewhere in the world on a daily basis.

As an exporter, you'll act as a middleperson, selling domestic goods for American manufacturers or producers to foreign buyers. Products can range from eggs to airplane engines and anything in between. You might deal with a customer in Turkey one week and another in Guatemala, the next. Acting on behalf of a manufacturer is the least expensive route to take, but you can also purchase products to resell or import goods from foreign shores to sell on your home turf.

The advantages to this business are that you're always doing something different, you meet lots of fascinating people and you get to travel to your heart's content. And one of the really exciting aspects of the export business is that most American manufacturers have no idea they can expand their trade exponentially by exporting. Once you show them the light, the possibilities are limitless.

The disadvantages are that you have to adjust your thinking and business style to the ideas and cultures of many different people, and you have to account for foreign currency fluctuations that may make your business transactions less lucrative than you had originally planned. You'll also occasionally run into contract fulfillment nightmares due to uncontrollable events like bad weather, shipping crises or foreign politics.

Essentials

You'll need a good working knowledge of letters of credit and other foreign payment policies, as well as an understanding of shipping terms and methods. You'll also need strong sales and marketing skills—you'll have to convince manufacturers to let you sell their products and then persuade buyers to purchase them. Good organizational and time-management skills are also a must. If you don't fulfill all the terms of a letter of credit by the day it's due, your buyer can refuse to pay you a centavo.

Tools Of The Trade

All you need to get up and running are a computer system, a laser printer and a fax machine.

Money Talk

Figure on start-up costs of $5,000 to $20,000, depending on how much you spend on travel and market research. (It's not easy, but it is possible to run an export business with minimal travel involved.) Expect to earn $30,000 to $200,000 or more. The amount you charge your customers depends on what structural arrangement you make, but you'll probably work on a commission of 10 percent to 15 percent for consumer goods and 15 percent to 20 percent for industrial products. These fees are based on the product cost from the manufacturer.

Pounding The Pavement

Your customers can be producers or manufacturers of any domestic goods you care to target. It's best to start in an industry you're already experienced in—if you know the grocery field, for instance, you might start by selling upscale convenience foods to French grocery distributors.

You'll work a two-step process here. First, once you've targeted your market, you'll need to convince manufacturers to let you sell their products. Send letters describing your services and the rewards of exporting, then follow up with phone calls requesting appointments. After you contract with these people, go on to your second step, selling the goods abroad. Send letters to sales reps or distributors, explaining your products and requesting an appointment to meet or talk by phone.

You can also place ads for your products on any of the plethora of free or fee-based Web sites that feature trade leads, which are import/export classified advertisements.

What's Next

You can find a fabulous array of materials on the Internet that will help you get started. Pore through all of them. You also can—and definitely should—get more help than you might believe possible through the Export Assistance Centers run by the U.S. Commercial Service. These centers are set up with the sole purpose of promoting American exports through companies like yours. Take advantage of them!

Organizations

- *The American Association of Exporters and Importers*, 11 W. 42nd St., 30th Fl., New York, NY 10036, (212) 944-2230, www.aaei.org
- *Association for International Business*, 1469 Rosena Ave., Madison, OH 44057, (440) 428-6163, www.earthone.com
- *The Federation of International Trade Associations*, 1851 Alexander Bell Dr., Reston, VA 20191, (800) 969-FITA (3482), www.fita.org

Books

- *Entrepreneur's Business Start-Up Guide #1092, Import/Export Business*, Entrepreneur Media Inc., 2392 Morse Ave., Irvine, CA 92614, (800) 421-2300, www.smallbizbooks.com
- *Exporting, Importing, and Beyond*, by Lawrence W. Tuller, Adams Media
- *Export-Import*, by Joseph A. Zodl, Betterway Books

- *Import/Export, How to Get Started in International Trade*, by Carl A. Nelson, McGraw-Hill

Cyber Assistance

- *U.S. and Foreign Commercial Service* (www.ita.doc.gov/uscs): Everything for the aspiring exporter—market research assistance, a trade events calendar and more. A must-surf!
- *Export Assistance Centers* around the country can be found on the Commercial Service Web site at www.ita.doc.gov/uscs. Their sole purpose is to help you—so let them!

Franchises

- *Transcom International*, 11261 Richmond Ave., #103, Houston, TX 77082, (800) 227-8417

SPECIALTY TRAVEL & TOURS

The Inside Scoop

If you think travel means a week at a Howard Johnson's and dinner in a diner with nothing more taxing—or interesting—to do than hang around the pool, think again. Tourists today can choose from a staggering number of specialty tours—everything from a trip down the Amazon studying ethnobotany with local shamans to surf camps à la The Beach Boys to walking, biking, hiking or chocolate-binge-ing tours. If you love travel and you can communicate your enthusiasm to others, then a specialty travel and tour business might be just the ticket for you.

You can conduct just about any type of tour you can dream up, but keep in mind that the closer you stick to home, the less expensive your start-up costs will be. If you live in an area that attracts visitors or business travelers, you can specialize in unusual tours like On the Town After Dark or Antiques Ahoy. You might go with backpacking or rafting adventure tours to outdoor areas close to home. Or you can sell worldwide adventures from your own armchair by advertising other companies' tours and taking commissions on sales.

If you've fallen in love with Paris or have an ongoing affair with Venice or Thailand or anywhere else exotic, you can package overseas tours as well, but your start-up costs will be much higher. The main point to remember with specialty tours is that you must have a niche, a plan that's tailored to a specific type of person or group. The old "If It's Tuesday, This Must Be Belgium" bus trip is not your goal. Instead you want to design tours for clients like seniors, families with small children, women traveling alone, music lovers or chocolate fiends.

The advantages to this business are that you meet lots of interesting people and you get to travel frequently and investigate hotels, restaurants and all sorts of fascinating spots in the name of work. What more could a travel aficionado want?

The disadvantages are that you're away from home a great deal, you'll occasionally be stuck for the run of the tour with a can't-be-pleased client, and you can face a lot of upfront costs. (You have to pay for hotel rooms before you've booked a single client.)

Keep in mind that industry regulations prevent you from writing airline tickets, but you can overcome this by establishing a relationship with a travel agency that will cut the tickets for you. Some will pay you a commission in the range of 10 percent; others will pay by referring clients to you.

Essentials

You must have a strong working knowledge of your tour terrain. This includes fluency in at least one language of the countries you'll travel to, up-to-date familiarity with hotels, restaurants and places of interest if you're doing cities, or trails and rivers if you're four-wheeling or rafting it, and of course local customs and currencies.

You'll also need excellent people skills for dealing with clients of all types (as well as innkeepers and other assorted purveyors along your route), solid organizational abilities, and the ability to roll with the punches. If something goes awry at the last moment, you've got to be able to find a fallback position in a hurry. And last, but definitely not least, you'll need terrific sales and marketing skills to sell your tours to customers.

Tools Of The Trade

The only things you really need to get up and running are a computer system, Internet access, a fax machine and a phone.

Money Talk

Send yourself off with start-up costs of $5,000 and up, depending on how much advertising you'll do at the outset. Printing and mailing costs for your brochures can be high, so get creative with what you can produce on a budget and negotiate heavily for services like photography and printing. Specialty travel and tour companies price their

A STAR IS BORN

Going Bananas

Who wouldn't want to travel with Wild Women Adventures? Their motto is "Insanity With Dignity," and their tours have names like "What's Mayan Is Yours" (an excursion to the Yucatan) and Erin Go Braghless (you guessed it— Ireland). Carol Rivendell and Martha Lindt are the Wild Women and their specialty travel company, in Sebastopol, California, had as its seed a desire to serve housewives and older women who want to travel on their own but not alone. But it has also found a market among young professionals too busy to plan their own vacations.

Rivendell, a former psychotherapist, and Lindt, a travel agent, met when their children were high school sweethearts. And while the kids have long gone their separate ways, Carol and Martha are into their fifth year as a business team.

They started with $5,000—a nice chunk, but not enough to compete with the snazzy brochures of established tour operators. So the partners developed their own niche. They costumed themselves as modern-day Carmen Mirandas (a look that's become their company logo), had a friend do their photography, and put their stamp on an inexpensive newsprint catalog.

Their first clients came from a mailing list of 3,000 names borrowed from a local comedian. Today, their list—compiled solely from people who asked to be included—numbers 22,000. They've also taken pains to solicit the interest of decision-sway-ers in the industry by sending out scads of travel-agent and media kits. And they've gotten lots of response from a fabulous Web site mastered by Lindt's daughter, Sarah Reyna, a profes-sional Web site designer, in exchange for babysitting and cook-ie-baking.

Their advice to newbies? Be prepared to give the busi-ness your all. You can find financing and ways to reach the right people, they report, but it takes dedication and tenacity. And a sense of humor. Zany and fun-loving are the company bywords, even when there's not enough time in the day. "This is hard work," says Rivendell, "but my God, it's fun."

services on a variety of elements. If your tour agenda is based on outside vendors—for instance lodging, tour guides, or outfitters—you'll most likely price your tour at your net rates plus about 20 percent. If you'll need to pay travel agents to book your tours, you'll add another 10 percent to that. Annual gross revenues for specialty travel and tour companies range between $50,000 and $500,000, with the higher rates going to companies that also act as travel agencies.

Pounding The Pavement

Your customers will vary according to the type of tours you design. You can target everybody from mountain climbers to wheelchair-bound adventurers to museum junkies.

Market your tours on the Internet with a Web site. Send your brochure to mailing lists of people who are already confirmed travelers (those who've already purchased tour packages) with similar interests. Advertise in national and special-interest publications. Get your tour written up in local publications. Donate a tour to be auctioned at a charity event in exchange for free advertising.

Then get creative. If you've packaged an art tour, for instance, send brochures to faculties and students at art colleges and societies and the fine arts departments of universities.

What's Next

Design your tour. Design your Web site and brochure, or have a graphic artist and Web site designer do it for you. Shop your competition to get a feel for prices.

Organizations

- *American Hotel & Motel Association*, 1201 New York Ave. NW, #600, Washington, DC 20005-3931, (202) 289-3100, www.ahma. com
- *American Society of Travel Agents*, 1101 King St., #200, Alexandria, VA 22314, (800) 275-2782, www.astanet.com. Check out the Web site, which contains busloads of information, including a listing of every travel-oriented professional organization under the sun.
- *United States Tour Operators Association*, 342 Madison Ave., #1522, New York, NY 10173, (212) 599-6599, www.ustoa.com

Books

- *Entrepreneur's Business Start-Up Guide #1386, Specialty Travel & Tours*, Entrepreneur Media Inc., 2392 Morse Ave., Irvine, CA 92614, (800) 421-2300, www.smallbizbooks.com

- *Home-Based Travel Agent: How to Cash in on the Exciting New World of Travel Marketing*, by Kelly Monaghan, Intrepid Traveler

- *How to Start a Home Based Travel Agency*, by Joanie Ogg and Tom Ogg, Tom Ogg & Associates

- *The Intrepid Traveler's Complete Desk Reference*, by Sally Scanlon and Kelly Monaghan, Intrepid Traveler

- *Start and Run a Profitable Tour Guiding Business: Part-Time, Full Time, at Home, or Abroad: Your Step-By-Step Business Plan*, by Barbara Braidwood, Self Counsel Press

The Inside Scoop

How to do you say "party of the first part" in Spanish? If you know the answer, or if you know someone who does, then a language translation service might be just the business for you. Language translators are in big demand these days. International commerce is growing as fast as the Internet, and while we may believe that English is the world's linguistic choice, it's not. So people who can translate documents from one language to another are in high demand.

As a language translator, you'll interpret all sorts of documents, from books to private letters to product labels, but your greatest source of revenue will be legal and medical companies. You can specialize in the one or two languages you speak fluently, or you can hire other linguists to translate dozens of other tongues. You don't actually have to speak anything other than English—you can function as the management and administrator for your bilingual freelance consultants.

The advantages to this business are that you can work at home, you can start part time, you'll deal with all sorts of interesting people and materials, and if you like the nuances of languages, it's always fascinating.

The disadvantages are that clients can be slow to pay, sometimes taking two to three months, and it can be difficult to price jobs because you often don't know the full extent of the work until you're well into it.

Essentials

You (or your consultants) will need a definite fluency in your specialty languages. High school French is not enough, especially if you'll deal with legal and medical documents. An understanding of medical or legal lingo is also a plus so that your translated materials come out sounding like the real thing. You'll also need good administrative and organizational skills.

Tools Of The Trade

Certification as a medical or legal professional is a plus but not a necessity—if you're a doctor, a nurse, an attorney, a paralegal or are otherwise well-versed in the lingo of the profession, you'll be way ahead of your competition. You'll need a computer with the usual office software, a laser printer, and a fax machine. There's a variety of translation software on the market, but since they tend to translate verbatim regardless of context, they don't really do the trick—in most cases you're better off without them.

Money Talk

We're talking start-up costs of $2,150 or less, depending on whether you'll be purchasing brand-new equipment or you already have it all. Once you get established, you can expect to earn annual revenues of $250,000 to $500,000. Translation services usually charge by the word, for instance, $240 to $350 per 1,000 words.

Pounding The Pavement

Your customers can be anyone who needs something translated, but your best sources will be the legal and medical communities. You can also target book publishers, government institutions like welfare agencies and immigration services, insurance companies, and import/export firms.

Direct-mail brochures to targeted businesses. Place ads in trade publications and introduce yourself to supervisors and administrators at local hospitals and institutions.

What's Next

Decide on your target market, start shopping for freelancers so that when you need help you'll be ready, and bone up on tax and legal issues relating to the use of independent contractors.

A STAR IS BORN

Success In Any Language

Like all true entrepreneurs, Tom West started his company, Intermark Language Translation Services Corp. in Atlanta, because he saw both a need and a way to fill it. As an attorney at the largest law firm in the city, West constantly came up against legal documents that had been translated—in the worst way. Translators were terrific at things like "The hotel is on the corner," but just couldn't cope with the whereofs, hereinbefores and other intricacies of legalese.

So in 1995, West—who holds a bachelor's degree in French, a master's in German and a minor in Russian—opened his own language translation service, geared toward the legal market. Although he started as a one-man operation, West has since hired an in-house Spanish translator, a project manager and a receptionist, and has seen his sales double each of the three years since he opened his doors. His client list includes Atlanta-area luminaries like Coca-Cola, The Home Depot and BellSouth.

West, 37, makes sure each legal document receives three passes—the first by a native speaker of the target language, the second by an editor who checks for linguistic accuracy, and the third by a proofreader who verifies formatting and that each paragraph has a corresponding paragraph in the translated version.

As for advertising, West gets most of his clients from word-of-mouth. When he started his company, he called to inform friends, colleagues and former classmates, and business just boomed from there.

West's start-up costs, which included a directory of translators purchased from the American Translators Association for $75, were minimal. The hidden cost of the business, he says, is in finding qualified people to do the work. Good translators are busy beyond belief, and it's up to you to develop relationships that will encourage them to work for you.

There are zillions of really bad translators, he says, and you can't compete with them—the well-meaning high school Spanish teacher or friend of a friend—because they'll work for free. "Your translators are your key to success," he advises. "Pay them promptly, keep them happy and treat them nicely."

Organizations

- *American Translators Association*, 1800 Diagonal Rd., #220, Alexandria, VA 22314-2840, (703) 683-6100, www.atanet.org
- *Northwest Translators and Interpreters Society*, P.O. Box 25301, Seattle, WA 98125-5642, (206) 382-5642, www.notisnet.org
- *Southern California Area Translators and Interpreters Association*, P.O. Box 802696, Santa Clarita, CA 91380-2696, (818) 725-3899, www.scatia.org

Books

- *Translation Services Directory,* ATA, 1800 Diagonal Rd., #220, Alexandria, VA 22314-2840, (703) 683-6100, www.atanet.org

Publications

- *The ATA Chronicle*, American Translators Association, 1800 Diagonal Rd., #220, Alexandria, VA 22314-2840, (703) 683-6100, www.atanet.org/chroniclemain.htm

Chapter eight

GREEN THUMB

If you've got that magic touch with plants—everything you water blooms magnificently, your lawn is the envy of your neighbors, strangers stop to admire your roses, and you've got container plants spilling over every flat surface of your home and yard, then this may be the Interest Category for you.

HERB FARM

The Inside Scoop

Herbs are tremendously popular these days—from the smallest shop to the largest discount warehouse, you'll find medicinal herbs, culinary herbs, and herbal teas, baths, candles and aromatherapy essences.

If you love the romance and mystique of herbs and you like gardening—and, as popular TV gardener Rebecca Kolls says, getting those hands dirty—then an herb farm might be just the business for you.

You'll plant and raise your herbs, then sell them to wholesale or retail customers. You can also sell container plants or herbal products like soaps or vinegars. Some herb farmers operate pick-your-own fields where customers can gather their own plants.

The advantages to this business are that it's just you and Mother Nature—this is real back-to-basics stuff, good for the body and the soul—and you can start from home (or more accurately, the field), part time if you like. You can start out small, growing your herbs in a large backyard or renting inexpensive land, but keep in mind that your profits will also be small unless you've got two-digit acreage.

The disadvantages are that you're at the mercy of the elements—if Mother Nature gets temperamental, there's not a lot you can do about it—and you can also end up at the mercy of invading agribusiness and the fickle public. If you've planted acres of echinacea and the public decides that some hitherto unheard-of herb is in this year instead, you'll have to develop new marketing techniques in a hurry.

Essentials

You'll need a solid working knowledge of growing and nurturing herbs. If you'll be working several acres or more, you'll need to know farming techniques as well—commercial growing is different from coaxing along a few plants in a backyard border.

You'll also need a firm grounding in the wholesale herb business—what's popular, who's buying it for what purposes, which herbs are best abandoned to agribusiness and which new herbs are likely to be the "in" product in the next few years. (Since it can take two years to reap the rewards of your labors, you'll need to forecast at least this far ahead.)

In addition to all this, you'll need top-notch sales and marketing skills to get your herbs in the marketplace and keep them there.

Tools Of The Trade

First and foremost, you'll need a good chunk of soil. If you've got acreage, you're ahead of the game. If not, you can often rent land inexpensively—try power companies with fallow land beneath their towers or property owners with unused acres in rural areas of your town or county. One thing to watch for is that wholesale buyers of natural products may require your farm to be on certifiably organic land—one on which nothing was previously grown using pesticides, herbicides or fertilizers. (This certification comes from a state agency or a private organization, depending on your state.)

Next you'll need seeds and growing supplies. If you live in a cold-weather locale, you may want to invest in a greenhouse. You'll also need a pickup truck or van to deliver your produce to customers.

Money Talk

Start-up costs for an herb farm—assuming you already have cleared land and your delivery vehicle—range from $5,000 to $10,000. Your annual revenues will fluctuate from season to season and region to region, depending on a wide variety of factors, including market prices around the world, the weather, what you'll be growing and your marketing skills. You can expect anywhere from $5,000 per acre to $30,000 per acre, but keep in mind that these are extremely variable figures. Whatever they are, you can add onto them if you sell potted plants or herbal products.

The prices you charge your customers will also vary. They'll depend on produce prices not only in your area but throughout the world (wholesale imports of some herbs can drive your prices into the ground, so do your homework before you plant), on weather fluctuations, and on what herbs you're growing. Prices for herbal products will also vary according to what you're selling, to whom and where. As a thumbnail, prices range from $1.50 per pound (which isn't really enough to earn a living from) to $45 per pound for expensive-to-grow crops like ginseng.

Pounding The Pavement

Your customers can be wholesale distributors buying for health product manufacturers, grocery chains and restaurants, or you can sell directly to these businesses yourself. You can target other SOHOs—artisans and crafters who work with herbs—as well as caterers; makers of beauty, health and skin care products; and natural-foods stores. You can sell potted plants to garden centers, florists and nurseries. And you can put your herbs directly in the public's hands by selling at farmers' markets and flea markets.

Your best bet for selling to other businesses large or small is to develop a niche—a specialty that's fresh and new in your area—so that instead of competing, for example, with every other dill grower, you've got an untapped market. You might specialize in varieties of mint or mystical herbs or native plants.

If you want to go the wholesale route, contact distributors (which you can locate through herb and specialty foods organizations). To sell directly to SOHOs, take samples of your herbs to them and ask for their business.

For farmers' and flea markets, contact the market organizer to find out about fees, then make space reservations—display space at some flea markets and swap meets can be very competitive, so don't wait until the last minute to make arrangements.

If you plan on a pick-it-yourself operation, advertise in local papers and put advertising/directional signs on roads leading to your farm. (Make sure to get permission from land owners and local zoning authorities.)

What's Next

Decide what your specialty will be and which market you'll target. Then research your market thoroughly. Make certain the herbs you've chosen will grow well in your area. Check with local zoning authorities to make sure your land is approved for farming.

Organizations

- *American Botanical Council*, P.O. Box 144345, Austin, TX 78714-4345, (512) 926-4900, www.herbalgram.org

- *Herb Growing and Marketing Network*, P.O. Box 245, Silver Spring, MD 17575, (717) 393-3295, www.herbnet.com and www.herbworld.com. This great organization offers seminars, conferences, business packs filled with information for the herb-growing newbie entrepreneur, and lots more!

- *International Herb Association*, P.O. Box 206, Mechanicsburg, PA 17055-0206

Books

- *Entrepreneur's Business Start-Up Guide #1282, Herb Farm*, Entrepreneur Media Inc., 2392 Morse Ave., Irvine, CA 92614, (800) 421-2300, www.smallbizbooks.com

- *Growing and Selling Fresh Cut Herbs (Making a Living Naturally)*, by Sandie Shores, Storey Books

- *Growing Your Herb Business*, by Bertha Reppert and Deborah Balmuth, Storey Books

- *Pay Dirt: How to Raise and Sell Herbs and Produce for Serious Cash*, by Mimi Luebbermann, Prima Publishing

- *HerbalGram, The Journal of the American Botanical Society and Herb Research Foundation*, American Botanical Council, P.O. Box 144345, Austin, TX 78714-4345, (800) 373-7105, www.herbalgram.org

EXTERIOR LANDSCAPER

The Inside Scoop

We all feel good when our world is green, filled with trees, shrubs and flowers as brilliant accents. Landscaping increases the tangible and intangible value of homes, encourages business at retail locations and enhances the productivity of corporations. But most people are intimidated by the very thought of greening their grounds and don't have the time to devote to it even if they have the talent.

If you like planting trees and flowers, transforming the world one project at a time, and you're not afraid of physical labor, then landscaping might be just the business for you. And there's plenty of it—according to the Professional Lawn Care Association, more than 22 million households spend $14.6 billion on professional landscape and lawn care services.

You'll carry out landscape architects' plans by purchasing plant materials, sprinkler systems, and decorative accents like boulders and river rock, and installing them. You can then contract with your satisfied commercial and residential customers to maintain your work with weekly watering, pruning, fertilizing and pest control services. And you can carry out seasonal projects as well—everything from winter holiday lighting and decorating to snow removal.

The advantages to this business are that your start-up costs are relatively low, you're outdoors every day, and if you like making things grow and the accomplishment of putting in a good day's physical labor, then this can be a rewarding field.

The disadvantages are that you're at the mercy of the elements—inclement weather can ruin your cash flow—and if you work commercial jobs where you're a subcontractor, the general contractor's cash flow problems can cause you nonpayment nightmares.

Essentials

You'll need a solid working knowledge of planting and maintaining a wide variety of trees, shrubs and flowers, as well as of sprinkler systems and nonplant materials like gravel, boulders and paving stones. A sense of logistics will also be valuable—the better route you map out of customer sites, the less time you'll spend on the road and the more efficient and cost-effective you'll be.

Tools Of The Trade

You'll need a power mower, edger, leaf blower, seed and fertilizer spreader and sprayer, an assortment of shovels and rakes, and a gasoline can for on-the-job refills (take care to use an approved container and follow safe storage and usage practices). You'll also want a pickup truck and perhaps a small trailer to carry it all in.

Money Talk

Assuming you already have the truck, you can get in the green with start-up costs of $500 to $1,500, depending on how many tools you already have and what you'll need to buy. Expect to make annual gross revenues of $60,000 to $80,000 or more, depending on how hard you want to work and how far you ultimately expand your services. Charge your customers $25 to $40 per hour or a flat fee per project or per month—you'll base this on the number of hours you expect to spend on each visit or on the project. Don't forget to figure in your travel time and your materials—most landscapers mark up materials 50 percent to 100 percent.

Pounding The Pavement

Your customers will be homeowners and businesses that want their properties beautified and kept looking good. Target commercial types like apartment and condominium complexes, hotels and motels, hospitals, large and small businesses and office parks, and government institutions. Architects, real estate developers and contractors building new homes or small tracts also make good customers.

Nab residential customers by going door-to-door with fliers or door hangers. (Don't place them in mailboxes—the U.S. Postal Service gets very upset about this.) Place ads in your local newspaper and in your neighborhood Yellow Pages.

For small-business commercial customers and architects, developers and contractors, go on-site to hand-deliver fliers or brochures and explain your services. You may not get any takers the first time you visit, but don't get discouraged. A repeat visit or two can often seal a deal. A direct-mail campaign of a brochure will work better for large corporations; follow up with a phone call.

You can also target real estate agents with noncurb-appealing sale or rental properties on their books. Take a Polaroid of the place, then give it to the realtor with suggestions of how you can spruce it up.

What's Next

Learn everything you can about your new business. Garden centers and home improvement warehouses often give clinics on planting trees and shrubs, sprinkler installation, and the like. Practice on your own home, or better yet, offer your services for free to a charitable organization if they can pay for materials—it's terrific free advertising. Get a resale license so you can purchase wholesale materials. Establish relationships with wholesale nurseries in your area. They can help with questions or problems and can also refer to you to new customers.

Weekend Warrior

GARDEN DESIGNER

There's more to gardening than just sticking plants in the ground. A beautiful garden—the kind that stops passersby for a second look—requires artistry, skill and imagination. If you've got the talent to bring plant palettes to life, why not share it with others as a garden designer? You can draw up designs for business or residential customers, deciding what to plant for each situation—sun, shade, heavy traffic, kids and pets, or people who want water, tropical, native or exotic landscapes. Start off by advertising in your local newspaper and leaving fliers with garden centers. **Start-up costs:** $500. **Expected annual gross revenues:** $10,000 to $15,000.

Organizations

- *American Horticultural Association*, 7931 E. Boulevard Dr., Alexandria, VA 22308, (800) 777-7931, www.ahs.org
- *Associated Landscape Contractors of America*, 150 Elden St., #270, Herndon, VA 20170, (800) 395-ALCA, www.alca.org
- *American Nursery & Landscape Association* 1250 I St. NW, #500, Washington, DC 20005, (202) 789-2900, www.anla.org. The site contains information on scholarships, professional services, publications and more.
- *Professional Lawn Care Association*, 1000 Johnson Ferry Rd. NE, Ste. C-135, Marietta, GA 30068-2112, (800) 458-3466, www. plcaa.org

Books

- *How to Start a Home-Based Landscaping Business*, by Owen E. Dell, Globe Pequot Press
- *Lawn Care & Gardening: A Down-to-Earth Guide to the Business*, by Kevin Rossi, Acton Circle Publishing Co.

Cyber Assistance

- *The Grow Zone* (www.growzone.org): How can you miss with pages like Cultivated Interests, Garden/Landscape Center, Nursery Associations and Conference Room?

INTERIOR LANDSCAPER

The Inside Scoop

If you're a plant lover—you've got sweet potato vines trailing over the kitchen counters and down the sides of the refrigerator, pots of geraniums in every window and baskets of ferns dangling from the ceilings—and you can't be dragged away from the garden department of any store, then an interior plant-scape (also called plant maintenance or interior landscape contractor) business is the one for you.

You'll feed, water, prune and doctor indoor plants on a weekly basis for residential and commercial customers—from small offices to major shopping malls. You'll also lease plants, caring for them along with your other green charges, replacing them at no extra cost if they become unhealthy, and provide seasonal plant décor from winter holiday poinsettias to spring tulips. You can also design hardscapes—indoor fountains, planters and other indoor garden-oriented amenities.

This can be a growing field, especially if you educate your clients about indoor air quality (IAQ), one of the newest health trends around. Plants, especially some varieties, scrub the air of environmental pollutants, from formaldehyde in carpet fibers to smoke and smog in our air.

The advantages to this business are that you can start part time, your initial costs are minimal, and if you like helping things grow, then you'll be in plant heaven every working day.

The only disadvantage is that customers may tend to perceive your service as a luxury rather than a necessity—if they decide to tighten their purse strings, you may be the first to go.

Essentials

Besides that green thumb, you'll need a working knowledge of indoor plants, their care and feeding, including what blooms in what season and which plants grow best under what lighting and humidity conditions. And if you'll be working on hardscapes, you'll need a knowledge of interior design and architectural elements as well.

Tools Of The Trade

All you really need are soil probes (regular size and perhaps a 4-footer for those towering indoor palms), watering cans, a pair of plant-snippers, plant foods and chemical insect controls, and a reliable vehicle to take you on your rounds.

Money Talk

Plant yourself in the business with start-up costs of less than $500. Expect annual gross revenues of $15,600 to $100,000 and up, depending on what you charge, what types of clients you have (major malls or small businesses), how many clients you have and, of course, how hard you want to work. Charge those clients $20 to $30 per hour, based on the number of plants, the amount of work you'll do (whether you're just watering and trimming or changing seasonal blooms, for instance) and your drive time.

Pounding The Pavement

Your customers can be residential and commercial, but businesses will provide a greater income with less drive time, especially if you sign up large corporations or office parks, or buildings where you can service a lot of clients in one stop. You can also target restaurants, hotels and institutions.

Hand-deliver brochures to prospective business customers. Place ads in local publications. Build up a referral network at garden centers and nurseries.

What's Next

Unless you're already an expert on indoor plants, study up on plant care. Find or design a handy carrying caddy for your tools and materials. Design a proposal for your services, pointing out the benefits of plants in the indoor environment and contact the Associated Landscape Contractors of America, which will provide you with a contract for your clients.

Organizations

- *American Horticultural Society*, 7931 E. Boulevard Dr., Alexandria, VA 22308, (800) 777-7931, www.ahs.org
- *Associated Landscape Contractors of America*, 150 Elden St., #270, Herndon, VA 20170, (800) 395-ALCA, www.alca.org
- *National Gardening Association*, 180 Flynn Ave., Burlington, VT 05401, (800) LETS-GROW

Books

- *All About Houseplants*, by Larry Hodgson, Susan Lauwers, Susan M. Lammers and Mariann Lipanovich, Ortho Books
- *The House Plant Encyclopedia*, by Ingrid Jantra, Firefly Books
- *The House Plant Expert*, by D.G. Hessayon, Sterling Publications

Cyber Assistance

- *The Garden Gate* (http://garden-gate.prairienet.org): All you'll ever need. Includes gardener's reading rooms, mailing lists, newsgroups, a teaching garden, garden shop, and more!
- *The Sun Room* (http://garden-gate.prairienet.org/sunroom.htm): Offers everything you could possibly want or need to know about indoor plants

Franchises

- *Foliage Design Systems*, 4496 35th St., Orlando, FL 32811, (800) 933-7351

The Inside Scoop

Everybody's ideal lawn is a swath of emerald green, each blade as precision-cut as a Marine drill sergeant's hair, and not a weed, bare patch or dog doodle in sight. But in today's two-income family and single-parent/breadwinner world, who has time to mind the lawn?

It could be you. As a lawn care professional, you can save the day by feeding, weeding, aerating and mowing the yards of not only residences, but businesses and institutions as well. And you can add to your income by rounding out your services from strictly lawn care to routine landscape maintenance. If you like working outdoors, making the world a greener and more beautiful place, and helping things grow, then this could be the business for you. According to the Professional Lawn Care Association, more than 22 million households spend $14.6 billion on professional landscape and lawn care services, so there's lots of room for growth.

The advantages to this business are that you can start on a shoestring, you're out in the fresh air every day with no ringing phones or clattering keyboards to interfere with the birdsong, and if you enjoy physical labor and the accomplishment of putting in a good day's work, then this can be a rewarding field.

The disadvantage is that you're at the mercy of the elements. You'll have to be on the job when it's 100 degrees and humid or 40 and foggy. And when it rains or snows, you can't tend lawns at all, which means your cash flow goes haywire.

Essentials

You'll need a good basic understanding of lawn care and of fertilizing and weed control products and techniques. A sense of logistics will also be a plus—the better route you map out of customer sites, the less time you'll spend on the road and the more efficient and cost-effective you'll be.

Tools Of The Trade

You'll need field tools, including an aerator, a power mower, an edger, a trimmer, a selection of rakes, a spreader for fertilizer and seed, a sprayer, and a small gasoline container for on-the-job refills. (Be sure to use an approved container and follow safe storage and usage practices.) You'll also need a vehicle to carry them in, a pick-up truck or other medium-duty vehicle and possibly a small trailer.

Money Talk

Assuming you already have the truck, you can get in the green with start-up costs of $500 to $1,500, depending on how many tools you already have and what you'll need to buy. Expect to make $25,000 to $50,000 or more, depending on how hard you want to work and how far you ultimately expand your services. Charge your customers $50 to $100 and up per visit, based on property size, for routine maintenance, plus additional fees for fertilizing, aerating or weed control. (Check your local competition for comparable prices.)

Pounding The Pavement

Your customers can be residential property owners or a wide variety of commercial properties—apartment and condominium complexes, hotels and motels, hospitals, large and small businesses and office parks. Government institutions make good sources of income as well.

Nab residential customers by going door-to-door with fliers or door hangers. (Don't place them in mailboxes—the U.S. Postal Service gets very upset about this.) Place ads in your local newspaper and in your neighborhood Yellow Pages.

For small-business commercial customers, hand-deliver fliers or brochures and explain your services. You may not get any takers the first time you visit, but don't get discouraged. A repeat visit or two can often seal a deal. A direct-mail campaign of a brochure will work better for large corporations; follow up with a phone call.

What's Next

If you're not already a lawn care expert, learn everything you can. Read up, talk to your local county extension service expert and

A STAR IS BORN

Keepin' It Green

Gene Sims spent 40 years manufacturing car radios, overseeing 52 men and 17 trucks. When he retired from the fast lane and moved to the resort town of Panama City Beach, Florida, six years ago, he turned back to his first love, gardening, and started growing Gene's Lawn Care—motto: Let Gene Keep It Green. His start-up costs, which included a truck, totaled about $14,000.

Sims keeps both his company and his customers in the green with what he counts as the essentials: honesty and service. But he's quick to point out that a good basic knowledge of horticulture is also imperative for a successful lawn-care and landscape maintenance company. "If you don't know bedding plants," he says by way of example, "you can kill 'em all real quick."

Not a problem for Gene's Lawn Care, which—with a crew of three to eight employees—handles not only lawns but landscape projects from routine maintenance to selecting and installing new plantings.

Sims runs a continuous ad in the service section of the local newspaper and has no trouble finding customers—in fact, he frequently fields midnight calls requesting a mow or landscape clean-up. The hard part, says the 65-year-old entrepreneur, is pricing yourself competitively. Gene's Lawn Care charges a basic rate of $35 an hour, less than the company could command in an urban area like Atlanta but more than the fly-by-nights with a lawn mower hanging out of the trunk who cruise beach neighborhoods.

With himself at the wheel of his pickup truck and his son primed to take over the daily duties while he slips into consulting mode, Sims is pleased with the way his company grows. "It's good work," he says, "and I enjoy doing it."

the lawn care pro down at your neighborhood garden center. Purchase an inexpensive vinyl magnetic-backed sign with your company name for your vehicle. Get the vehicle as clean and sharp as you can—potential customers will not be impressed by a rattle-trap truck. Design and build storage racks for your equipment. Investigate uniforms for yourself and any partners or employees—the professional look will increase business.

Organizations

- *Professional Lawn Care Association*, 1000 Johnson Ferry Rd. NE, Ste. C-135, Marietta, GA 30068-2112, (800) 458-3466, www.plcaa.org

Books

- *Entrepreneur's Business Guide #1198, Lawn Care Business*, Entrepreneur Media Inc., 2392 Morse Ave., Irvine, CA 92614, (800) 421-2300, www.smallbizbooks.com
- *Lawn Care & Gardening: A Down-to-Earth Guide to the Business*, by Kevin Rossi, Acton Circle Publishing

Cyber Assistance

- *Cyberlawn* (http://opei.mow.org): Fact-packed site developed by the Outdoor Power Equipment Institute—includes earth-friendly yard-care tips, lawn-care tips, a mower "repair shop," and even an opportunity to ride the cybermower
- *The Lawn Institute* (www.lawninstitute.com): Bills itself as a nationally recognized authority on turf grass—site contains lawn tips, a lawn newsletter and more

Franchises

- *Nutri-Lawn*, 5397 Eglinton Ave. W., #110, Toronto, ON, M9C 5K6, CAN, (800) 396-6096, www.valuenetwork.com/nutri-lawn. An ecology-friendly company.
- *Spring-Green Lawn Care Corp.*, 11927 Spaulding School Dr., Plainfield, IL 60544, www.spring-green.com

Chapter nine

HEALTHY & "WELL"THY

I f you've always wanted to be, or already are, involved in the medical field—your favorite TV shows are "ER" and "Chicago Hope," you subscribe to *Prevention* magazine, and check in to Dr. Koop's Web site on a daily basis—then this could be the Interest Category for you.

SENIOR HOME CARE AGENCY

The Inside Scoop

Here's the problem: A senior parent wants to live in his own home, maintaining his independence, but he has trouble bathing, fixing meals and remembering to take his medications. The solution: You. As owner of a senior home care agency, you'll send a qualified, compassionate person out to assist with the daily tasks of living.

This is a burgeoning field. According to the U.S. Census Bureau, as of the year 2000, there will be more than 3 million Americans aged 85 and older. With more and more seniors out there needing assistance and more and more two-income families, there's nobody to give mom or dad a helping hand. And with health-care costs rising by the moment, hospitals are discharging patients earlier than ever, sending them home too ill or too weak to fend for themselves. So senior home care is rewarding, not only financially but personally as well.

As a senior home care agency operator, you'll act as a referral service—much like a nanny placement service—locating cheerful, reliable, honest and kindly people to place in seniors' homes on a temporary or long-term basis. Your caregivers will be independent contractors paid directly by the patient or his family and though they must have the qualities listed above, they don't need medical training—just good common sense.

The advantages to this business are that you can start part time and you have the satisfaction of filling a real need, helping seniors lead more independent lives and taking some of the burden from worried family members.

The only disadvantages are that you can occasionally feel overwhelmed when you've got anxious clients and no one to send out to fill their needs. In addition, seniors can sometimes be cantankerous and difficult to work with—you may find clients who run through caregivers like Kleenex.

Essentials

You'll need terrific people skills—the ability to determine the suitability of potential caregivers and the magical quality of knowing which caregiver to pair with which client. Organizational and administrative skills are also a must because you'll be coordinating people, times and places all at once.

Tools Of The Trade

You don't need a medical background, but you should have the materials and knowledge to give your caregivers a good grounding in CPR, first aid and senior care professionalism. Make sure you don't position yourself as an employment agency or nursing registry because you'll need to be licensed for either of these—use independent contractors paid by the patient or his family. You'll want a computer with inkjet printer and the usual software.

Money Talk

Pencil in start-up costs of $2,150—which you can reduce to about $500 for initial advertising if you already have a computer. Once you get established, you can expect annual gross revenues of $75,000 to $250,000—if you're based in a more affluent area, you'll be able to command higher fees and therefore make more. Charge your clients $10 to $15 per day. (They'll pay the caregiver $7 to $10 an hour.) And once you get a case, you generally keep that case until the patient either passes away or has to be hospitalized on a long-term basis.

Pounding The Pavement

Your clients will be seniors and their families. You can place ads in local newspapers, but perhaps your best bet will be to establish

WELLNESS INSTRUCTOR

Fueled by baby boomers who aren't into actually aging, holistic health and wellness are popular topics today—and as our society grows older in spite of itself and lives longer, they'll continue to be popular. Take advantage of this trend, and teach and motivate people by being a wellness instructor. You'll give seminars and workshops on the physical—like drinking lots of water and eating healthy—to the spiritual, like stress management and empowerment. In some states, you may need certification, so be sure to check first. Then send brochures to businesses' human resources departments, advertise in your local newspaper and post fliers at community centers. **Start-up costs:** $500. **Expected annual gross revenues:** Up to $25,000.

your services throughout the medical community, which can provide referrals. Send sales letters and brochures to local hospitals and doctors specializing in geriatrics, cardiology and other diseases that affect seniors, local health-care agencies and senior centers, and even emergency medical services like paramedics. Follow up with phone calls to reinforce your image. Get your business written up in local publications.

What's Next

Start setting up your network of caregivers by placing ads in local newspapers and bone up on the tax and legal issues of hiring independent contractors.

Organizations

● *National Association for Home Care*, 228 Seventh St. SE, Washington, DC 20003, (202) 547-7424, www.nahc.org

Books

● *Entrepreneur's Business Start-Up Guide #1369, Home Health-Care Agency*, Entrepreneur Media Inc., 2392 Morse Ave., Irvine, CA 92614, (800) 421-2300, www.smallbizbooks.com

● *How to Start and Manage a Home Health Care Business*, by Jerre G. Lewis, Lewis & Renn Associates

Business Opportunities

- *Friend of the Family*, 880 Holcomb Bridge Rd., #160-B, Roswell, GA 30076, (770) 643-3000, ext. 200, www.afriend.com

Franchises

- *Home Instead Senior Care*, 604 N. 109th Ct., Omaha, NE 68154, (888) 484-5759, www.homeinstead.com
- *Homewatch Caregivers*, Homewatch International, 2865 S. Colorado Blvd., Denver, CO 80222, (800) 777-9770, www. homewatch-intl.com

MEDICAL CLAIMS BILLING

The Inside Scoop

Medical billing is one of the hottest businesses going these days—and with good reason. Thanks to the new baby boomlet and the increasing longevity of those of us already well into adulthood, more and more Americans are swelling the ranks of health-care seekers. And people are more health-conscious than ever before. Couple these points with the fact that doctors and other health-care providers are finding it increasingly difficult to earn a living from their services. Medicare, private insurance companies, and health-care groups such as HMOs have all seemingly conspired to make billing—and getting paid—a nightmare.

But if you have a medical or dental background and you like working with computers, then you can save the day with a medical billing service. You'll enter patients' charges into your specially designed software, then send these bills (or claims) to insurance companies via electronic data processing, the same type of system that sends your credit card information from the department store or gas station to the bank.

Some medical billing services offer "one-stop shopping," expanding their services to include handling all aspects of the doctor's billing, including charging and collecting from uninsured patients and collecting old debts.

Medical claims that are filed electronically are processed twice as fast as claims that are mailed to the insurer, so doctors get paid faster and more accurately. And with your billing expertise, you can quickly solve problems—like rejected claims—that may arise.

The advantages to this business are that you can work at home, you can start part time, the field is poised for greater growth as the years go by, and if you enjoy problem-solving in general and the medical field in particular, then this can be a lucrative and rewarding business.

The disadvantages are that the business can be extremely complex if you don't have a sufficient grounding in medical or dental practices and terminology, and diagnosis and procedure codes (which are what you base charges on) are frequently changed by government health-care agencies.

Essentials

You should have a solid working knowledge of the medical or dental fields—if you've worked as a nurse or a medical or dental assistant, or any other health-care professional, you'll have the awareness of terminology and procedures to take you to the top in a hurry. If you don't have this knowledge and experience, you can still succeed in medical billing, but the road will be much more difficult. You'll also need strong organizational and time-management skills— you'll have to be able to process claims and solve billing problems quickly.

Tools Of The Trade

You'll need a computer system with a laser printer, a fax machine, medical billing software, and an arrangement with an electronic clearinghouse, which checks your billings for errors, then forwards them to insurers. You should also have a car for picking up clients' billing materials, but this is not a must. Some medical billers have their clients fax everything to their home offices.

Money Talk

Bill yourself start-up costs of about $3,000. You can expect annual revenues of $20,000 to $100,000. The amount you'll charge your clients will depend on the going rate in your region of the country, but it's usually 5 percent to 7 percent of the amount billed per month, or $1.50 to $3 per claim.

Pounding The Pavement

Your clients can be any health-care providers you care to target—doctors of every specialty, dentists, oral surgeons, podiatrists, psychologists, ambulance services, pharmacists, prosthetics providers and nursing homes. You'll do best to start off with the specialty you

A STAR IS BORN

Prescription For Profits

Felicia Thomas spent almost 12 years on a hospital post-op surgical floor. When an on-the-job injury permanently sidelined her career in scrubs, she parlayed her knowledge of the health-care field and start-up costs of $13,000 to $15,000 into a medical billing business, San Diego-based Healthcare Management Services. Thomas, a homebased mother of two, found it hard going at first, but today, less than 18 months into her new career, she has 10 clients—enough that she's stopped taking on new business.

"Getting that first client is the toughest," Thomas advises. "If you don't have a client, then you have no basis, no credibility for [doctors] to rely on you. This is a big thing that they're giving up. A lot of doctors have a hard time giving up the financial end of things."

So how did the San Diego entrepreneur get those doctors to hand over the reins? With a variety of marketing techniques. "When one thing didn't work," says Thomas. "I tried another. I don't give up easily."

The former nurse reeled in her first doctor with a fill-out-and-return survey and garnered two more medicos as referrals from the first one. Other clients came, thanks to a postcard mailing, her company Web site, and a vendor table Thomas and a colleague set up at a chiropractors' seminar. And then there's the 10 percent price break on the monthly billing of their choice that Thomas gives to doctors who refer other doctors.

Lest you think all this was easy, be aware that it took Thomas five months of persistent cajoling to get that first client. "Some people are looking for a get-rich-quick scheme," she warns. "This is not the type of business to do that. You can be successful and make good money at this, but like any business, it takes time to generate a positive influx of income."

know—if you've worked in a cardiology office, start by selling your services to cardiologists.

Send letters and brochures to providers you've targeted. Follow up with phone calls requesting appointments. You may have to work hard to get your first client, but persistence pays off. Once you get that first provider, word-of-mouth will help speed your marketing efforts. Doctors are a gossipy bunch—they'll rapidly spread news of your abilities.

What's Next

Shop around for a software package and clearinghouse. There are lots out there—make sure you choose one that's compatible with your skills and experience. If you don't have a medical or dental background, take classes and seminars offered by local colleges and various organizations. Sign on as a temporary employee of a billing service to learn the ropes.

Organizations

- *American Association of Healthcare Administrative Management,* 1200 19th St. NW, #300, Washington, DC 20036, (202) 857-1179, www.aaham.org
- *National Electronic Biller's Alliance*, 2226-A Westborough Blvd., #504, San Francisco, CA 94080, (650) 577-1190, www.nebazone.com

Books

- *Directory of Medical Management Software*, Resource Books, 175 N. Buena Vista, San Jose, CA 95126, (800) 995-8702
- *Entrepreneur's Business Start-Up Guide #1345, Medical Claims Billing Service*, Entrepreneur Media Inc., 2392 Morse Ave., Irvine, CA 92614, (800) 421-2300, www.smallbizbooks.com
- *Making Money in a Health Service Business on Your Home-Based PC*, by Rick Benzel, McGraw-Hill

Publications

- *The Journal of Medical Practice Management*, Williams & Wilkins, Journal Customer Service, 351 W. Camden St., Baltimore, MD 21201-2436, (800) 638-6423, www.wwilkins.com
- *Medical Economics Magazine*, 5 Paragon Dr., Montvale, NJ 07645, (800) 223-0581, www.medec.com

Business Opportunities

- *Claimtek Systems*, 222 SE 16th Ave., Portland, OR 97214-1488, (800) 224-7450

- *Pacific Medical*, 9921 Carmel Mountain Rd., #321, San Diego, CA 92129, (800) 815-6334, www.pacificmedical.com

- *Santiago SDS Inc.*, 1801 Dove St., Newport Beach, CA 92660, (800) 652-3500

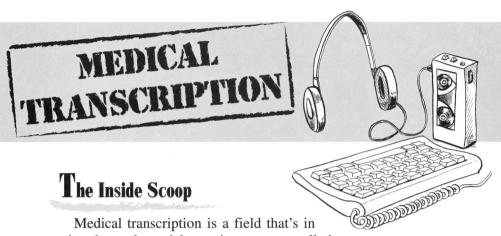

MEDICAL TRANSCRIPTION

The Inside Scoop

Medical transcription is a field that's in major demand—and becoming more so all the time. Since health insurance companies often require transcripts of medical procedures before they'll pay for them, doctors need somebody to translate their dictated reports into professional-looking documents.

And that could be you. If you like the fascination of the medical field and the feeling of accomplishment that comes with turning out a professional product that's badly needed, then this might be the business for you.

As a medical transcriptionist, you'll sit at your computer, earphones on your head, jamming to the sounds of surgeons detailing operations (or other medical professionals giving a play-by-play of other procedures), then send the completed reports by modem back to the doctor or hospital. The great thing about this is that you don't have to leave home—you can receive dictation over the phone and send it back via e-mail. (Of course, there are also lots of jobs using the traditional dictaphone, too.)

Time is of the essence in this field. If you can offer a 24-hour—or less-than-24-hour—turnaround, work second- and third-shift hours and occasionally put in weekends or all-nighters, then you'll be an all-star.

The advantages to this business are that there's far more demand than there are transcriptionists to fill it, so you'll have plenty of work, you can operate from home, and if you enjoy working in a professional field, this can be a worthwhile venture.

The disadvantages are that the faster you work, the more money you make, so you might end up tied to your keyboard all day, every day with earphones clamped to your head and a case of carpal tunnel syndrome on the horizon. (To help counteract this, you can invest in an ergonomic keyboard and wrist rests.)

Essentials

You must have a strong knowledge of medical terminology and excellent spelling, grammar and punctuation skills. The ability to interpret sometimes garbled dictation from doctors with a variety of accents, dialects and speech patterns is also important. You'll also need the self-discipline to sit at your keyboard uninterrupted for long hours and remain focused—goofs can spell disaster in this business.

Tools Of The Trade

You'll need a computer system with a laser printer (you'll sometimes print your reports), a fax machine, a dedicated phone line, a dictaphone, word-processing software and special medical transcription software. You'll want a library of reference books, including a medical transcription style guide, a medical dictionary, drug reference books and various medical-terminology guides.

Money Talk

Dictate start-up costs of about $3,000. As an established medical transcriptionist, expect annual gross revenues in the range of $40,000. You'll charge your clients by the line (which is estimated to be about 65 characters long). Line rates vary nationwide, so you'll need to check comparable prices in your area, but as a thumbnail, an average rate would be about .18 per line, or about $2 per minute of dictation.

Pounding The Pavement

Your clients can be doctors, hospitals (including medical records departments, information offices, radiology and pathology departments and emergency rooms), other health-care providers like clinics and psychologists, and attorneys working disability or malpractice cases. Send sales letters to these prospects, then follow up with a phone call. You can also place ads in local medical professional publications and call transcriptionists to ask for overload work or referrals.

What's Next

If you don't have medical transcription experience, start learning. Take classes at local colleges or technical schools. Start building your reference library.

Organizations

- *American Association for Medical Transcription*, P.O. Box 576187, Modesto, CA 95355-6187 (shipping address), 3460 Oakdale Rd., Ste. M, Modesto, CA 95355-9691, (209) 551-0883, www.aamt.org
- *Medical Transcription Industry Alliance*, 77 Broadway E., #7, Seattle, WA 98102, (800) 328-3333, www.mtia.com

Books

- *Entrepreneur Business Start-Up Guide #1392, Medical Transcription Service*, Entrepreneur Media Inc., 2392 Morse Ave., Irvine, CA 92614, (800) 421-2300, www.smallbizbooks.com
- *The Independent Medical Transcriptionist*, by Donna Avila-Weil and Mary Glaccum, Rayve Productions
- *Medical Transcription Guide: Do's and Don'ts*, by Marilyn Takahashi Fordney and Marcy Otis Diehl

Publications

- *Journal of the American Association for Medical Transcription*, P.O. Box 576187, Modesto, CA 95355-6187, (209) 551-0883, www.aamt.org

CyberAssistance

- *HandiLinks to Medical Transcription* (www.handilinks.com): Jam-packed with helpful sites and other stuff for the professional
- *mt desk* (www.mtdesk.com): More links to more great sites than you can imagine. An absolute must-surf!

ChaPter ten

HOUSE SMARTS

You're the one everybody calls on when the bathroom faucet drips all night, the kitchen cabinets need replacing, or they've bought that older house that's a home repair nightmare. If you're a home repair expert and you love nothing better than hammering, sawing, drilling and painting, then this is the category for you. If you can't paint a room without painting yourself as well, and you hammer your thumb instead of the nail, but you're the one everybody asks for decorating advice, then this can be your category as well.

APARTMENT PREP SERVICE

The Inside Scoop

When tenants vacate apartments, they usually fail to clean up after themselves. Even the tidiest tenant can leave a trail of normal wear and tear—carpets that need cleaning, nail holes to be filled and walls to be painted. And apartment managers and other assorted landlords rarely have the time or the inclination to handle the tasks.

But if you like transforming shabby to shiny and you're not afraid of a little elbow grease, then you can answer an apartment manager's prayers with an apartment prep service. You'll scrub bathrooms, kitchens and baseboards, wax floors and shampoo carpets. You'll toss out junk—you'd be surprised at what people leave behind—and you'll patch holes, paint, and replace cracked windows, broken towel bars and off-track closet doors—whatever it takes to get that unit looking spic, span and sharp to show to the next prospective tenant.

The advantages to this business are that you can start on a shoestring, you often find interesting treasures among the former tenant's trash, it's recession- and trend-proof, and if you like the glow of accomplishment that comes from putting in a good day's physical labor, then you'll have a long and satisfying career. It's also gratifying—landlords and managers faced with a tenant mess are always appreciative when you come in to save the day.

The only disadvantages are that because most people move out at the end of the month, jobs can tend to stack up all at once, and that this is labor-intensive stuff. You'll definitely put in a good day's work.

Essentials

You'll need experience in patching and painting, plus a few other fix-it skills like replacing mirrors or doors, and the ability to do a sparkling cleaning job in a relatively short time. You'll also need a sense of logistics to take you from one job to another efficiently.

Tools Of The Trade

You'll need a caddy of cleaning supplies, a vacuum cleaner, carpet shampooer, mop, broom and dustpan, rolls of rags or paper towels, scrub brushes and sponges, rubber gloves, rolls of garbage bags, a stepstool or a small ladder, flea spray, a general-purpose bug spray, and carpet deodorizer. You'll also want paint brushes, rollers and trays, putty knives, spackle, window putty, a glass knife, and a caddy of tools like hammers, screwdrivers and wrenches. And you'll want a pager so clients can get in touch with you quickly.

Money Talk

Prep yourself with start-up costs of about $500. Expect to make annual gross revenues of $25,000 to $37,500. You'll charge your clients $100 to $150 and up per job, depending on the size and range of the work—not including paint and other noncleaning materials, which you'll charge to your clients.

Pounding The Pavement

Your clients can be managers or owners of large or small apartment complexes, individual landlords who own rental properties, and real estate agents charged with managing rental properties or selling vacant ones.

Send your brochure to apartment managers or owners and realtors, and follow up with a phone call. Or stop in and introduce yourself—this works even better. If you don't get a job immediately, check back. Persistence pays off. You can target individual landlords by calling "for rent" ads in the newspaper and asking if you can send them a brochure and card for future reference.

What's Next

Gather your tools and supplies. Check into uniforms—a polo or T-shirt with your company name embroidered on the pocket or screen-printed on the front enhances your professional image and will increase business.

Organizations

● *California Apartment Association*, 980 Ninth St., #2150, Sacramento, CA 95814, (800) 967-4222, www.ca-apartment.org

● *Houston Apartment Association*, 10815 Fallstone Rd., Houston, TX 77099-3496, (281) 933-2224, www.haaonline.org

Note: Your state or urban area probably has an apartment association as well. Check your local Yellow Pages.

Books

● *Cleaning Up for a Living: Everything You Need to Know to Become a Successful Building Service Contractor*, by Don A. Aslett, Betterway Publications

● *Everyday Home Repairs (Black and Decker Home Improvement Library series)*, Creative Publishing International

● *New Complete Do-It-Yourself Manual*, by *Reader's Digest*

The Inside Scoop

If you could see the average home from a baby's point of view, you could find all sorts of trouble to get into—electrical outlets and cords, poisons in cupboards, interesting plants to eat, and more. Since most of us adults don't go around on our hands and knees, we don't see these potential hazards—or realize other home dangers like scalding water or reachable plastic bags. According to the National Center for Injury Prevention and Control, each year between 20 percent and 25 percent of all children sustain an injury severe enough to require medical attention, missed school and/or bed rest. And with nearly 4 million births in one recent year, there are plenty of babies around.

You can avert catastrophes with a baby-proofing service. You'll tour homes, installing safety latches, catches and other safety devices and alerting parents to potential hazards like poisonous plants and other materials.

The advantages to this business are that you can work from a home base, you can start out part time, and you'll provide a needed, appreciated service.

The disadvantages are that your target market is basically limited to households with young children who have the income to afford your services, and that once you service them you're unlikely to get their repeat business.

Essentials

You'll need a strong knowledge of what kind of trouble babies and small children can get into and how to avert it. You'll need good people skills to work with parents, some of whom may be on the overanxious side. And you'll need the confidence to install child-proofing latches and other safety devices while mom, dad and assorted grandparents are hovering over your shoulder.

Tools Of The Trade

You'll need basic tools like screwdrivers, wrenches and a cordless drill, as well as a tidy supply of baby-proofing devices. And since this is a business that hits about as close to customers' homes and hearts as possible, you'll want to be sure to carry liability insurance.

Money Talk

Baby yourself with start-up costs of $500 to $750 to cover advertising and initial baby-proofing devices. You can expect annual gross revenues of $30,000 to $60,000 per year. You'll charge your clients $10 to $40 an hour, or you can bid by the job—be sure to add in a fee for the devices.

Pounding The Pavement

Your customers will consist mostly of parents and grandparents of babies and toddlers, but you might also target businesses that find babies on board—look for ones that have children's play areas set up

Weekend Warrior

HOUSE-SITTER

You can help vacationers or businesspeople leave town with light hearts with a house-sitting service. You'll pop in every day to collect the mail, feed Puss or Rover, water the plants, pick up newspapers, adjust the heat or air conditioning if necessary, and give the place the once-over for any signs of trouble. All you need to get started is a set of references from friends and neighbors and a reliable vehicle to take you on your rounds, although you may want to be bonded or carry insurance. Advertise by leaving fliers on homeowners' doorsteps and placing ads in your local newspaper. **Start-up costs:** $500. **Expected annual gross revenues:** $5,000 to $10,000.

in a corner so toddlers can play while mom, for instance, shops or visits the doctor.

Place ads in local papers and get yourself written up in local publications. Send brochures to pediatricians. Introduce yourself to business owners and leave brochures. Go on a local radio chat show to talk about baby-proofing.

What's Next

Learn everything you can about baby-proofing. Read articles and books, talk to emergency room staff, poison control centers and pediatricians. Check out the baby latches and other devices at your home improvement center and stock up on them, plus a caddy to carry them in.

Organizations

● *American Academy of Pediatrics*, 141 Northwest Point Blvd., Elk Grove Village, IL 60007-1098, (847) 228-5005, www.aap.org

● *National Center for Injury Prevention and Control*, Mailstop K65, 4770 Buford Hwy. NE, Atlanta, GA 30341-3724, (770) 488-1506, www.cdc.gov/ncipc

● *National Safety Council*, 1131 Spring Lake Dr., Itasca, IL 60143-3201, (800) 285-1121, www.nsc.org

Books

● *On the Safe Side: Your Complete Reference to Childproofing for Infants and Toddlers*, by Cindy Wolf, Whirlwind Publishing

HANDYMAN

The Inside Scoop

If you're the type who can (and likes to) do just about anything around the house—mend a leaky faucet, nail down those sagging shingles, paint a wall, unstick a sticking door, repair a broken cabinet or build a garbage can enclosure, then this might be just the business for you.

You'll be on-call in your neighborhood for all those jobs that aren't quite big enough to hire an expensive contractor but are beyond the homeowner's expertise or time constraints. This is a business with room for growth: According to the U.S. Census Bureau, Americans spent nearly $43 million on home maintenance and repairs in a single recent year.

The advantages to this business are that you can work from home, you can start on a shoestring, you're always doing something different, and it's gratifying. People are delighted when you can save them money by doing the job yourself and appreciative of skills that they don't possess.

The only real disadvantage is that you'll occasionally bump up against that customer who isn't satisfied no matter what you do or how you do it.

Essentials

You'll need a variety of home-repairs skills—everything from minor plumbing to minor electrical to painting and carpentry. You'll want people skills because you'll be dealing with a variety of personalities on their home turf, and a good sense of logistics to help you determine which jobs to schedule in what order.

Tools Of The Trade

In some states, you'll need a contractor's license, so be sure to check with your local contractor's board or commerce department before you start. You'll want to be bonded. And you'll need the handyperson's stock-in-trade: hammers, screwdrivers, pliers, wrenches, grip vises, flashlights, a cordless saw, a stepstool and ladder, and paint brushes and rollers. You should also have a pager so customers can reach you during the day and a pickup truck for making house calls.

Money Talk

Assuming you already have the truck, you can pencil in start-up costs of $500 to $1,000, depending on how many tools you already have and what you'll want to go out and buy. Expect to make annual gross revenues of $30,000 to $60,000. You'll charge your clients $10 to $40 an hour, or you can bid by the job.

Pounding The Pavement

Your customers will be mostly homeowners, but you can also target owners or managers of small apartment buildings or condominium complexes who don't have a maintenance person on staff, and small shopkeepers and real estate agents who may need help with a vacant property.

Deliver fliers detailing your services to potential customers by tucking them under doormats or making them into door hangers. (Don't place them in mailboxes—the U.S. Postal Service gets very upset about this.) Place ads in your local newspaper and in your neighborhood Yellow Pages.

For small-business commercial customers, hand-deliver fliers or brochures and explain your services. You may not get any takers the first time you visit, but don't get discouraged. A repeat visit or two can often seal a deal.

What's Next

Check to make sure you don't need a contractor's license or special permit. Get bonded. Design and make or purchase a caddy for your tools. Look into a uniform—a polo shirt or jacket with your company name on the pocket will give you a professional appearance and help land business.

Organizations

- *National Association of the Remodeling Industry*, 4900 Seminary Rd., #320, Alexandria, VA 22311, (703) 575-1100, www.nari.org

Books

- *Everyday Home Repairs (Black and Decker Home Improvement Library series)*, Creative Publishing International
- *New Complete Do-It-Yourself Manual*, by *Reader's Digest*

A STAR IS BORN

Living On A Fix-It Income

If you need something fixed in Panama City Beach, Florida, the man to call is Clarence Keith, a k a Mr. Fixit. With occasional after-school assistance from his sons Paul and Justin, Keith runs a one-man handyman service that keeps him on the go six days a week and sometimes on Sundays as well. During the resort community's hectic spring and summer seasons, Mr. Fixit makes nine to 10 service calls a day; in fall and winter he averages about three.

Keith stepped into his Mr. Fixit shoes three years ago after a 20-year career in the military and four years of retirement due to poor health. When he got back on his feet, he realized he was happier working than lounging around with a remote control. He signed on as second-in-command for a local handyman service called Mr. Fixit, and when the owner moved to Japan, Keith took both the title and the reins.

Keith, 51, does no advertising—all his business comes via word-of-mouth. He builds in additional steady income—and assures customer loyalty—with service contracts that give clients a price break and guarantee semiannual maintenance work on heaters and air conditioners.

The secrets to a successful handyman business? "Don't overprice yourself out of a job," Keith advises. "Don't overload yourself. You need good communication and work habits, and you need to know what you're doing."

- *Quick Home Maintenance: Protect Your Family's Most Important Investment*, Luxart Communications

Franchises

- *Handyman Connection*, 230 Northland Blvd., #229, Cincinnati, OH 45246, (800) 466-5530, www.handymanconnection.com
- *House Doctors Handyman Service*, 6355 E. Kemper Rd., #250, Cincinnati, OH 45241, (800) 319-3359

HARDWOOD FLOOR REFINISHER

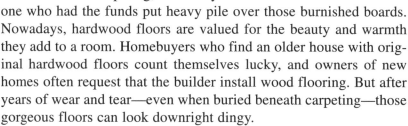

The Inside Scoop

Fifty or 60 years ago, if you had hardwood floors it meant that you couldn't afford carpeting, and everyone who had the funds put heavy pile over those burnished boards. Nowadays, hardwood floors are valued for the beauty and warmth they add to a room. Homebuyers who find an older house with original hardwood floors count themselves lucky, and owners of new homes often request that the builder install wood flooring. But after years of wear and tear—even when buried beneath carpeting—those gorgeous floors can look downright dingy.

If you like working with wood, restoring ugly ducklings to their rightful titles of flooring beauties, then a hardwood floor refinishing business might be for you.

The advantages to this business are that you can work from home, you can start part time with relatively low costs, and you get the deep-down glow that comes from giving new life to fine wood.

The disadvantages are that the equipment is heavy, your customers will probably expect you to move furniture to clear the room, and there's a lot of hands-and-knees work involved.

Essentials

Hardwood floor refinishing is an art—you should know how to read wood, whether it's healthy or not, suffering from moisture or dryness, and how it lives in the home it's in. You'll need a good working knowledge and solid skills with your equipment and materials, including polyurethanes, varnishes and stains.

Tools Of The Trade

You'll need a drum floor sander, an edger, a buffer with steel wool pads, and a reliable vehicle like a pickup truck to get you and your equipment to jobs.

Money Talk

Assuming you've already got the truck, you can plan on start-up costs of just under $12,000, most of which will go for your equipment. You can expect annual gross revenues of $50,000 and up, depending on how popular hardwood floors are in your area and how hard you want to work. You'll charge your clients $1.75 to $2 per square foot, plus an additional fee—about 25 cents per square foot—for added services like dark stains.

Pounding The Pavement

Your customers will be home and apartment owners, remodeling contractors and interior designers. You can generally figure that homes and apartments built prior to the late 1950s will have hardwood floors—target neighborhoods of these homes and leave fliers on doorsteps or as door hangers. Send fliers to interior designers and contractors, then follow up with phone calls to reinforce your com-

Weekend Warrior

WALLPAPER HANGER

Wallpaper is a perennial favorite in the home-decorating world. But not everybody has the knack for applying it. If you do, then you can hang loose with a wallpaper-hanging business. You'll remove old wall coverings if they exist, then install the new—from borders to chair rails to ceilings or dormers. You'll work with owners of homes, apartments and businesses, as well as interior designers and contractors to dress up those interiors. So grab those wallpaper tools, make up fliers and business cards, and leave them at wall-covering and decorating centers as you introduce yourself and ask for referrals. **Start-up costs:** $250. **Expected annual gross revenues:** $10,000 to $20,000.

pany in their minds. Leave cards or fliers at neighborhood hardware or home improvement stores (larger warehouse-type centers don't usually allow this).

Get your company written up in the real estate or home section of your local newspaper. Network in your community.

What's Next

Establish a relationship with the folks at your local home improvement stores and warehouses. They can be a good source of advice and terrific referrals for new business.

Organizations

● *Floor Coverings Installation Contractors Association*, P.O. Box 948, Dalton, GA 30722-0948, (706) 226-5488

HOME INSPECTION

The Inside Scoop

Purchasing a home is a big-time expense for most people and comes complete with worries, not only about the mortgage, but also about possible defects. The average home buyer has no idea whether that dream abode is indeed a dream or a nightmare of cracked foundations, leaky roofs, electrical hazards or bursting water pipes ready to fall to pieces.

But if you have construction or remodeling experience and you like diagnosing house ailments, then you can give that buyer sweet dreams—or at least let him know what he's up against—as a home inspector. You'll work mostly for buyers, but also for sellers and with real estate agents, clambering around in attics, crawl spaces and basements, peering at plumbing and electrical components, air conditioning and heating systems, and checking out decks, pools and landscaping elements. You'll then provide a written report or checklist of your findings. If the news is bad, the buyer can back out of the deal, renegotiate the contract, or arrange to have the seller correct any defects before the sale is finalized.

In these days when everybody seems to be lawsuit-mad, your service can solve problems before they arise, making the seller and realtor as happy as the buyer. And this business is poised for growth—real estate disclosure laws make inspections more important than ever, and mortgage lending firms and institutions often require inspections before handing out loans.

The advantages to this business are that you're always out and about, and you get to see lots of different homes and exercise your mind, solving where-did-that-water-stain-come-from type mysteries.

The disadvantages are that you can potentially be on the receiving end of flak if a problem you didn't catch surfaces after the sale. (Protect yourself with errors-and-omissions insurance.) If you've got claustrophobia or no head for heights, you won't like climbing ladders or through crawl spaces. And as a final minus, while you can do well financially with a home inspection service, it takes quite a while to build up a clientele—be prepared to both market aggressively and wait out the slow times.

Essentials

You'll need extensive knowledge of homes and how they work (or don't work)—foundations, walls, floors, roofs, plumbing, electricity, heating and air conditioning. You also must be able to diagnose major-appliance problems; outdoor components like pools, drainage, decks and landscaping; and invisible ailments like radon and lead-based paint. And you should be familiar with building and zoning codes and ordinances in your area.

You'll also need people skills to work with high-anxiety home sellers, overanxious home buyers, and real estate agents who may fear your findings will gum up a potentially sealed deal.

Tools Of The Trade

Most states don't require a license, but you may want to join the American Society of Home Inspectors for start-up credibility. You'll need a ladder that reaches to most roofs in your area, flashlights, screwdrivers, an ice pick for testing for dry rot or termites, electrical diagnostic tools like circuit testers and volt meters, a moisture meter, water pressure gauge, gas leak detector and carbon monoxide detector.

You'll also need a checklist on which you can make detailed notes and a computer system with a laser or inkjet printer and the usual software on which to write them up. And don't forget the errors-and-omissions insurance as well as liability insurance and bonding.

Money Talk

Home in on start-up costs of $2,400 to $3,000. Annual gross revenues for established home inspectors range from $50,000 to

$100,000 per year. Charge your clients $150 to $400 per inspection, depending on the size and age of the home and the going rates in your area.

Pounding The Pavement

Your clients will be home buyers and real estate agents, mortgage lenders and attorneys who deal with real estate transactions, with the occasional home seller thrown in for good measure.

Your best bet is to target realtors, attorneys and mortgage companies by sending your brochure, then following up with a phone call to cement your image in their minds. Give talks to real estate professionals on the benefits of your services. Place ads in the Sunday real estate sections of local papers. Get your business written up in local publications.

What's Next

If you don't have home inspection or comparable construction experience, start learning. You can take courses at local colleges or check in with professional organizations. Sign on for a short stint with a working home inspector to learn the ropes.

Organizations

● *American Society of Home Inspectors Inc.*, 932 Lee St., #101, Des Plaines, IL 60016, (800) 743-ASHI, www.ashi.com. Be sure to check out the online library, which contains links to every facet of home construction imaginable.

Books

● *10 Most Common Questions Asked About the Home Inspection Business and More*, by Stanley C. Harbuck, Heur Evectic Inc.

● *Entrepreneur's Business Start-Up Guide #1369, Home Inspection Service*, Entrepreneur Media Inc., 2392 Morse Ave., Irvine, CA 92614, (800) 421-2300, www.smallbizbooks.com

● *The Home Buyer's Inspection Guide: Everything You Need to Know to Save $$ and Get a Better House*, by Warren Boroson and Ken Austin, John Wiley & Sons

● *Real Estate Home Inspection: Mastering the Profession*, by Russell Burgess, Dearborn Publishing

Franchises

- *The BrickKicker Home Inspections*, 849 N. Ellsworth St., Napierville, IL 60563, (800) 821-1820, www.brickkicker.com
- *HouseMaster*, 421 W. Union Ave., Bound Brook, NJ 08805, (800) 526-3939, www.housemaster.com
- *Pillar to Post*, 14502 N. Dale Mabry Hwy., #200, Tampa, FI, 33618, (800) 294-5591, www.pillartopost.com

HOUSE PAINTER

The Inside Scoop

One of the hallmarks of a well-kept home or prosperous business is a fresh, professional coat of paint. But most people hate painting—it takes a lot of time and skill to do the job right—plus you have to spread drop cloths over everything, climb around on ladders or scaffolding, and hope you don't get paint in your hair.

But if you like painting—you love the smell of latex and oils and the transformation as a dingy room or building becomes clean and new—and you've got the talent and experience to deliver a first-class job, then this could be the business for you.

The advantages to this business are that you can work from a home base, your start-up costs can be relatively low, and if you like the feeling of accomplishment that comes from a good day's physical labor, it can be both rewarding and lucrative.

The disadvantages are that, when you're doing exterior jobs, you'll have to work with Mother Nature. If it's blistering hot or biting cold, once you've started a project you've got to finish it, and if it rains, it throws your schedule out of kilter. And this is a business where you can run into difficulties if you work on a construction project for a general contractor—if he runs into cash flow problems, they can affect you.

Essentials

You'll need experience in painting interiors and exteriors and in working with different types of paints and primers. You'll also need some people skills in dealing with various personalities and the ability to estimate a job and come out on the winning end.

Tools Of The Trade

You can start off with a couple sizes of ladders, an assortment of brushes, rollers and paint trays and perhaps a sprayer and a breathing mask. As you grow, you can branch out to heavy-duty sprayers and compressors and a set of scaffolding. You'll also need a pickup truck to carry you and your equipment to jobs.

Money Talk

Assuming you already have the truck, paint yourself (not into a corner!) with start-up costs of $500 to $1,000, depending on what tools you already have and what you'll want or need to purchase. A good range of annual gross revenues for a one-person house painting service is $50,000 to $75,000. You can charge your customers by the job, by the square foot or—on interiors—by the room. Check the going rates in your area and make yours comparable. And make sure that when you bid jobs, you consider the existing condition of the project as well as your materials and all the prep work you'll have to do—from sanding to covering up shrubs or furniture. Otherwise, as a spokesperson for the Painting and Decorating Contractors of America puts it, "The only way to make a small fortune is to have started off with a large one."

Pounding The Pavement

Your targets will be homeowners, apartment buildings and condominium complexes, businesses large and small, interior designers, and real estate agents who may need help with a vacant property.

You may want to specialize in certain types of painting—homeowners and interior designers will go for decorative treatments like sponge-painting, faux aging or stenciling—or, if you live in a historic area, you can specialize in "painted ladies," those glorious, gaudy Victorians, Colonial homes, or whatever suits your neighborhood. Using authentic historic colors for antique homes is very popular these days, so you can offer color consultation and expertise as part of your historical service.

To sell to this type of client, send brochures to historic home associations or introduce yourself to homeowners and contractors. To target other types of prospects, send brochures; leave fliers on homeowners' doorsteps; and network with interior designers, contractors and real estate agents.

You can also place ads in local papers. If you specialize in decorative-painting techniques, get your company written up in local publications, give talks to local groups and volunteer yourself as a guest on a local radio chat show.

What's Next

Decide if you'll be a specialist or a generalist. Gather your tools and materials. Introduce yourself to local paint and home-improvement stores—they can be excellent referral sources and also help with any questions you may have.

Organizations

● *Independent Professional Painting Contractors Association of America*, c/o Heinz K. Hoffman, P.O. Box 1759, Huntington, NY 11743, (516) 423-3654

● *Painting and Decorating Contractors of America*, 3913 Old Lee Hwy., #33B, Fairfax, VA 22030, (800) 332-PDCA, www.pdca.com

Books

● *Making Money With Your Creative Paint Finishes*, by Lynette Harris, North Light Books

Cyber Assistance

● *USA Painter* (www.usapainter.com): Calls itself "Everything Painting Online" and it is, with industry links, painter community boards, paint-talk archives and more

Franchises

● *Certa Propainters Ltd.*, 1140 Valley Forge Rd., Valley Forge, PA 19482, (800) 452-3782, www.certapropainters.com

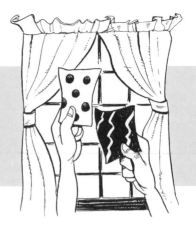

The Inside Scoop

If you love interior decorating—your home draws admiring comments from visitors, you've got décor magazines stacked on coffee tables and nightstands, home design shows playing on the television all day (and night), and you're a home furnishings shopaholic—then this could be the business for you.

As an interior designer or decorator, you'll help clients make their home or work spaces comfortable, attractive reflections of their interests and personalities. You'll deal with architects, contractors, painters, wallpaperers and stencilers, and purchase all the elements that go into the home's décor, including window and wall coverings, furniture, linens, and accent pieces.

The advantages to this business are that you can work from home, start-up costs are relatively low, it's challenging and creative, and if you're a decorating junkie, it provides the opportunity to redecorate over and over without tearing your own house apart and spending a fortune.

The only real disadvantage is that you've got to work with lots of personalities and tastes. If your client insists on Southwestern décor, that's what you'll have to go with, even if you detest it. You'll also occasionally run up against the client who can't be pleased or the one who can't stop making changes long after the job should have ended.

Essentials

You'll need a strong design and color sense and a good working knowledge of furnishings, fabrics and wall coverings. You should also be aware of design trends and traditions. Good people skills are important and organizational abilities are a must—you'll be coordinating painters and other contractor types and furniture and furnishings deliveries, and you'll sometimes be on a ready-in-time-for-the-daughter's-wedding or other special-event deadline.

Tools Of The Trade

Some states require an interior design license—check with local professional organizations to find out local regulations. You'll need a computer system with a laser printer and the usual software, a fax machine, sample books of fabrics and wall coverings, and a tape measure. You can purchase a number of interior-design software programs that let you print out floor plans, 3-dimensional room designs and even change decorating colors. If you're a computer person, shop around for one that suits you.

Money Talk

Design start-up costs of $3,500 or less, depending on how many sample books you need and what prices you can negotiate for them. (Some vendors will give them out as freebies; others require $20 to $60 per book.) Expect annual revenues of $30,000 to $50,000. Charge your clients $40 to $125 per hour, or you can figure out a flat fee per job. Since shopping is part of your services, you'll add buying fees onto your rates. You can tack 20 percent onto the price of any materials and furnishings you purchase, or you can purchase the goods at wholesale prices, charge your clients the retail price, and keep the difference. Since all this can get sticky, make sure you spell out everything in a contract before you start. Once you get established, you can expect annual gross revenues of $60,000 to $187,500.

Pounding The Pavement

Your clients can be residential or commercial property owners. You can specialize in types of properties like restaurants, hotels or offices, or you can work with all these and residences, too. Or you can specialize in the type of work you do—instead of completely redoing an entire home, you can do shoestring redesign, redecorating a single room using the owner's existing furnishings in new ways.

Network at your chamber of commerce and other local professional organizations. Send brochures to architects and contractors, especially those building spec homes who need a decorated model; follow up with phone calls. Place an ad in your local Yellow Pages. Volunteer yourself as a guest on a local radio chat show and as a speaker at women's clubs.

A STAR IS BORN

Designer Details

Heidi Wianecki is an artist and interior designer whose work has appeared in magazines, on television, and in the homes of a loyal following. And she attributes it all to her dad. Growing up, she says, she had the luxury of a father who constantly said "No." She wanted a fancy headboard, for example, but her dad nixed the idea. So she painted one on the wall, which led to her doing her own room as well as those of her girlfriends.

Wianecki, who is a fine artist as well as a self-professed "doodler," finds inspiration for her interiors in scavenged materials she translates into eclectic furnishings—lampshades fashioned from beads and sea glass; ceilings paneled in old, painted doors; and tables with croquet mallet and tennis racquet supports.

All of the Pacific Palisades, California, resident's work comes via word-of-mouth—she does no advertising. Clients who've seen her decorating style want the same look for their own homes. "Start out by making your own house fabulous," Wianecki counsels. "Let people know you're into doing interiors, and then business will build from there."

The homebased mother of two frequently does projects on an hourly basis, giving clients' homes a beauty makeover by re-arranging the furnishings they already have on hand in a fresh, new way. Her ideas are so well-received that most of her clients stay with her for years, through new babies, adolescent re-dos and all the other changes in family life. "You get involved in people's lives," Wianecki says. "Most of my clients I never stop working with." One advantage to working on an hourly basis, she says, is that if you come up against a personality conflict, you can finish the hour and leave.

"I have a vision and I go for it," Wianecki says of her ideas in art and design, both of which are self-taught. Her advice for newbies who want to follow their own vision as a designer? Don't sweat the sales stuff. "It's so easy to create a mood,? she says. "You're not selling yourself; you're sellingh a product that you make."

What's Next

Join a local professional design organization. Find out if you need certification in your area. Take classes and seminars; read everything you can. Sign on as an employee of a going concern to learn the ropes. Establish contacts with wholesalers and with local wall-covering and fabric shops and home improvement centers—they can be a good source of referrals as well as materials. Put together a portfolio of your work—you can showcase your home or do one for a friend or a charitable organization free of charge.

Organizations

● *American Society of Interior Designers*, 608 Massachusetts Ave. NE, Washington, DC 20002-6006, (202) 546-3480, www.asid.org

Books

● *How to Prosper As an Interior Designer: A Business and Legal Guide*, by Robert L. Alderman, John Wiley & Sons
● *The Interior Design Business Handbook*, by Mary V. Knacksedt and Laura J. Haney, John Wiley & Sons
● *The Interior Designer's Marketing Workbook*, by Jennifer Dowdall and Melani Berry, Bery byLines

Business Opportunities

● *Décor & More Inc.*, 900 Main St. S., Bldg. 2, Southbury, CT 06488, (800) 477-3326

Franchises

● *Decorating Den Systems Inc.*, 19100 Montgomery Village Ave., #200, Montgomery Village, MD 20886, (800) DEC-DENS, www.decoratingden.com
● *Décor-At-Your-Door International*, P.O. Box 1089, Pollock Pines, CA 95726, (800) 936-3326, www.decor-at-your-door.com

Cha**p**ter eleven

HOW TO SUCCEED IN BUSINESS

If you find the world of business fascinating—you like the excitement of nurturing a new company into prosperity, the thrill of competition with other corporate entities and the mechanics of the 9-to-5 world—but you want to be your own boss and play by your own rules, then this is the Interest Category for you.

The Inside Scoop

Entrepreneurship is in, with more and more Americans starting their own businesses: According to the U.S. Small Business Administration, more than 564,000 new firms got up and running in a single recent year. But to get the most from a start-up—from knowing where you're headed to obtaining financing to planning that perfect marketing campaign—the small-business newbie needs a business plan. Most people don't know how to write one (considering it a sort of killer combo, like a term paper melded with an IRS tax package), yet banks and other lenders demand a business plan before they'll consider a loan.

If you've got business experience, you know how to pen a business plan and you like working with other people to make their dreams reality, then you can write your own success story as a business plan consultant.

You'll work with start-up companies seeking financing or investors, or who simply want a business plan to use as a guide. You'll also work with established companies that are looking for new or additional financing, want to franchise, or want to form a merger or acquisition with another firm.

The advantages to this business are that you can work at home, you'll always be working on a different and interesting type of business, you get to exercise your creativity and your business skills, and you get the excitement and satisfaction of helping in the birth of a new and potentially lucrative business entity.

The disadvantages are that you can be subject to the vagaries of the economy—when times are lean, you may not get as many takers for your services—and you may occasionally run into the clients whose start-up dries up and they can't pay you. (You can help compensate for this by requiring 50 percent of your fee up-front.)

Essentials

You'll need a solid grounding in business basics from finances to marketing and in the mechanics of a good business plan. You'll also need good business writing skills, the ability to manipulate figures and super communication skills. You'll need to work closely with your clients to interpret their ideas and produce plans custom-made for their businesses instead of boilerplates that go nowhere.

Tools Of The Trade

A computer system with the usual office software, a laser printer and a fax machine are all must-haves, as is special business-plan-writing software or some other spreadsheet software for working out financials.

Money Talk

Plan on start-up costs of $2,200 to $3,200, depending on whether you've already got your computer set up and if you choose to join a couple of professional organizations. Expect annual revenues of $50,000 to $100,000. Charge your clients $2,500 to $5,000 for each plan, depending on the length of time you'll need to research and write it. You can rewrite or edit business plans your clients may have had on a dusty shelf for $100 an hour or a flat fee based on your projected completion time. Another option is to charge your clients a small fee for writing the plan, then take an equity interest in the company as additional payment.

Pounding The Pavement

Your customers will be new businesses of all descriptions as well as up-and-running firms seeking new directions or financing. Target their owners by networking among bankers, venture capitalists, attorneys specializing in business affairs, accountants, and at your local

A STAR IS BORN

Planning For Success

In 1996, with 15 years in the sales and marketing division of a pharmaceutical firm under his belt, Steve Crow decided he'd had enough. Being a company man involved lots of stress, strain and time away from his family. So Crow segued his experience in writing sales and marketing plans into self-employment as a business plan writer. He had recently met someone who needed help with a business plan and pitched in. "I had an absolute ball," Crow recalls. "And [I decided] this was something I could do."

With minimal start-up costs that went toward business cards, letterhead and a brochure that he spun out on the computer and laser printer he already owned, he was up and running. And he's got plenty to keep him busy: With his Mundelein, Illinois, company, A Better Business Plan, he usually has four to eight plans in the works at a time. His normal fee tops $68 an hour, and a typical business plan brings in up to $4,000.

For Crow, 42, finding clients is not a problem. He names two primary advertising sources: The Yellow Pages is the first. With 600 listings under "Business Consultants" in the Chicago area book, it's no accident that his company comes in first on the page—Crow chose the name for its at-the-front alphabetical properties. It's also descriptive of what his company does so potential clients don't have to guess what type of "consulting" it might be.

The homebased father of two counts as his other advertising source another well-calculated plan. When he started the company, he identified key people within his county to get in touch with and scheduled an appointment with the director of the local Small Business Development Center. That introduction spawned a series of seminars at the center, which led to seminars at the local chamber of commerce. "Those seminars have generated clients almost continuously," Crow reports. And clients who come to him from his talks soon refer others.

His advice for newbies is to do a few business plans before you start to determine if you really like the work. You have to be good with words rather than mediocre, willing to wade through financials, and able to see the global view of the client's business as well as focus on specific areas. "You end up as a consultant," Crow says, "holding their hand as they build their business. You supply the questions they don't know to ask."

chamber of commerce. You should also introduce yourself to the staff at small-business incubators and other SOHO assistance centers.

Place ads in your local Yellow Pages and don't forget to network among friends and associates.

Get yourself written up—and write articles for—the business section of your local paper. Give talks at professional and civic organizations. Teach courses at community colleges and alternative learning centers.

What's Next

If you don't have any business plan experience, learn everything you can by reading, taking classes and—of course—writing your own business plan. Write a few plans for other businesses free of charge as samples for your portfolio and ask your clients to refer you to others. Shop around for a good software package and familiarize yourself with it.

Books

● *The Complete Book of Business Plans: Simple Steps to Writing a Powerful Business Plan*, by Joseph A. Covello and Brian J. Hazelgren, Sourcebooks Trade

● *Entrepreneur's Business Plans Made Easy: It's Not as Hard as You Think!,* Entrepreneur Media Inc. (available at all major bookstores and online at www.amazon.com and www.barnesandnoble.com)

BUSINESS SUPPORT SERVICES

The Inside Scoop

Every business needs those unsung heroes or heroines behind the scenes, the ones who do the word processing, filing and bookkeeping. But most SOHOs don't have the funds—or sometimes even the space—to accommodate assistants.

If you've got the secretarial right stuff, you can be a small-business person's knight or knightness by providing business support services. You'll take on all those office tasks—word processing, filing, bookkeeping and even desktop publishing.

The advantages to this business are that you can work at home, you get an insider's view of lots of different businesses, you're always doing something different, and your clients are appreciative of your services. Plus, with more and more small businesses out there, this field is poised for growth. And it's recession-sturdy—companies that might no longer be able to afford in-house staff will still need help, and that's you.

The only disadvantage is that each client thinks his job is top priority, and you may have times when you'll have tasks piled up, each screaming "me first!"

Essentials

You'll need top-notch secretarial skills, including impeccable spelling, grammar and punctuation. Many businesspeople skim over these tasks—part of your job will be to translate C- English into polished prose. You should also have good communication skills for dealing with a variety of different people, and what doctors call "triage," the ability to decide which projects need immediate attention and which can be set aside for later.

Tools Of The Trade

You'll need a computer system with a laser printer, a fax machine, a copier and a sharp selection of software packages, including word processing, desktop publishing and accounting. You'll also want storage space for each client's letterhead and envelopes, plus blank and draft paper, extra printer and fax cartridges, and files for copies of clients' ongoing work.

Money Talk

Pencil in start-up costs of about $3,000. Once you get established, you can expect annual gross revenues of $30,000 to $45,000 and up depending on how hard you choose to work. You'll charge your clients $20 to $30 per hour, or you can quote flat fees for particular projects.

Pounding The Pavement

Your customers will be small and homebased businesses of every type you can imagine. Place ads in your local Yellow Pages and newspapers. Network at your chamber of commerce. Introduce yourself and leave brochures at banks, insurance agencies, accounting firms, attorneys specializing in business—anybody who will have small-business customers they can refer to you.

Give talks at local professional and civic organizations and get your business written up in local publications.

What's Next

If you don't already have a computer and software, start shopping around. Then get yourself up to speed with these tools. It's hard to bang out a 30-page report in two days if you're still trying to figure out what the F12 key does.

Books

● *Start Your Own Secretarial Service Business*, by Joann Padgett (editor), Prentice Hall Trade

Franchises

- *The Office Alternative*, 5151 Monroe St., #200, Toledo, OH 43623, (800) 843-1040
- *Your Office USA Inc.*, 13777 Ballantine Corporate Pl., #250, Charlotte, NC 28277, (888) 950-1700

CAREER & PERSONAL COACH

The Inside Scoop

If you're the one everybody turns to for advice—the optimistic, goal-oriented cheerleader of your friends' and co-workers' successes—and if you like helping people on the road to business and personal accomplishment, then this could be the business for you.

As a career and personal coach—a combination mentor, cheerleader, sounding board and advocate—you'll work with clients to help them achieve success in their business and personal lives. You'll spend a half-hour to an hour per week listening to their ups and downs and providing both business and personal goal orienteering and guidance. You might work with people in transit from one career or lifestyle to another, with SOHO start-ups or with employee teams at large corporations.

Coaching is a hot new business, with the demand for coaching and coach training more than tripling in a single recent year. *U.S. News and World Report* recently rated career and personal coaching as one of the country's hottest consulting activities. The largest consumers of coaching services are baby boomers who, having reached midlife, have also reached the realization that to achieve all those rainbow-colored dreams they started out with, they need to start taking immediate action. Gen Xers are also coaching consumers but not to the extent that boomers are.

The advantages to this business are that you can work at home, you can start part time and you can be a part of people's lives, helping them grow financially, emotionally and spiritually.

The disadvantage is that you may end up juggling quite a few clients at a time—you'll have to take care not to get them confused or burn out on other people's problems.

Essentials

All you really need is people skills—the ability to listen to your clients, help them brainstorm through problems and provide cheerleading coupled with good business and personal advice. You should also, of course, have a knowledge of how various businesses work—it's hard to give advice on how to handle business situations if you've never been in one and don't know anything about corporate or entrepreneurial environments.

Tools Of The Trade

You don't need formal training or a license, but you can get lessons on A+ coaching through various facilities around the country. Although it's not required, certification as a psychologist or counselor is a major bonus, and experience in human resources, resume writing or other career development fields can also lend credence to your list of credentials. Besides your own skills and experience, you'll need a computer, a laser printer and a fax machine.

Money Talk

Coach yourself through start-up costs of about $3,000. After you become established, in one or two years, you can expect annual gross revenues of $40,000 to $500,000. Charge your individual clients $250 to $500 per month for one half-hour phone call or meeting a week, plus some freebie e-mail advice. Bill corporate clients $1,000 to $10,000 per month, depending on the size of the group and how much time you'll put in.

Pounding The Pavement

Your clients can be corporate types experiencing downsizing, start-up entrepreneurs, or large companies that sign you on as an employee enabler. Target the downsized and corporations by sending brochures to human resources departments; follow up with phone calls to set appointments. About-to-retire military people also make good targets.

You can reach SOHOs, as well as your other targets, by giving seminars and workshops, writing articles for business publications and sending press releases to local newspapers. Network among professional and civic groups in your area. Introduce yourself to the staffs at business incubators. If you live near a college, post fliers on bulletin boards. And if you're near a military installation, place ads in on-base newspapers.

What's Next

If you feel you need formal training, start school-shopping—the best way to find coach-training programs is through your favorite search engine on the Internet. Enter "career-coach training" and get hunting. Practice on friends for free, then send them out to spread the word about your services.

Organizations

- *Coach University* (www.coachu.com): A fee-based training organization rather than a nonprofit professional one, but with scads of information on its Web site

Books

- *24 Hours to Your Next Job, Raise or Promotion (Career Coach Series),* by Robin Ryan, John Wiley & Sons
- *Take Yourself to the Top: The Secrets of America's #1 Career Coach*, by Laura Berman Fortgang, Warner Books

The Inside Scoop

If you're a business expert—you're a whiz at marketing, reorganization, setting up franchises, retooling the company image, or any number of other specialties—then you've got the right stuff to be a business consultant. Instead of reporting in to the office every day as a company man or woman, you'll work on as an independent contractor on special projects for a number of clients.

The advantages to this business are that you can work at home and you get the excitement and pacing of the corporate world without having to live it on a 9-to-5 basis.

The disadvantages are that it can take a while to build your business, you may have to travel more than you'd like, and you may occasionally face employees who feel you're a threat to their cozy world.

Essentials

You'll need a strong background in your area of expertise coupled with stellar marketing skills to convince potential clients of your worth. You'll also need excellent communication and people skills—you'll be going into the company as an outsider, which can be good or bad, depending on the interpersonal culture of the company.

Tools Of The Trade

You should have top-notch credentials in your specialty—you've held prominent positions, can cite professional certification, belong to pertinent organizations, have written books or articles, or taught courses or workshops. You should also have a reference network—

colleagues or other businesspeople who can attest to your expertise and business smarts. Besides what's in your head, you'll need the standard office setup—a computer, a laser printer, a fax machine and the usual office software.

Money Talk

Pencil in start-up costs of about $3,000, plus—unless you already belong—up to an additional $1,000 for professional organization dues. Setting rates for consulting work, according to the National Association of Business Consultants, is more of an art form than a science, but once you get established you can expect gross annual revenues of $30,000 to $150,000. You'll need to consider the length and complexity of your assignment, competitive prices in your specialty and the type of contract (flat rate or time and materials), and then negotiate with your client. As a thumbnail, you can shoot for $50 to $250 per hour or $300 to $1,500 per day.

Pounding The Pavement

Network among professional and civic organizations in your area and among present and former colleagues. Write articles for the business section of local publications. Give talks to business groups and seminars or workshops at local colleges. Place an ad in the Yellow Pages. Put up a Web site.

Weekend Warrior

RELOCATION CONSULTANT

Planning a move to a new part of the country can be a scary experience. How do you decide where to settle without knowing what neighborhoods or schools are like; how far away shopping or medical services are; or whether you'll find things like child care, swim teams or libraries? You can help transferees of large corporations or institutions solve these issues as a relocation consultant. You'll scout out the answers around town, then relay them by phone or fax. Solicit business by sending brochures to large corporations with local and regional branches as well as institutions like hospitals and colleges. **Start-up costs:** $700. **Expected annual gross revenues:** $15,000.

What's Next

Prepare your business brochure, listing your experience, certifications, references and the expertise you can bring to clients.

Organizations

- *Consultants' Network*, 57 W. 89th St., New York, NY 10024, (212) 799-5239, www.consultants-mail.com
- *National Association of Business Consultants*, 9438 U.S. Hwy. 19 N., #101, Port Richey, FL 34668, (800) 390-8024, www.nabc-inc.com

Books

- *Entrepreneur's Business Start-Up Guide #1151, Consulting Service*, Entrepreneur Media Inc., 2392 Morse Ave., Irvine, CA 92614, (800) 421-2300, www.smallbizbooks.com
- *How to Run Seminars and Workshops: Presentation Skills for Consultants, Trainers and Teachers*, by Robert L. Jolles, John Wiley & Sons

Business Opportunities

- *The Wright Track*, P.O. Box 3416, Oak Park, IL 60303, (800) 779-6093. Specializes in advisory services for small businesses

EMPLOYEE TRAINER

The Inside Scoop

If you're a born teacher and motivator—when you speak, people sit up and listen instead of doodling fighter planes or making out grocery lists—then you'll get inspired as an employee trainer. You'll give specialized sessions on your area of expertise, which can be anything from language or math skills to getting the most from company employees or their customers through leadership, self-motivation or sales motivation.

This is a hot new field, and growing hotter. Outsourced training expenditures are expected to more than triple to a whopping $318 billion by 2001. The most popular training topics include customer service and creative problem-solving, but they can also encompass internal communications and even math or reading 101.

The advantages to this business are that start-up costs are minimal, it's creative, and when you communicate new ideas and techniques and see them take root in someone else's mind, it's fulfilling.

The disadvantages are that you'll need to market aggressively—convincing companies to use your services can be an uphill battle. Also, you may have to do quite a bit of traveling.

Essentials

You'll need not only a knowledge of the topic you're teaching, but also the innate talents of a good instructor: the ability to explain your subject clearly and make it interesting, and to inspire. You'll also need excellent sales and marketing skills to merchandise your services.

Tools Of The Trade

You should have the businessperson's basics—a computer with a laser printer, a fax machine and the usual software—and you may want to invest in a copier so you can run off materials for your students. And depending on your subject matter and your personal style, you may want a dry-erase easel, board and markers.

Money Talk

Train yourself in start-up costs of less than $3,000. You might want to add up to another $1,000 for professional organization and networking dues. Annual gross revenues for established employee trainers range from $100,000 and up—as a newbie, you can expect to make $30,000 and up. Charge your clients $100 to $150 per hour or $600 to $1,000 per day.

Pounding The Pavement

Your customers will depend on the topics of your workshops or seminars. Just about any business could benefit from a course on customer relations or marketing techniques, but if your subject is advanced spreadsheet software, you'll be wasting your time targeting, for instance, companies with an employee base of telemarketers.

Direct-mail brochures or letters of introduction to prospective companies, then follow up with phone calls. Network among professional and civic organizations in your community. Give seminars and workshops at local colleges and give talks at business associations. Write articles for business publications. Place an ad in your local Yellow Pages.

What's Next

Decide what your specialties will be, then start writing up seminars and workshops and gathering student materials.

Organizations

- *American Society for Training and Development*, 1640 King St., Box 1443, Alexandria, VA 22313-2043, (800) 628-2783, www.astd. org. Web site contains links to more professional organizations, associations, seminar promotions and other assorted goodies than you can imagine. A must-surf.

Books

- *101 Ways to Make Training Active*, by Melvin L. Silberman, Pfeiffer & Co.
- *Basic Training for Trainers: A Handbook for New Trainers*, by Gary Kroehnert, McGraw-Hill
- *Effective Training Strategies: A Comprehensive Guide to Maximizing Learning in Organizations*, by James R. Davis and Adelaide B. Davis, Berrett-Koehler

Publications

- *Training & Development Magazine*, American Society for Training and Development, 1640 King St., Box 1443, Alexandria, VA 22313-2043, (703) 683-8100, www.astd.org

Franchises

- *Crestcom International Ltd.*, 6900 E. Belleview Ave., Englewood, CO 80111, (888) CREST-COM, www.crestcom.com. Crestcom provides management, sales and office personnel training.
- *Sandler Sales Institute*, 10411 Stevenson Rd., Stevenson, MD 21153, (800) 669-3537. Sandler provides sales and sales management training.

EXECUTIVE ORGANIZER

The Inside Scoop

The average businessperson faces a daily avalanche of information—e-mail, snail mail, faxes, memos, reports, revisions, agendas, addenda, ad infinitum—and is nearly swept under by the sheer mass of all this stuff. Did you know that most executives spend the equivalent of five weeks a year hunting for papers in their own offices? And this doesn't mean they've found them.

If you're a neat freak with a passion for order—your desk is a model of efficiency, all your files are color-coded and coordinated, your phone memos are neatly prioritized, and you don't have to call up every document on your computer to find the one you want—then you can save the day as an executive organizer.

You'll work with businesspeople and their employees to bring order to chaos. You'll streamline paper flow, set up filing systems, clean up and organize desks and work spaces, rearrange schedules, delegate tasks, and even create quiet times to maximize office efficiency. If you're a computer person, you can turn your talents to organizing Windows desktops and document storage, too.

The advantages to this business are that you can start part time, it's creative, you can explore the business worlds of lots of different people, and once you get going, you can earn extra income giving seminars. You can also—as most professional organizers do—take on tasks in private homes as a personal organizer.

The disadvantage is that if you do your job properly, you won't get much repeat business, so you'll always be looking for new clients.

Essentials

The key ingredient here is, of course, organizational ability, which you must be able to apply to other people's situations. You'll have to diagnose how an office works as well as how it should work and then apply that diagnosis to do-able solutions for your clients. You'll also need to be an organization-oriented shopper with a keen knowledge of what furniture, accessory, software and office supply products are in the marketplace so you can make recommendations.

Tools Of The Trade

All you really need to get started is yourself and a planning book, but once you get up and running, you'll want a computer, a laser printer and a fax machine, along with the usual office software. You may also want special time-management and form-design or desktop-publishing software.

Money Talk

Get yourself organized with start-up costs of $500 to $3,000, depending on whether you purchase the computer setup. Once you get established, you can expect annual revenues of $40,000 to $60,000, although this can vary according to how corporate your clients are and how major your metropolitan area is. Charge your clients $150 to $200 per hour, depending on the size of the task and the going rates in your area. You can also charge a flat or per-diem fee for a particular job, say, weeding through an executive's desk or redoing a filing system.

Pounding The Pavement

Your clients can be any corporation, executive or small-business owner. Rein in these prospects by networking with business consultants, interior designers and architects, and professional and civic organizations. Place ads in the business section of your local paper and in the Yellow Pages.

Write articles and press releases for local publications. Give seminars and workshops at local colleges and alternative learning centers, and give talks to local business groups.

Join professional organizing associations—these can be terrific sources of referrals.

What's Next

Start networking. Launch your workshops and seminars. Volunteer your services to a charity auction—this nets lots of free publicity.

Organizations

● *National Association of Professional Organizers*, 1033 La Posada, #220, Austin, TX 78752, (512) 206-0151, www.napo.net

Books

● *Everything's Organized*, by Lisa Kanarek, Career Press

● *The High-Tech Personal Efficiency Program: Organizing Your Electronic Resources to Maximize Your Time and Efficiency*, by Kerry Gleeson, John Wiley & Sons

● *Organized to Be the Best! New Timesaving Ways to Simplify and Improve How You Work*, by Susan Silver, Adams Hall Publishing

● *Organizing for the Creative Person*, by Dorothy Lehmkuhl and Dolores Lamping, Crown Publishing

EXECUTIVE RECRUITER

The Inside Scoop

If you think headhunting refers to the grocery shopping practices of cannibals in darkest Borneo, then you've never been exposed to the world of the corporate job search. But if you know that—in the business world, anyway—headhunting is another term for executive recruiting, and if you've got sales and people skills in big supply, then this could be the business for you.

As an executive recruiter, you'll match job candidates with potential corporate employers. Sometimes you'll start with an executive looking for a new position; on other occasions a company with a slot to fill will initiate the search. While an employment agency generally works with lower-echelon prospects, executive recruiters—as the name implies—concentrate their efforts on higher-level posts, filling management, and professional and technical spots. You can specialize in a particular industry or you can be a generalist.

And there's plenty of work—according to the U.S. Bureau of Labor Statistics, nearly 2 million executive, administrative, managerial, professional specialty and technical support employees actively sought new jobs in one recent year. And in executive search, these people are just the tip of the iceberg—most of your successes come from recruiting those already happily employed.

The advantages to this business are that you can work at home or anyplace else where you can access the telephone, your start-up costs are low, and you get the satisfaction, when everything goes right, of delivering matches made in corporate heaven.

The disadvantages are that you'll spend 98 percent of your time on the phone—if you like phone calls, this is wonderful; if not, you'll burn out in a snap. Competition is fierce in this business, and you only get paid when you make a successful match.

Essentials

You'll need A+ people skills—that matchmaker's talent for innately knowing who will mesh exactly with whom—coupled with the business acumen to assess a candidate's skills and level of experience against the requirements of the position. You have to be a stellar salesperson because you are, after all, selling—candidates to companies and vice versa. If you specialize in a particular industry, you'll also need up-to-the-nanosecond knowledge of its trends and technology. And last but definitely not least, you'll need the salesperson's thick skin—you'll have to do a lot of trolling for clients, and you'll net a lot of "no thanks" along the way.

Tools Of The Trade

You don't need special licenses or permits to be an executive recruiter, but an employment agency does, so take care that you don't mislabel yourself. Some states prohibit meeting candidates or client companies in a home setting, so check into this before you launch your home office. (You'll conduct the vast majority of your business by phone anyway.)

You'll need the basic office setup—a computer, a laser printer, a fax machine and the usual office software—plus a database program for tracking clients and candidates and plenty of filing space for the hundreds of resumes you'll have on tap. And you'll want one of those nifty telemarketer's headsets so your ear doesn't go numb from hours spent jammed against the earpiece.

Money Talk

Plan on start-up costs of about $3,200. Once you become established, you can expect annual revenues of $40,000 to $150,000 or more. Charge your corporate clients 20 percent to 40 percent of the first year's salary for the person you place. (In this business, it's always the company who pays the tab, never the candidate.) Most homebased executive recruiters charge 25 percent, which gives them

A STAR IS BORN

Headhunter Central

Ralphe Vawter has been a headhunter for 35 years. He claims no specialties in any one industry but has concentrated heavily on financial services for the last 10 years. As the sole proprietor and employee of Vawter and Co., a Gulf Breeze, Florida, executive search firm, the 72-year-old is semi-retired but still going strong. Vawter had minimal start-up costs. "It's more in the head," he reports, "than in the hardware," the hardware being a dedicated phone line and a computer system.

"I'm an old geezer," Vawter says, "so I'm not actively recruiting clients." But they seem to be recruiting him—of two client firms he's served for 20 years, one has given him 40 assignments and the other more than 20. And he's just successfully placed a candidate in a $500,000-per-year post—a definite feather in any recruiter's cap.

What do you, as a would-be headhunter, need to attain the same lofty heights? "Stick-to-it-iveness," Vawter advises. "The instincts of a natural ferret, painstaking research work, written and oral communication skills, and being naturally nosy and inquisitive."

Add being terrific on the telephone to all that. To place a candidate for a $150,000 position, Vawter explains, it would not be uncommon to make 150 contacts in 60 to 70 different companies and produce a first batch of 10 to 15 potential takers. Then you'd interview former employers, colleagues and friends, and delve into college records, digging deeper and deeper until coming up with three candidates to present to the prospective employer.

And as a full-time headhunter, you'd work on something like six searches at a stretch, putting in 50- to 55-hour weeks. Vawter, who's not averse to the occasional cruise, puts in an average of 25 hours a week and does no advertising. He gets all his work from repeat customers. "That's the measure of success," he says, "if they invite you back."

a competitive edge and nets out about the same as large headhunting firms, which have to take office and employee overhead off the profits.

Pounding The Pavement

Depending on whether you specialize and in what industry, your clients can be anything from a five-star hotel desiring an executive chef to an oil company looking for a petroleum geologist to a software company desperately seeking a CEO.

Look through trade and business publications for companies advertising for executives (or chefs or whatever), then call to offer your services. Direct-mail brochures to clients in your specialty, then follow up with phone calls. Network at trade shows and professional organizations and with present and former colleagues. Establish relationships with other executive recruiters—often they'll have a client for whom you have the ideal candidate, or vice versa, and you can share the placement fee.

What's Next

If you don't have executive search experience, hire on with an up-and-running firm to learn the ropes. If you do, get out there and get recruiting.

Organizations

- *International Association of Corporate and Professional Recruitment*, 1001 Green Bay Rd., #308, Winnetka, IL 60093, (847) 441-1644, www.iacpr.org
- *National Association of Executive Recruiters*, 20 N. Wacker Dr., #550, Chicago, IL 60606, (312) 701-0744, www.naer.org

Books

- *Ask the Headhunter*, by Nick A. Corcodilos, Plume
- *Entrepreneur's Business Start-Up Guide #1228, Executive Recruiting Service*, Entrepreneur Media Inc., 2392 Morse Ave., Irvine, CA 92614, (800) 421-2300, www.smallbizbooks.com

RESUME WRITER

The Inside Scoop

What's the first thing a person needs (besides persistence and thick skin) when they go job-hunting? A really good resume. That, plus a good cover letter, is what separates the wheat from the chaff when prospective employers pore through paper piles of hopeful applicants. Unfortunately, most people have no idea how to write a winning resume—and in fact consider penning a resume on a par with writing a term paper.

If you have a flair for the written word and a way with people, you can come to the rescue with a resume service. You'll interview your clients to find out where they've been, what they've done and where their talents lie, then design and write a resume that showcases them from both business and personal viewpoints. In addition to resume writing, you can add other services like writing cover letters, providing career counseling or interview rehearsals.

The advantages to this business are that you can work at home, you can start part time, you meet lots of interesting people in all avenues of life, and you get the satisfaction of helping people better themselves and their lives.

The disadvantages are that people usually want their resumes yesterday, so you'll have to work quickly and still turn out a professional product, and that if you work with a college student market, your work can be seasonal. (You can compensate by handling both students and businesspeople.)

Essentials

You'll need a solid knowledge of what makes a good resume in terms of both format and content—and then a copywriter's creativity for making each one stand out from the crowd. You must have excellent grammar, punctuation and spelling skills and tiptop people talents. (One reason people have a hard time writing their own resumes is that they can't see what's special in their own backgrounds—drawing this out will be your job.) Understand that you'll have your clients' career and financial future, at least in part, in your hands; with this business comes a lot of responsibility.

Tools Of The Trade

You'll need a computer with a laser printer, a fax machine, a copier and word-processing software. Because you'll be interviewing clients in your home, you should also have a comfortable setting in which to work with them—in this case, the kitchen table or corner of the bedroom is not appropriate.

Money Talk

Write yourself start-up costs of about $3,000. Resume services typically charge by the hour and rates can range from $40 to well over $100. Most resumes require at least two hours total—including the client interview, the actual writing, and then a review of the finished product with the client. You can expect annual gross revenues of $60,000 to $112,500 per year and up.

Pounding The Pavement

Your clients can be just anybody who wants a job, whether or not they're currently employed or in what capacity. College students are a terrific target market—when they near graduation, they have to go to work somewhere—and those at the sophomore and junior level need resumes to land internships. Graduate students also make good sources of business. Beyond the student zone, you can target mid- and upper-level management and professional types as well as empty-nest or suddenly single moms.

Target the college market by placing fliers on bulletin boards all over campus or by mailing brochures to lists you can rent from the school. Offer a finder's fee to clients who refer other business. (College kids always need money, so this is a good incentive.)

Nab business clients by networking in local professional and civic organizations, introducing yourself to the staff at local business incubators, unemployment offices and disability retraining facilities. Post fliers on public library bulletin boards and at copy centers.

Give seminars and workshops—always a good source of clients—and place ads in the Yellow Pages and in local newspapers.

What's Next

Practice by writing a few resumes, which you can use in your portfolio. Offer to do them free of charge in exchange for word-of-mouth advertising from satisfied customers.

Organizations

● *Professional Association of Resume Writers*, 3637 Fourth St., #330, St. Petersburg, FL 33704, (800) 822-7279, www.parw.com

Books

● *101 Best Resumes,* by Michael Betrus and Jay A. Block, McGraw-Hill

● *Resumes for Dummies*, by Joyce Lain Kennedy, IDG Books Worldwide

VIRTUAL HUMAN RESOURCES CONSULTANT

The Inside Scoop

Back in the days of Ebeneezer Scrooge, an employer could treat (or mistreat) his employees just about any way that suited him. But in our more enlightened—and lawsuit-mad—world, businesses must tread carefully to make certain they don't accidentally step on employees' toes. And this causes problems for small and midsized companies that don't have the time, the staff or the expertise to deal with all those complex and constantly changing human resources issues.

If you're a human resources expert, you can solve these problems with a virtual human resources service. You'll do it all, from writing employee handbooks to handling personnel forms to setting up and administering 401(k) programs.

The advantages to this business are that you can work at home and the field is recession-proof. The worse things get financially, the greater a company's tendency to outsource—and since this is work that can't legally be ignored, you'll always be in demand.

The disadvantage is that laws and regulations in this industry change on a routine basis, so you've got to make sure you're up to speed at all times. And if you're not a by-the-book type, you'll be miserable filling out forms and reporting to Uncle Sam every day.

Essentials

You'll need a solid up-to-date knowledge of human resources issues and how to handle them, an aptitude for accounting and record-keeping, and the sales skills to sell your services to your clients.

Tools Of The Trade

You'll need a good computer setup with a laser printer, a fax machine and the usual office software. You'll want to have a stock of personnel forms, files and other record-keeping materials, reference manuals, and filing cabinets and handy storage space.

Money Talk

Pencil in start-up costs of less than $3,000, plus up to another $1,000 for professional association and networking dues. Once you're established, you can expect gross annual revenues of $45,000 to $60,000. You'll charge your clients on a contract basis, either per project, per day or per employee—find out what the going rates are in your area and make yours comparable.

Pounding The Pavement

Your customers will be small and midsized businesses that either have no human resources departments or might prefer to downsize and outsource to you. Direct-mail your brochure and sales letters to these firms, then follow up with phone calls.

Network among professional and civic organizations in your area. Write articles for the business section of local publications. Give talks to business groups. Introduce yourself to bankers, accountants, attorneys specializing in small business, insurance agents—anybody who deals with small and start-up businesses and can give you referrals.

What's Next

If you don't have human resources experience, go out and get it. Read everything you can get your hands on. Sign on for a tour of duty with an outsourcing company or with the in-house human resources department of a large firm to learn the ropes.

Organizations

● *Northeast Human Resources Association*, 1 Washington St., #101, Wellesley, MA 02481, (781) 235-2900, www.nehra.com

- *Society for Human Resource Management*, 1800 Duke St., Alexandria, VA 22314, (800) 283-7476, www.shrm.org. The society's Web site contains a wealth of information for the HR professional. Check it out!

Books

- *Managing Human Resources: Productivity, Quality of Work Life, Profits*, by Wayne F. Cascio, McGraw-Hill Text

Business Opportunities

- *Resource Associates Corp.,* 31 Hickory Rd., Mohnton, PA 19540, (800) 799-6227, www.rac-tqi.com

ChaPter twelve

KIDS' STUFF

I f you're a kid at heart—you'd still play with Barbies and Big Wheels if you thought no one was looking, you love dress-up and make-believe, reading stories aloud, and milk and cookies—and you like sharing your enthusiasm for life and learning with the tots-to-teens brigade, then this is the Interest Category for you.

CHILD CARE

The Inside Scoop

Not that long ago, outsourced child care was virtually unheard of. Moms were June Cleaver types who lived in the kitchen and were on tap 24 hours a day. Now that the typical mum is a working woman, child care is what during World War II they used to call an essential industry—a job the nation can't manage without.

If you love kids, you're a Big Wheels and Barney fan, and you've got patience to spare, then you can help parents in your area hit the workplace with easy spirits with a child-care service. You'll care for kids in your home, providing a safe and loving environment as well as snacks and meals. Some child-care services offer child development activities; others provide extended or 24-hour service for parents who work the late shift. Still others combine senior care with the tot set, giving both generations the chance to enjoy and learn from each other.

The advantages to this business are that you can work at home; your start-up costs are low; if you have kids of your own, you can work and care for them all in one; and you get the joy of watching little people grow.

The disadvantages are that you're tied to home—it's hard to run out for a quart of milk with four toddlers in tow—and you'll occasionally have to deal with parents who can't seem to pick up their kids on time. (You can counteract this by charging stiff fees, say $10 for every 5 minutes that they're overdue.)

Essentials

You'll need a genuine affection for the crayon set—if you haven't got it, you'll burn out quickly—as well as patience squared and the mind-set to enjoy being at home all day with only tots to talk to. You should also have a good working knowledge of child care, child development and psychology. (You needn't be a trained pediatrician, but you'll have to know the basics, things like the difference between teething and an illness-induced fever and at what age children learn to share.)

Tools Of The Trade

Depending on your locale, you may need licensing, certification, inspection or some combination thereof. Be sure to check before embarking on your business. Even if it's not required, you should take courses in CPR and pediatric first aid.

You'll need to install safety devices in your home, including smoke detectors (if you don't already have them); fire extinguishers; first-aid kits; gates around pools, spas or other hazards; stairway gates; outlet covers; and safety latches on cabinets and cupboards containing any potentially dangerous substances or materials.

Once safety's accomplished, you'll want to think entertainment. Stock up on development-oriented toys, kid videos, tot-sized tables and chairs, and arrange adequate sleeping quarters for your prospective charges.

Money Talk

This is a shoestring start-up—if you've got kids of your own and all the Tools Of The Trade just described, you can pencil in costs of $500 or less. If you'll need to purchase this stuff, you can add another $1,000.

Pounding The Pavement

Your customers will be working parents and grandparents with preschoolers to be cared for. Post fliers on church or temple bulletin boards and place ads in their newsletters. Network among friends and neighbors; have your spouse or significant other spread the word at work and at professional and civic organizations. Place an ad in your local newspaper.

You can also target local businesses. Send letters extolling the benefits of paying for employees' child care with you—you're close at hand so employees won't be late arriving or early leaving work, and with your exceptional care, there's no lost productivity worrying about Junior.

What's Next

Read child care and development articles and books. Get your house childproofed and prepped. Call about licensing or certification. Stock up on apple juice and bake some cookies.

Organizations

● *National Child Care Association*, 1016 Rosser St., Conyers, GA 30207-5275, (800) 543-7161, www.nccanet.org

Books

● *Entrepreneur's Business Start-Up Guide #1058, Child Care Services*, Entrepreneur Media Inc., 2392 Morse Ave., Irvine, CA 92614, (800) 421-2300, www.smallbizbooks.com

● *How to Start and Run a Home Day-Care Business*, by Carolyn Argyle, Citadel Press

● *Profitable Child Care: How to Start and Run a Successful Business*, by Nan Lee Howkins, Facts on File Inc.

● *Start Your Own At-Home Child Care Business*, by Patricia Gallagher, Mosby Yearbook

Franchises

● *Wee Watch Private Home Day Care*, 105 Main St., Unionville, ON, L3R 2G1, CAN, (905) 479-4274, www.weewatch.com

CHILDREN'S PARTY PLANNER

The Inside Scoop

Remember when you were a kid and your birthday party was one of the highlights of the year? Plain old cake and ice cream seemed pretty slick, but if you were lucky enough to have a mom who went all out with themed parties—pirates or princesses or the circus—you were the envy of every kid on the block.

Today's moms and dads, the kids of not so long ago, want to give their own kids memorable parties, too, but with a two-income household, it's difficult to find the time to plan and organize all this stuff. And even moms or dads who don't work often feel that a really creative party is beyond their capabilities.

But if you love to party with the pre-teen set and you've got creativity-plus, then you can be the life of the gala with a children's party planning business. You'll plan the theme, provide costumes (unless guests arrive wearing their own), décor, food, favors and other assorted goodies, entertainment, and clean up afterward so parents can enjoy the festivities instead of running themselves ragged. And you can do more than birthday parties—go all out with Halloween, Christmas, Chanukah, end-of-school and end-of-summer parties—whatever you can dream up and sell.

The advantages to this business are that your start-up costs are low, it's creative and it's always fun—heck, you get to go to birthday parties every working day!

The disadvantages are that since most kids' birthday parties are weekend events, you may run into scheduling problems, and at least at first, you may find that you spend an excessive amount of time planning each gig—but you'll be having fun.

Essentials

Besides that all-important creativity, you'll need the organizational skills to pull everything together and do it smoothly so that everyone has fun. You should also know what kids like today so that you can plan parties around the cartoon character or hit movie of the hour. And you'll need to be a people person who can make sure that no shy child gets left out of the fun and no sensitive parent gets miffed at being left out the picture.

Tools Of The Trade

All you really need is a planning book and a telephone. If you specialize in a certain type of party, like dress-up tea parties or wild animal parties, you'll want to lay in a stock of costumes and makeup for guests to put on.

Money Talk

Pencil in start-up costs of $500 to $1,000, depending on how much initial advertising you plan on doing. You can expect to earn annual gross revenues of $22,000 to $30,000—you can up these figures if you add other services that customers will use on weekdays or weeknights like mother-daughter teas or father-son football afternoons. Charge your customers $150 to $200 per party, depending on comparable rates in your area.

Pounding The Pavement

Your customers will be parents and kids who just wanna have fun. Send brochures to moms and dads in your area. Write fun, informative articles for local newspapers. Place ads in the Yellow Pages and in local publications. Network among the kiddie set and post fliers (with the owners' permission) at dance and karate studios and other children's hang-outs.

Donate a party to the lucky winner of a charity auction—always good publicity—and give free parties to friends who'll spread the word. Be sure to take pictures for your portfolio.

A STAR IS BORN

It's Their Party

What little girl wouldn't love a birthday party where she reigns as princess complete with tiara, where guests and hostess alike are treated to makeup and manicure sessions, get to dress up in fancy costumes, and partake of an elegant cake in the shape of a teapot? That's the idea behind Little Princess Tea Parties, and the brains behind the idea belong to sisters-in-law Joy and Dawn Yates of Gainesville, Virginia.

Joy, 26, and Dawn, 32, were stay-at-home moms with four kids between them when they began their party program in May 1997. A $500 budget went to purchase thrift-shop prom and wedding dresses, shoes, gloves, and a variety of hats so each "lady" at every party is properly attired for tea. For the occasional boy partygoer, the partners also bought suit jackets, vests and ties, and the rest of the funds went toward makeup, tea supplies and crafts.

The Yateses stay busy on weekends with tea parties but have expanded their repertoire to include manners and etiquette courses at community centers as well as mother-daughter teas for church groups, which are held on midweek afternoons. "We have big cups for moms," reports Joy, "and little cups for children."

The charge for these dainty events? It's $60 for a one-hour, six-week course on etiquette and manners, $16 per mother-daughter for teas, and $170 per birthday party. "I set my price at what I would pay," Joy explains. "We hit every ethnic group, every religion and every walk of life, so no mother has to tell her child it's too expensive."

The Little Princess concept was an instant success—in more ways than one. By fall of their first year, Joy and Dawn had received nine calls from women wanting a franchise so they could do the same thing. Like all good princesses, they listened to what their "subjects" wanted and have just begun marketing Little Princess franchises.

Joy's advice for the newbie? "Do your homework," she says. "Get a feeling for your area." Allow mental preparation time, too, for your new venture—the Yateses spent five months on their project before officially opening for business.

What's Next

Start brainstorming party ideas. Read kids party-planning books and tour party supply warehouses to see what's in store.

Books

- *The Children's Party Handbook: Fantasy, Food, and Fun*, by Alison Boteler, Barrons Educational Series
- *The Kids' Pick-a-Party Book: 50 Fun Party Themes for Kids Ages 2 to 16*, by Penny Warner, Meadowbrook Press
- *Let's Have a Party! The Winning Entries in the Nationwide Children's Birthday Party Contest*, by Larry Zisman, Honey Zisman and Jordana LeBlanc, St. Martin's Press

Franchises

- *Little Princess Franchise Development Corp.,* P.O. Box 411, Gainesville, VA 20156, (800) 489-0-TEA (489-0832), www. princesstea.com

The Inside Scoop

A new baby in the house is a living, breathing miracle. It's also sleepless nights and days that pass in a haze of exhaustion and new worries for new moms and dads. But if you love being around that most exciting of new life forms, participating in the joy a new baby brings to a home, then this could be the business for you. And there's plenty of business to be had—in one recent year alone, nearly 4 million babies were born in the United States.

With a doula service (also called postpartum care service or postpartum doula to distinguish it from a birth doula or labor assistant), you'll coach on breast-feeding, baby's first bath, cries in the night, and diaper duty—whatever it takes to help parents cope with the demands a brand-new infant can make on a household.

The advantages to this business are that you can start on a shoestring and you get all the fun of being around a new baby without going through the hard parts—from labor pains to worrying about college educations—yourself.

The disadvantages are that you won't get a lot of repeat business from satisfied clients (not for at least another nine months), and although you may quickly begin to feel like a member of the family, once they get on their parental feet, your job will be over and you'll move on. Another disadvantage is that babies usually come unannounced, sometimes weeks early. And once you've promised yourself to new parents, it's up to you to be there when the baby arrives. (The best way to compensate for this is to have at least one partner or independent contractor you can send out if you're tied up with another family.)

Essentials

As a doula, you should have a genuine feel for new parents and babies, as well as experience with infants. While you won't be a nurse or nanny, you'll need to know how to help new moms with breast-feeding, change diapers, deal with colic and handle the other minor crises of new babyhood that can send parents into a panic.

Tools Of The Trade

This is a shoestring operation. Accreditation and certification are available—but not necessary—from the National Association of Postpartum Care Services. If you're a nurse, medical assistant or other health professional, you're a step ahead as far as credibility, but all you really need to get started are your own innate abilities and a reliable vehicle or public transport to carry you to your assignments. And since you're dealing with people's most precious possessions, you'll want to carry liability insurance and have pediatric first aid and CPR certification.

Money Talk

You can get started for about $150. Once established, a two-person doula service can expect annual gross revenues of $60,000 and up. You'll charge your clients $15 to $20 per hour, with higher fees for care of twin and other multiple infants. Most clients have their doula on hand four to five hours a day for one to two weeks, though some will enjoy you so much they'll stretch the time out for months. For those short-termers, be sure to request at least a 10-hour minimum and insist on a minimum of eight hours for overnight stays.

Pounding The Pavement

Your clients will be new parents. Advertise your services by giving free parenting talks to prenatal classes, then passing out brochures that describe your services. You'll also want to leave brochures with hospital maternity centers, obstetricians, pediatricians and new-parent support groups in your area. And don't forget grand-parents—a doula service is a terrific new-baby gift!

What's Next

Read up on infant care so you'll have plenty of material for your talks, and if you're a little rusty, volunteer your services for free to get back in the swing.

Organizations

● *National Association of Postpartum Care Services*, P.O. Box 1012, Edmonds, WA 98020, (800) 45-DOULA, www.webspan.net/~callahan/napcs2.html

Books

● *Baby Basics: A Guide for New Parents*, by Anne K. Blocker, Chronimed Publishing

● *Baby Care for Beginners*, by Frances Williams, HarperCollins

Cyber Assistance

● *Baby Bag Online* (www.babybag.com): All sorts of stuff for new parents (and assistants)—recipes, health advice, parenting stories and more

● *Baby Zone* (www.babyzone.com): Everything for the new parents and their assistant—baby names, baby gear, fatherhood pages for new and expectant dads, chats and boards, tips, hints, helps—you name it. Check it out!

HOME TUTOR

The Inside Scoop

When kids can't keep up with schoolwork because they don't understand the subject matter, a world of difficulties opens up—low grades, low self-esteem that can lead to behavioral problems, friction on the home front, and the danger of falling behind socially and academically.

If you like kids of all ages, you can communicate concepts and ideas, and you've got a good grounding in at least one subject, you can save the day—and the kid—as a home tutor. This is a field with room for growth: The U.S. National Center for Education Statistics estimates that by 2008, more than 70 million young people (kindergarten through college) will be enrolled in public and private schools.

As a home tutor, you'll work with your pupils on a one-on-one basis to bring them up to speed and even beyond. You can specialize in teaching younger kids elementary reading and math skills, coach high school and college kids on subjects from Spanish to algebra to English, or spur your pupils to succeed on SAT or MCAT (medical school entrance) exams.

The advantages to this business are that you can work from home, you can start part time and on a shoestring, and you get the satisfaction of helping kids grasp the concepts you're teaching and shine—in your eyes, their parents' and their own.

The only disadvantage is that you're unlikely to get rich, but that's speaking in terms of money. What you'll gain in satisfaction just might be riches enough.

Essentials

While experience as a professional teacher is a plus, it's not a necessity. What you will need is a good basic understanding of the subject or subjects you'll be tutoring plus the innate teaching talents to communicate ideas and concepts clearly and effectively. You should have enthusiasm for your subjects and your students—you can't inspire anyone to excel at geometry if you're bored silly by it.

Tools Of The Trade

In most states, you don't need licensing or certification, so getting up and running is quick and easy, but if you're a present or former teacher, you've got a plus as far as credibility. Be sure to check before you embark on your business. Your students will bring their own textbooks, but you may want to offer a selection of reference materials or teaching aids.

Money Talk

You can start on the proverbial shoestring—less than $500 for advertising and a few teaching aids. Charge your clients $25 to $35 per hour, depending on the going rates in your area and whether you're teaching phonics or medical-student-level physiology. You can expect annual gross revenues of $37,500 to $52,500.

Pounding The Pavement

Your clients can be grade-school kids or college seniors or anybody in between who needs help turning textbook trauma into school success, but the biggest demand these days seems to be in the high-school-and-up range.

If you're targeting the younger set or high school kids, introduce yourself to school staffs and leave brochures or fliers, place ads in local papers and Yellow Pages, and post fliers at kid-oriented spots like dance or karate schools, public libraries and community centers.

For college students, post fliers on bulletin boards, distribute them to frat and sorority houses, and place ads in college publications. You can also introduce yourself or send brochures to professors of the subjects you specialize in.

What's Next

Decide what subjects you'll teach. If you feel a bit rusty or unsure of your skills, practice on kids of friends or neighbors for free. This will help you work out the bugs of your technique with the added bonus of netting you terrific word-of-mouth advertising.

Organizations

● *National Tutoring Association*, P.O. Box 154, Ashley, PA 18706, (800) 621-2930, http://nta.jsu.edu
● *National Tutoring Foundation*, P.O. Box 1181, Wilkes-Barre, PA 18703, (800) 621-2930

Books

● *Becoming an Effective Tutor*, by Linda B. Myers and Phil Gerould (editor), Crisp Publications
● *The Practical Tutor*, by Emily Meyer, Oxford University Press

Franchises

● *The HONORS Learning Center*, 5959 Shallowford Rd., #517, Chattanooga, TN 37421, (423) 892-8000, www.yp.bellsouth.com/honors
● *Kumon Math & Reading Centers*, Glenpointe Ctr. E., 300 Frank W. Burr Blvd., 2nd Fl., Teaneck, NJ 07666, (800) ABC-MATH, www.kumon.com

KIDS' TAXI SERVICE

The Inside Scoop

Kids these days have schedules just about as hectic as their parents—school, soccer practice, Little League, ballet lessons, orthodontist appointments, after-school care—it can leave working parents with no time to work in between all these drop-off and pick-up assignments.

But if you're a kid-lover who likes to be on the go, you can save the day with a kids' taxi service. You'll transport Babs and Junior to wherever they need to be, leaving parents free to win the bread. With nearly 16 million families with children under age 18 and both parents in the workforce, this is a business with plenty of potential.

The advantages to the kids' taxi service are that you'll forge relationships with the kids you drive on a routine basis, and you get the satisfaction of knowing you're helping your clients' lives run more smoothly.

The disadvantage is that this is a heavy-responsibility job—not only are you in charge of highway safety, but it's up to you to make sure kids get safely into the facility where you've delivered them. You can't just drop them like a bus driver and take off.

Essentials

Unless you want to end up like Fred Flintstone, who collapsed after one day of driving a school bus, you'll need nerves of steel. You can't be distracted by giggling or minor wars in the back of the van or by imminent car sickness up front. At the same time you'll need to love kids and understand their need to be treated as people rather than parcels.

You'll also need a good sense of logistics to figure out how to get two different passengers to opposite ends of town for appointments at the same time.

Tools Of The Trade

You'll need a reliable van with seating for six or more, adequate insurance, and a cellular phone to keep mom and dad apprised of traffic or other scheduling delays or changes. You should also be certified in pediatric first aid and CPR.

Money Talk

Pencil in start-up costs of $10,000 to $15,000, most of which will go toward a good used van—if you already have one, you're dollars ahead. Expect to earn annual revenues of $15,000 to $41,000 per year. Charge your clients $100 to $200 per month for one trip per day and $200 to $300 for round trips, based on a five-day week. (Don't expect tips from your passengers, unless you like chewing gum.)

Pounding The Pavement

Your clients will be the working parents in your area, plus a smattering of stay-at-home moms who don't drive or have access to a car. Introduce yourself and leave fliers at day-care and after-school cen-

Weekend Warrior

CHILD I.D. SERVICE

Give parents peace of mind and help protect their children with a child I.D. service. You'll provide fingerprints, color photographs and a form detailing special information like birthmarks, scars or medical conditions. You can solicit business from schools, day-care or after-school centers, church groups and community organizations. Remember when you advertise and perform your service that your purpose is not to frighten people—especially children—with horror stories, but to help them be aware, informed and as safe as possible. **Start-up costs:** $1,000. **Expected annual gross revenues:** Up to $20,000.

ters, community centers, public libraries, pediatric and orthodontic offices, grade-school offices, and kid-oriented facilities like dance, gymnastics and karate studios.

Get your company written up in local publications and run ads in your local newspaper. Donate one free month of service to a charity auction—this is terrific publicity.

What's Next

Make sure your van is in A-1 condition, including seatbelts, and give it a beauty makeover with a thorough clean and polish. If it needs new paint, go for it—parents aren't likely to trust a driver with a rattletrap vehicle. Have your company name painted on the sides or have a vinyl/magnetic sign made. Make sure your phone number is clearly visible to other drivers—this will be a good source of on-the-road advertising.

Books

● *Drive to Survive: Using Professional Racing Techniques for Better, Safer Everyday Driving*, by Kenneth E. Vose, Prentice Hall Trade

Cyber Assistance

● *Automobile Association of America* (www.aaa.com): The venerable auto driver's assistant online

Chapter thirteen

LET ME ENTERTAIN YOU

You're the life of the party—the one who makes holidays merry, birthdays memorable and who can be counted on to enliven even fussy Aunt Ethel's annual get-togethers. If you've got a feel for fun and a flair for the festive, and you're also blessed with a major helping of organizational oomph, then this is your category.

BALLOON BOUQUETS

The Inside Scoop

Everybody loves balloons. They're big, bright, bold and colorful, and when you're holding one by a string, you feel almost as if you're lighter than air, too. As a surprise delivery, they make a terrific alternative to flowers. And they're the perfect party decorating strategy.

If you've got creativity and a sense of fun, you can soar with a balloon bouquet service. You'll design and deliver balloon arrangements for all occasions—white and gold for weddings, black for that over-the-hill 40th birthday party, green and white for St. Patty's Day bashes. You can tie gifts to your bouquets—candy, stuffed animals, decorative tins of coffee and cookies—let your imagination be your guide, and make up both standard and custom presentations.

You can also make a really big splash by providing hundreds of balloons en masse for grand openings, sales presentations, inaugurations, graduations and just about any other celebrations you can dream up.

The balloon bouquet business's advantages are that you can start part time, you can work at home, your start-up costs are relatively low, and if you're a creative person who likes conjuring up themes and packaging and putting them all together, it's a lot of fun. And it's gratifying—everybody's delighted to receive a fancy bouquet, especially with gifts attached.

The disadvantage is that you'll have a lot of competition, not only from other balloon bouquet services, but also from florists and gift basket services that deliver balloons, too. (You can compensate for this by finding a special niche market and by coming up with new and creative ways to use your products.)

Essentials

A balloon bouquet—or wreath, rainbow or cloud—can be elegant, whimsical or sporty, but any way you go, it needs to look smart; you can't just toss together a hodgepodge of colors and gifts and stick on some ribbon. You'll need a flair for the creative and the design ability to pull it all together into an attractive package. You'll also need to be a savvy marketer who can sell those unique bouquets to a variety of clients and customers.

Tools Of The Trade

You'll need a supply of helium tanks, an assortment of colorful, fun and elegant ribbons, and as many kinds of balloons as you can lay your hands on. In most states, you'll need a liquor license if you plan to attach that fine wine, and you'll want a resale license so you can buy gifts and supplies at wholesale prices.

You'll want a hot glue gun and a work space large enough to spread out your materials and assemble your bouquets. (Keep in mind that a business client may order 100 or more bouquets at a time.) You'll also need a delivery vehicle with plenty of balloon room to cart all those clever gifts around in. And don't forget a credit card processing machine so you can take orders over the phone.

Money Talk

Start-up costs, including your initial gift and supplies inventory, can run as low as $3,200. You can expect annual gross revenues of $25,000 to $35,000 and up, depending on how creative and sales-savvy you are. Balloon bouquets sell for anywhere from $5 to $50, depending on what they're attached to.

Pounding The Pavement

Your clients can be just anybody who might buy florists' bouquets, gift baskets, or any other sort of delivered gift. Individuals will make up a large part of your sales, but be sure to target business customers, who can be a terrific source of repeat business. Start off with travel and real estate agents, innkeepers, apartment complexes, car and boat salespeople, public relations firms—or any other corporate clients who'll want to make their customers feel they're walking on air.

Don't forget clubs and organizations—they're always throwing dinners, teas, parties and assorted awards banquets for which clouds of balloons make a stunning statement.

You can net these clients and customers with creative marketing. Send brochures to businesses and organizations, then follow up by setting appointments to show your bouquets or a professional portfolio of your designs. To attract retail customers, place ads in local newspapers, send press releases to local and national publications, offer yourself as a guest on a local radio chat show, and donate a few bouquets to other businesses' grand openings or for fund-raisers in return for free publicity.

You should also send brochures to wedding and event planners and caterers, all of whom can take advantage of your services or refer their own clients to you.

What's Next

Shop the competition to find out what sorts of bouquets and other arrangements they sell, what their prices are and, if possible, what types of customers they sell to. Shop for gifts and supplies at craft, gift and novelty trade shows and through wholesalers you can find in the Yellow Pages or online.

Organizations

- *Gift Association of America*, 612 W. Broad St., Bethlehem, PA 18018, (610) 861-9445
- *The National Specialty Gift Association*, P.O. Box 843, Norman, OK 73070, (405) 329-7847

Publications

- *Giftware Business*, 1 Penn Plaza, New York, NY 10019, (800) 255-2824 (for subscriptions)

The Inside Scoop

If you're the premier party-giver in your crowd—friends and family can't wait for an invitation to your house because you've always got something new and exciting in store—then you can have a ball as an event planner.

You'll work for private and corporate clients, creating, planning and organizing everything from bar mitzvahs to new-product unveilings, company picnics to murder mystery dinners, sales meetings to Valentine's balls. You'll do it all, from designing the theme to sending invitations to arranging the site, the entertainment and the caterer. And you'll negotiate with vendors and suppliers to make sure your client gets the most for his money.

Event planning is a field with room for growth. While it used to be that a company could impress clients or sales teams with a tray of donuts or cold cuts and a slide show, in today's sophisticated world it takes a splashy event to do the trick. And on the personal front, few people today have the time—or the energy—to plan and organize anything more than a cup of coffee and a pie from the frozen food case at the supermarket. What that means is that there's plenty of work out there for you.

The advantages to the event-planning business are that it's creative, challenging, and if you specialize in corporate events, you'll probably have your weekends free for yourself. If you're a people person, what could be better?

The disadvantage is that crises can and will occur, so it can be stressful, hours can be long, and unless you request deposits from your clients, cash flow can be a problem.

Essentials

As an event planner, you must be organized and detail-oriented to a fault. You've got to have a major creative streak to come up with new ideas and the planning skills to be able to implement them. And you'll need to be a people person, capable of dealing with everybody from temperamental or flighty entertainers to the stodgy company president.

Tools Of The Trade

To get up and running you'll need a computer with the usual office software, a laser printer, a fax machine and desktop publishing software for developing corporate proposals. And don't forget a phone, a calendar and a planning book.

Money Talk

Plan on start-up costs of $1,500 to $3,000. You can expect annual gross revenues of $25,000 to well into six figures. Charge your clients 10 percent to 15 percent of the event's budget, a flat fee for the event, or an hourly rate that you can determine by the estimated cost of the event and by the going prices in your area.

Pounding The Pavement

Your clients can be individuals, companies, or groups like charities, associations and organizations. Place ads in your local Yellow Pages and newspapers.

Establish relationships with local event-oriented vendors: florists, photographers, sound-system rental companies, videographers, caterers, hotels and country clubs, and musicians. Leave your brochures with them and ask for referrals. And don't forget advertising agencies and public relations firms.

Plan a small event for free for a local charity in exchange for free publicity. If you've got the inside scoop on a corporate event in your area—an up-and-coming grand opening, sales meeting or product unveiling—send a sales letter and your brochure, then follow up with a phone call.

A STAR IS BORN

You Say You Want A Celebration

You say you want a celebration? You name it and Naomi Kolstein can provide it. As president of Naomi's World of Entertainment Inc. in New Hempstead, New York, Kolstein is an event planner extraordinaire. Just check out the company Web site, which provides the event-ready client with a dazzling array of entertainment possibilities—custom-written murder mysteries, treasure hunts, Art of the Bug Lady, human bowling, and transforming your guests into Sumo wrestlers. Then, of course, there's the more traditional stuff like celebrity look-alikes, magicians and singers.

"We try to be as creative as possible and to exceed the client's expectations," Kolstein says. And she has—all over the world, arranging everything from a birthday bash in Switzerland to a corporate dinner in New York.

It's not all entertainment, though. A big part of event-planning is the details. Kolstein's tasks include selecting sites, preparing menus, lining up speakers, decorating meeting facilities and arranging sound systems. "Our job is making sure that when we say 'Take the third left after the highway,' it really is the third left," Kolstein says. "We are the entire backup system for every event, making what is a lot of work and a lot of detail appear effortless at the time of the function. It's fun to work behind the scenes, and it's a real thrill to see everything come together. But it's incredibly hard work."

Kolstein started for just under $1,000 and has built a six-figure business. Her advice to newbies is to try to really understand your clients' needs and deliver the best possible package. "Cutting corners doesn't work," she says. "People count on you to make their event dazzle. Whether it's a corporate function or a bar mitzvah, it's a very special event in their lives. You need to give equal care to large and small clients."

What's Next

Start shopping around for vendors and suppliers. Introduce yourself, find out what types of services and products are available, and what prices are like.

Organizations

- *International Society of Meeting Planners*, 1224 N. Nokomis NE, Alexandria, MN 56308, (320) 763-4919, www.iami.org/ismp.html
- *International Special Events Society*, 9202 N. Meridian St., #200, Indianapolis, IN 46260-1810, (800) 688-ISES (4737), www.ises.com

Books

- *Entrepreneur's Business Start-Up Guide #1313, Event Planning Service*, Entrepreneur Media Inc., 2392 Morse Ave., Irvine, CA 92614, (800) 421-2300, www.smallbizbooks.com
- *Planning Successful Meetings and Events*, by Ann J. Boehme, Amacom

Publications

- *Event Solutions*, Virgo Publishing, Box 40079, Phoenix, AZ 85067-0079, (602) 990-1101

Cyber Assistance

- *Event Solutions* (www.event-solutions.com): Online version of *Event Solutions* magazine, absolutely packed with articles, links, educational information and other terrific stuff. A must-surf.

INDEPENDENT RECORD LABEL

The Inside Scoop

If you've always wanted to be in the music business, you groove to the club and album scene, but you can't sing a note and your instrumental talents are limited to a hunt-and-peck rendition of "Heart and Soul," take heart. You can do the Dick Clark thing as head of your own record (or more properly nowadays, CD) label. You'll be a mover and shaker: According to the Recording Industry Association of America, music influences every culture on our planet to the tune of $38 billion annually, with the U.S. recording industry accounting for a full one-third of the world market.

As a recording whiz, you'll locate talent, choose the songs, style and format for your first album, then do everything the Capitol Records execs would do—rent a studio, hire an engineer and producer, have the tracks mixed and mastered, arrange for cover art, and have your CDs pressed. You'll also be the advertising and marketing department, working with distributors, getting your band gigs on the road, and making sure your CDs and posters are displayed in stores. Then you'll turn around and do the whole thing over again with your next album.

The advantages to this business are that it has a definite cachet and sounds not only glamorous but way cool. (The reality is that it's more hard work than hard-core cool, but everybody doesn't have to know this.) If everything goes right, you can make a sizable amount of money, and, of course, you get to be in the music biz every working day.

The disadvantages are that, while you can earn oodles, you're far more likely to merely make a living and you'll work long, grueling hours at a lot of tasks that are definitely uncool.

Essentials

This is entrepreneurship of the first order—you'll need to be a major go-getter, willing and able to carry out every aspect of getting your CDs from gleam-in-your-eye to on-the-charts reality. You should have a good working knowledge of how the music business operates, from recording studios to distribution channels. You can't be a wimp when it comes to pushing your product. And you'll need the innate ability to recognize talent when you hear it and to know what will appeal to a significant listening audience.

Tools Of The Trade

You'll rent the recording studios and hire out production, mixing, mastering and pressing, so all you really need are your own abilities and plenty of chutzpah.

Money Talk

Your start-up costs should run from $5,000 to $25,000, depending on how long you use the studio, engineer and producer; what kind of deal you negotiate; and how many CDs you have pressed. As a

Weekend Warrior

HOME ENTERTAINMENT/ CAR STEREO INSTALLER

If you're one of the rare few who can hook up all those wires and cables at the back of the television, VCR, cable box, CD player and stereo system and make the whole thing work, then this is the business for you. You'll work at customers' homes, putting together new systems or adding new components they've purchased, or hooking things back together after a move. You can also make money as well as music by installing customers' car stereo systems. Leave fliers with cooperative electronics sales stores and place ads in your local newspaper. **Start-up costs:** $250. **Expected annual gross revenues:** Up to $20,000.

record label mini-mogul, you can expect to earn revenues of $20,000 to $150,000 and up.

Pounding The Pavement

As with the book-publishing industry, you generally don't sell directly to the ultimate consumer, the person who pops that CD into his player and cranks up the sound on a sunny afternoon. Therefore, you'll need to work out a deal with distributors.

Some smaller record labels do sell directly to listeners at flea markets and swap meets and through mail order. And even if you go through a distributor, you can sell directly to music stores as you canvass your territory, making sure they're carrying your album.

What's Next

You need a really great concept and an even better band or artist. Start planning your idea and scouting for talent while boning up on the ins and outs of the biz.

Organizations

● *Association for Independent Music*, P.O. Box 988, 147 E. Main St., Whitesburg, KY 41858, (800) 607-6526, www.afirm.org. Be sure to check out the mentoring program—if you're a member, you can sign up online!

● *National Academy of Recording Arts and Sciences*, 3402 Pico Blvd., Santa Monica, CA 90405, (800) 423-2017

Books

● *How to Make and Sell Your Own Recording*, by Diane Sward Rapaport, Jerome Headlands Press

Publications

● *Billboard*, BPI Communications, 1515 Broadway, 11th Fl., New York, NY 10036, (212) 536-5240

Cyber Assistance

● *Recording Industry Association of America* (www.riaa.com): Check out this site for information on topics like piracy, censorship and Web licensing, and, of course, membership in the association.

Business Opportunities

- *EZCD.com.* Not really a biz op, EZCD.com will put your band's song in their music library, where listeners can hear a sample. If they like it, the company will put your tune on a custom CD created for the customer. Bottom line—you get paid when they choose your melody.

MOBILE DISC JOCKEY

The Inside Scoop

If you've always wanted to be a radio personality, spinning records (or CDs) and entertaining your audience with your own patented brand of patter, then this could be just the business for you.

As a mobile disc jockey, you'll roll to party locations, set up your equipment on-site and fill the night (or day) with music. You'll provide entertainment at all sorts of events, from weddings to office parties to open houses and birthdays. You'll also make sure guests are having fun, encouraging would-be wallflowers to get out there and boogie, teaching line dancing or the Watusi, and initiating bunny hops or conga lines.

The advantages to this business are that, first and foremost, it's fun—if you're an extrovert with an ear for music, you can't do much better unless you're a live musician. It's creative, you can start part time, you get to party while you work, and while you won't make a fortune, your earnings will be more than respectable.

The disadvantages are that most people want to have a party on the weekends and as only one person, you can only be one place at a time, which will limit the amount of money you can make. Also, since most gigs take place on weekends, in the evenings and on holidays (Valentine's Day, New Year's Eve and Halloween, for example), this business can take a major bite out of your social life.

Essentials

You've got to be an onstage, people kind of person who can not only entertain a crowd but draw others out and help them have fun, too. You should have an appreciation for lots of kinds of music—you can't refuse to play either Perry Como or Pink Floyd if that's what your clients and their guests want to hear—plus up-to-the-nanosecond music-industry knowledge of what's new and hot. And you'll need the skills and experience to operate all that equipment smoothly and easily.

Tools Of The Trade

You'll need a sound system—CD player, mixer, speakers, amplifier, a microphone—and a major collection of music of all kinds. You should also have a vehicle suitable for carrying all this around in, and liability insurance and a policy to cover your equipment in transit.

Money Talk

Sound out start-up costs of $15,000 to $22,000. If you can't afford equipment to start off with, you may be able to rent a radio station's remote location outfit. Expect to earn $30,000 to $150,000 per year, depending on a lot of factors, including your geographic region, how aggressively you market yourself and how hard you want to work. You'll charge your clients $50 to $200 per hour of play time, based on going rates in your area.

Pounding The Pavement

Your clients will be anybody who wants to party or help others have fun—couples or individuals, associations and organizations, corporations, and wedding and event planners.

Send brochures to wedding and event planners and even caterers, who may refer you to other party planners. Place ads in your local Yellow Pages and newspapers. Post fliers on bulletin boards around colleges and frat and sorority houses.

What's Next

Go through your music collection to see where you might fall short on favorites for certain types of gigs—have you got, for instance, the kind of songs the older relatives of the bride will like?

Take notes on how other mobile DJs and entertainers work a crowd. Practice your own techniques—help out at the parties of friends or neighbors for free. You'll get the experience and also free publicity.

Organizations

● *American Disc Jockey Association*, 297 Rte. 72 W., Ste. C-120, Manahawkin, NJ 08050-2980, (301) 705-5150, www.adja.org

Books

● *The Mobile DJ Handbook: How to Start and Run a Profitable Mobile Disc Jockey Service*, by Stacey Zemon, Focal Press

Franchises

● *American Mobile Sound Franchise Corp.*, 600 Ward Dr., Ste. A-1, Santa Barbara, CA 93111, (800) 788-9007, www.amsdj4u.com

● *Complete Music*, 7877 L St., Omaha, NE 68127, (800) 843-3866, www.cmusic.com

REUNION **O**RGANIZER

The Inside Scoop

If you're the one your family or group relies on to keep everybody together and in touch—the one who plans all the holiday celebrations and knows who's moved where, and who's had a baby or gotten married—then this could be the business for you.

As a reunion organizer, you'll be a combination event planner and private detective, hunting down missing members of high school and college classes, large families, groups and associations, then planning and organizing the bash of the decade. To find those missing members, you'll pore through phone directories and computer databases and contact school and civic records departments and friends, neighbors and relatives.

Reunion-organizing is a growing field—with all those baby boomers being joined by Generation Xers just reaching high school reunion age, there's no dearth of potential customers. And since just about everybody is out in the workforce these days, no one has the time to spend on tracking down former classmates or associates and then attending to all the details of the event. Which leaves lots of work for you.

The advantages to this business are that you can work at home, it's creative, challenging and rewarding—you get to help people have fun and renew old ties every time you plan a reunion.

The disadvantage is that hunting down people to attend events can be time-consuming and, if you can't locate someone, frustrating.

Essentials

As a reunion organizer, you'll have to be obsessive about locating attendees—you can't give up the search after one glance in the local phone book—as well as creative about ways to broaden your search. You'll also need to be extremely detail-oriented and organized—people will be traveling from all over the country to attend events you arrange and counting on you to pull it all together.

Tools Of The Trade

You'll need a computer with the usual office software, a laser printer, a fax machine, a calendar, a planning book and a phone.

Money Talk

Organize yourself with start-up costs of $1,500 to $3,000. A good reunion organizer can make annual revenues of $60,000 to $120,000. Charge your clients $5 to $10 per attendee and try to work with groups large enough to make the effort worth your while.

Pounding The Pavement

Your customers can be the Class of X for high schools and colleges, groups and associations, and large, far-flung families. Your best bet for selling to these groups is to establish yourself in your community. Introduce yourself to and leave brochures with vendors in event-planning industries who can refer people to you—caterers, hotels, florists, printers and photographers. Find out who's in charge of the reunion committees for your own high school or college class or those of your friends and relatives, then call and introduce yourself and your services.

What's Next

Start establishing yourself with vendors around town, not just to get referrals but to learn who's offering what and at what prices to help in planning your reunions.

Books

- *Family Reunion Handbook*, by Tom Ninkovich, Reunion Research
- *The Family Reunion Planner*, by Donna Beasley and Donna Carter, MacMillan General Reference

- *So That's Who You Used to Be! A Reunion Planning Guide*, by Patricia M. Bauer, Patricia McKee Bauer

Business Opportunities

- *Reunions With Class*, P.O. Box 5040, Colorado Springs, CO 80931, (719) 390-1112

The Inside Scoop

Most women anticipate their wedding day for years, probably long before their first kiss. But it's hard to plan those dream nuptials these days— both the bride and her mother (the one traditionally responsible for wedding planning) usually work, which leaves them scant time or energy for all the hundreds of details that go into planning the big event.

But this doesn't mean an end to rose petals, orange blossoms and happily ever after. You can make dreams come true as a wedding planner (also called a bridal consultant). You'll work with the happy couple on an hourly basis, lending advice on a few issues, or you'll plan and orchestrate the entire event, from deciding how many guests to invite to helping choose a site and someone to officiate on the big day.

Wedding planning is big business these days and getting bigger. More than 2 million couples tied the knot in 1998, with that number expected to continue to rise through 2012. And because many of those couples are marrying later than ever before—having spent years as working singles—they've got the funds to put on major productions. That means lots of work with plenty of income for you.

The advantages to this business are that you can start part time with low costs, it's creative and challenging, and you get to be an active participant in one of the most glamorous, exciting and romantic aspects of anyone's life over and over again.

The disadvantages are that it can be competitive and seasonal. And since weddings are usually planned six months or more in advance of the event, yet you don't get paid until the big day, your cash flow can be pretty dismal. (You can compensate for this by requiring a retainer upfront and then having couples make pre-wedding payments.)

Essentials

This is a business where you've got to be extremely organized and detail-oriented. It's up to you to pull everything together, and you can't forget to order the cake or put that deposit on the ballroom. You also have to be creative and able to meet challenges, advising the bride and groom on what they can get for their budget and inventing ways to give them the wedding of their dreams even if they can't afford their original ideas or the site their hearts are set on is already booked solid.

You'll need a good working knowledge of what goes into planning a wedding, including resources and price ranges for everything from invitations to photographers to orchestras. And since weddings are emotional for everyone involved, you have to be able to keep your cool, help soothe ruffled feathers and suggest compromises.

Tools Of The Trade

All that's really necessary to get started is a calendar, a planning book, a phone and your list of resources.

Money Talk

You can get started for less than $500. A good wedding planner can earn gross annual revenues of $50,000 to $75,000, handling 30 to 40 weddings a year. You'll charge your clients 10 percent to 15 percent of the wedding budget.

Pounding The Pavement

Your clients will be brides and grooms eager to make their wedding the event of a lifetime. Attract their business through ads in your local Yellow Pages, in the society or wedding section of your local paper and in special bridal supplements. Establish a relationship with local wedding-oriented vendors—florists, photographers, bridal shops, videographers, caterers, hotels and country clubs, bakeries and cake decorators, jewelers and musicians. Leave your brochures with them and ask for referrals.

What's Next

Plan a few weddings or anniversary parties for friends and relatives free of charge. It's good practice and great free advertising.

Organizations

● *Association of Bridal Consultants*, 200 Chestnutland Rd., New Milford, CT 06776-1404

● *American Society of Wedding Professionals*, 268 Griggs Ave., Teaneck, NJ 07666, (800) 526-0497

● *June Wedding Inc.*, 1331 Burnham Ave., Las Vegas, NV 89104-3658, (702) 474-9558, www.junewedding.com

Books

● *Affairs of the Heart: How to Start and Operate a Successful Special Event Planning Service*, by Nancy D. Gluck, Humbug Associates Inc.

● *Entrepreneur's Business Start-Up Guide #1330, Bridal Consultant*, Entrepreneur Media Inc., 2392 Morse Ave., Irvine, CA 92614, (800) 421-2300, www.smallbizbooks.com

● *The Everything Wedding Book*, by Janet Anastasio and Michelle Bevilacqua, Adams Media

- *Planning a Wedding to Remember: The Perfect Wedding Planner*, by Beverly Clark, Wilshire Publishing
- *The Portable Wedding Consultant: Invaluable Advice From the Industry's Experts for Saving Your Time, Money and Sanity*, by Leah Ingram, NTC/Contemporary Publishing

Cyber Assistance

- *The Wedding Channel* (www.weddingchannel.com): It's designed more for brides than bridal consultants but has choice tidbits of tips, fashions, advice and more.

ChaPter fourteen

ONE SINGULAR SENSATION

Everybody wants to look and feel good. But not everybody knows how. If you're the one friends and family beg for fashion advice, the one who gives makeup and hair tips and always looks classy, this might be the category for you. If you're most comfortable in sweats and shorts, you know how to make exercise count and you like helping others get fit, then this could be your category, too. In short, if you know what it takes to be one singular sensation, read on and take advantage of the look good/feel good boom.

IMAGE CONSULTANT

The Inside Scoop

If you're the one everybody turns to for dress-for-success assistance—you know what's in and what's out, how to make even the plainest Jane sparkle, and how to dress for every occasion from lunch at McDonald's to dinner at the White House—then this could be just the business for you.

As an image consultant, you'll give clients—men as well as women—beauty makeovers to help them land better jobs, find a mate, shine at their weddings or just feel better about themselves. You'll coach them on the right wardrobe style for the image they want to project and even weed out closets or go on shopping expeditions. You'll also give hair and makeup advice, color-consulting, and updated versions of Mom's "don't slouch, shoulders back" instructions for self-confidence.

You can also work with corporate clients by recommending new employee uniform styles, or by teaching multicultural etiquette or body-language basics for better sales and customer relations. Or you can work with clients facing the media spotlight to help them look and act their best.

The advantages to the image consulting business are that you can work at home, you can start part time with low costs, and it's creative and satisfying—when you help someone achieve a better job or media success or just feel good about themselves, it can be heady stuff.

The disadvantages are that this is not a business that sells itself—you may have to work at educating people about your services—and it's not recession-proof. Since everybody except actors and models generally thinks of looking good as a nicety rather than a necessity, your business may be the first to go if the economy takes a tumble.

Essentials

As an image consultant, you'll need an innate sense of style and up-to-the-second knowledge of fashion, hair and makeup trends—and how to apply that makeup—in personal and corporate settings. You'll also want to know the latest trends and conventions in big- and small-business conduct.

Since you're dealing with people on one of the most personal levels, you'll need a really good closet-side manner—the ability to point out negative traits and suggest changes without hurting their feelings.

And last but definitely not least, you'll have to be a walking advertisement of your own advice. This is a practice-what-you-preach business—you'll have to look polished, professional and dressed for success on all public occasions.

Tools Of The Trade

If you've got a background in fashion or modeling, broadcasting, or cosmetology, you've got it made, but none of these is a necessity. All you really need to get started are mirrors, makeup, color swatches, and fashion books and magazines. You may want to purchase, either during start-up or after your business gets going, computer software that gives your clients a virtual beauty makeover before they take the actual hair-cutting plunge.

If you plan on going the corporate route, you may also want to invest in a video camera and VCR so clients can judge their before-and-after speech and body language performances.

In some states, you need a cosmetology license to work on clients' skin, so if you plan to offer makeup services be sure to check with your state board of cosmetology. If you can't apply makeup to your clients yourself, you can supervise while they do their own.

Money Talk

This can be a very low-cost start-up. If you won't be going the corporate or computer route, you can pencil in costs of about $500, although you may want to add up to another $500 for professional-organization and networking dues. If you're going to purchase all the bells and whistles, plan on an additional $750. Once you've become established, you can expect annual gross revenues of $25,000 to $75,000, depending on the going rates in your area, how hard you choose to work, and whether you've got a corporate or private clientele. You'll charge your clients by the hour at typical fees of $25 to $150, or by the seminar or workshop, with fees ranging from $750 to $2,000.

Pounding The Pavement

Your clients can be individuals who want to look sharp for a big social occasion, are looking for a new or better job, or because of divorce, empty-nest syndrome, midlife crisis or some other milestone, have decided it's time to turn over a whole new leaf. Your clients can also be corporations who may hire you to train groups of executives or employees or to give the company dress code a face lift.

Place ads in local publications and offer coupons in direct-mail coupon books. Network in professional and civic organizations. Introduce yourself to wedding consultants, caterers and event planners, who can refer you to their clients. Give workshops and seminars for private and corporate clients.

You should also target public relations agents who may refer their clients to you. Send PR people your brochure, then follow up with a phone call to cement your service in their minds.

Weekend Warrior
MOBILE HAIRDRESSER

Almost every female loves having her hair professionally cut, colored, permed or styled. But with today's hectic pace, it's hard to find the time to sit in a salon and be pampered. If you're a whiz with scissors and rollers, you can take your expertise to your customers as a mobile hairdresser. (You'll need to be licensed so, if you're not already, be sure to check with your state before your start.) Send brochures to the human resources departments of large companies that can set up lunch-time appointments for employees and to administrators at hospitals, hospices and nursing homes who can refer patients to you. Distribute fliers to workers in office complexes and advertise in your local newspaper. **Start-up costs:** $1,000. **Expected annual gross revenues:** Up to $20,000.

What's Next

Do a few free consultations for friends and associates. You'll get experience, word-of-mouth advertising (which is the best kind), and before-and-after pictures for your portfolio. (Always get permission to use photos.)

Organizations

● *The Association of Image Consultants International*, 1000 Connecticut Ave. NW, #9, Washington, DC 20036, (800) 383-8831

Books

● *Always In Style: The Complete Guide for Creating Your Best Look: Style, Bodyline, Wardrobe, Color, Hair, Makeup,* by Doris Pooser, Crisp Publications

● *Fabulous You! Unlock Your Perfect Personal Style,* by Tori Hartman, Berkley Publishing

● *Looking Good: A Comprehensive Guide to Wardrobe Planning, Color & Personal Style Development,* by Nancy Nix-Rice, Palmer Pletsch Publishing

Business Opportunities

● *Color 1 Associates Inc.*, 2211 Washington Cir. NW, Washington, DC 20037, (202) 293-9175

MAKEUP ARTIST

The Inside Scoop

If you've got a way with makeup—you know how to create magic with powders, lipsticks and shadows and you like transforming Cinderellas into princesses—then this could be the business for you.

As a makeup artist, you'll help clients look their best for weddings or other special events, give beauty makeovers to people who want to update their everyday images, or you might specialize in helping people disfigured by accident or illness look and feel good again. If you live in an area with a viable film industry, you can also become a makeup artist to the stars (or star-hopefuls) by working on TV or movie projects.

The advantages to this business are that you can start part time and on a shoestring, and you get the rewards of helping people feel good about themselves.

The disadvantage is that your income can fluctuate depending on how many clients you happen to have at a stretch.

Essentials

As a makeup artist, you'll need the skills and talent to turn a plain Prudence into a dazzling Diana as well as the teaching skills to send your clients home with tips on how to achieve everyday glamour results for themselves.

Tools Of The Trade

In some states, you need a cosmetology license to work on clients' skin, so be sure to check with your state board of cosmetology. Other than that, all you need is makeup, brushes and sponges, and your own innate talents.

Money Talk

Make yourself up start-up costs of about $500. You can expect annual gross revenues of $20,000 to $30,000 and up—you'll need to exercise creative marketing to better your income.

Pounding The Pavement

Your clients can be just about anybody who wants to look good, although they'll likely be female. You can target brides by establishing relationships (be sure to leave brochures and business cards) with wedding-oriented businesses like bridal consultants, bridal shops and caterers. Work up referral networks with event and party planners, too, along with public relations agents.

Nab clients who want a beauty makeover by placing ads in local Yellow Pages and newspapers and leaving brochures at hair salons, trendy boutiques and dress shops. Give workshops for women's groups or experiment with home parties à la Mary Kay—but keep in mind that if you sell your beauty products, you'll need a resale license.

If you plan to work with disfigured clients, introduce yourself and leave brochures with plastic surgeons and oncologists (doctors who specialize in cancer).

What's Next

Give a few free makeovers to friends and neighbors—it'll give you experience and word-of-mouth advertising, the very best kind.

Organizations

- *National Cosmetology Association*, 3510 Olive St., St. Louis, MO 63103, (800) 527-1683, www.nca-now.com

Books

- *The Art of Makeup*, by Kevyn Aucoin, HarperCollins
- *Color Me Beautiful's Looking Your Best: Color, Makeup and Style*, by Marry Spillane and Christine Sherlock, Madison Books
- *DK Living: Classic Makeup & Beauty*, by Mary Quant and Dave King, DK Publishing

MOBILE MASSAGE

The Inside Scoop

In today's fast-paced world, we all lead hectic lives. It's only too easy to get frustrated, frazzled, overwrought and over-stressed. We've got not only people demanding our attention, but also things—ringing phones, beeping pagers, and indignantly squealing computers, fax machines and microwave ovens—making relaxation a hazy daydream.

But if you've got that healing touch—you can unbunch tense muscles and calm jangled nerves—then you can make dreams of relaxation a reality with a mobile massage service. You'll drive to homes or offices; bring in your massage chair or table, soothing oils and restful music; and give your clients 7- to 20-minute on-site treatments. You can even—with permission from the proper authorities—set up on the beach, at shopping malls and at airports.

The advantages to this business are that your start-up costs are minimal and you get the glow of satisfaction from making the world—at least temporarily—a more relaxing place for your clients.

The disadvantage is that massage can be hard work. You'll use plenty of muscle, and you'll be on your feet throughout each session.

Essentials

You'll need to have a background in massage therapy, an affinity and empathy for people, and a restful nature. (You can't help your clients relax if you're scattered, tense or jangled yourself.)

Tools Of The Trade

Some states require massage therapists to be licensed—check with the American Massage Therapy Association to find out if yours is one of them. You'll need a portable massage table or chair, a selection of scented candles and oils, a stack of clean towels, and a CD or cassette player plus some relaxing music to pop into it.

Money Talk

This is a minimal start-up business—plan on costs of about $1,000. Massage therapists in major metropolitan areas charge from $35 to $60 per hour; those working in smaller regions usually price their services at $25 to $50 an hour. Keep in mind that massage is physically and emotionally demanding, so you—like most massage therapists—will probably work far less than a 40-hour week. Expect annual gross revenues of $20,000 to $40,000.

Pounding The Pavement

Your clients can be overworked executives and home office entrepreneurs, stay-at-home moms, and weekend (or weekday) athletes who've overdone the aerobics workout.

Send sales letters and brochures to the human resources departments or health and safety coordinators of large corporations and small-business owners in your area.

Leave fliers or brochures at health clubs and spas; swim, running and biking clubs; fitness centers; athletic shoe and clothing shops; vitamin and nutrition shops; and with chiropractors who can refer you to their patients.

Give seminars to professional and civic groups and volunteer yourself as a guest on a local radio chat show. Get yourself written up in local publications. Donate a few sessions to a charity fund-raiser in exchange for publicity.

What's Next

If you don't have a massage background, take classes (most can be completed in nine months to one year) and get your certification.

The Language Of Touch

Julie Donnelly knew nothing about massage 11 years ago. As a newly divorced former housewife, Donnelly did know that she needed a way to support herself and fund her travel bug. She discovered therapeutic massage on a weekly sailing expedition when the bowman, suffering a pinched nerve, asked her to knead it out. After several such informal sessions, Donnelly was hooked on massage as a way to earn a living, help other people and travel the world—all at the same time.

Although Donnelly had to take courses in anatomy, physiology and massage technique to attain her New York state license, she didn't need a college education or years of experience. Her new skills were portable, requiring only a massage chair or table, her own two hands and an ability to communicate that didn't need a common tongue. "Pain is the same all over the world," she says. "The language of touch is universal."

The 53-year-old grandmother has practiced massage on a cruise ship, on the dock in St. Thomas, Virgin Islands, and now operates the Julstro Muscular Therapy Center in Chestnut Ridge, New York. (Donnelly coined the name "Julstro" for a new massage technique she's pioneering to help people with carpal tunnel syndrome.)

Donnelly spends 20 or more hours a week on massage therapy—though she says 15 hours would be healthier—at an office she shares with a colleague, charging clients $60 per hour. She also makes monthly calls to an insurance agency, where she performs custom half-hour massages tailored to each employee's sore spots. The agency's employee sick time has plummeted. "And [the massage treatments] bring up employee loyalty like you can't imagine," says Donnelly.

She does no advertising. She kick-started her business by volunteering to do massages at the end of marathons and bike races, where she soon became the "unofficial official massage therapist." She also volunteered to give $1 massages for recipients of the local Meals on Wheels program. The program got the money and Donnelly got an unbeatable opportunity to hand out business cards plus a write-up in the local paper.

Other than her training, Donnelly's start-up costs were minimal—she found a used massage table and reupholstered the top to make it "new."

Get liability insurance and have your company name and phone number painted on your vehicle.

Organizations

- *American Massage Therapy Association*, 820 Davis St., #100, Evanston, IL 60201, (847) 864-0123, www.amtamassage.org. Features a great Web site with all sorts of detailed information on becoming a massage therapist. Check it out!

- *National Certification Board for Therapeutic Massage and Body Work*, 8201 Greensboro Dr., #300, McLean, VA 22102, (800) 296-0664, www.ncbtmb.com

PERSONAL TRAINER

The Inside Scoop

Health and fitness are very big issues today—everyone wants to look good, feel better and live longer. And while most of us would be perfectly happy sitting around all day eating chocolates and doing the couch-potato channel-surf, we know we should be out there exercising at least a few hours every week.

If you like working out—feeling your blood pump, your muscles strengthen and getting those endorphins going—and you're good at encouraging others to get fit, then this could be the business for you.

As a personal trainer, you'll instruct clients on proper exercise techniques, design regimes based on their goals, and analyze progress in body weight, muscle development and weight training. While many of your clients will be interested in shaping up and losing weight, you can also help people with specific problems like arthritis to build other muscles to compensate or those who want to rebuild or retrain their bodies after accidents or illness.

You can work with your clients in their homes, at a health club where you have a membership, or—like a certain bodybuilder type on television—on a scenic beach with hard bodies flashing in the background.

The advantages to this business are that you have the potential to make a very good living and you have the satisfaction of helping people become healthier and happier.

The disadvantages are that you can't just supervise—you'll need to do a fair amount of strenuous exercise yourself to demonstrate techniques—and because your clients generally won't be as interested in fitness as you are, they'll lose interest (and you'll lose at least a few clients) on a routine basis.

Essentials

Besides being physically fit and healthy yourself, you'll need terrific motivational skills to help your clients push beyond their physical and mental boundaries and keep at it week after week.

Tools Of The Trade

You'll need certification as a personal trainer. In addition, most personal trainers have a college degree in physical therapy, physical education, exercise physiology, sports medicine or related fields—this is particularly important if you'll be working with people recovering from illness or injuries. You may want to purchase assessment tools like fat calipers, but this depends on your (and your clients') personal tastes—some people don't want to know how fat they are; they just want to get rid of it. As for exercise equipment, you can let your clients purchase their own.

Money Talk

Get fit with start-up costs of about $500. You can expect annual gross revenues of up to $60,000 or $70,000 if you're willing to work hard. You'll charge your clients $25 to $100 per session, depending on your area. It's best to insist on a minimum number of sessions, say 5 to 10, and if you like, you can give your clients a discount for going for a certain number of sessions up front.

Pounding The Pavement

Your clients will be people who want to lose weight, gain muscle, recover from illness or injury, or just get into better shape. Sell yourself by leaving fliers or brochures at health clubs and spas; swim, running and biking clubs; fitness centers; athletic shoe and clothing shops; and vitamin and nutrition shops. Place ads in local newspapers. Introduce yourself and leave brochures with chiropractors, orthopedic surgeons and doctors of sports medicine.

Give seminars to professional and civic groups and volunteer yourself as a guest on a local radio chat show. Get yourself written up in local publications. Donate a few sessions to a charity fund-raiser in exchange for publicity.

What's Next

Start networking among friends, neighbors and relatives.

Organizations

● *The American Council on Exercise*, 5820 Oberlin Dr., #102, San Diego, CA 92121-3787, (800) 825-3636

● *American College of Sports Medicine*, P.O. Box 1440, Indianapolis, IN 46206-1440, (317) 637-9200

● *The National Strength and Conditioning Association*, P.O. Box 9908, Colorado Springs, CO 80932-0908, (719) 632-6722, www.nsca-lift.org

Books

● *The Business of Personal Training*, by Scot O. Roberts (editor), Human Kinetics Publishing

● *The Personal Trainer's Handbook*, by Teri S. O'Brien, Human Kinetics Publishing

Cyber Assistance

● *Teri O'Brien Fitness Systems* (www.onlythebest.net): This terrific site is hosted by radio fitness celeb O'Brien, "Chicagoland's Optimum Performance Coach." It's packed with tips, recom-

Weekend Warrior

SEAMSTRESS/TAILOR

If you've got a flair for working with fabric, you can sew up profits for yourself and fill a need for your customers as a seamstress or tailor. You'll do simple alterations—everything from hemming skirts or slacks to taking in (or letting out) waistbands to replacing lost buttons—as well as design and make custom clothing. Establish relationships with dress boutiques, menswear shops and dry cleaners who can refer customers to you, and advertise in your local newspaper. **Start-up costs:** $1,000. **Expected annual gross revenues:** Up to $20,000.

mended reading, a message board, couch potato confessional, and more.

Business Opportunities

● *Geri-Fit Ltd.*, P.O. Box 444, Hudson, OH 44236, (888) GERI-FIT, www.gerifit.com

Cha**p**ter fifteen

PAYING THE PIPER

So you're the financial whiz in your circle, the one everybody goes to for help with their income tax forms, figuring out how all those nasty bills add up and what went wrong with the check register. (Why *did* all those checks bounce?) If you like working with figures, making sense of legal forms, and adding up dollars and cents, then you can make your own dollar sense with a business in this rewarding category.

The Inside Scoop

Most people tend to consider the issue of owing money from a personal level—being late on the rent or credit card bills or cable TV service or whatever—and consider it an unpleasant state of affairs. For businesses, having customers who owe money is not only unpleasant but can cause serious cash flow problems and even force them to close their doors. Of course, they can hire a collection agency—but most big-time firms are only interested in going after the big accounts that promise big money.

But you can save the day with a homebased collection agency. You'll track down elusive debtors using the same skip-tracing techniques private detectives employ, then make arrangements with them to pay off those old bills. You can also specialize in finding errant parents who owe child support or people who have health-care debts.

Debt collection is big business: According to the American Collectors Association, outstanding consumer installment debt totaled $1 trillion in one recent year and new accounts totaling approximately $122 billion were placed for collection with professional agencies. So there's plenty of work for you!

The advantages to this business are that you can work at home, it's always challenging, you get to solve mysteries every day, and helping people repair their credit problems while getting your clients their hard-earned money can be quite rewarding.

The disadvantages are that nobody's going to like you—your debtor subjects will yell, lie and even blame you for their troubles—and dealing with people's problems day in and day out can be depressing. You'll have to take care not to start looking at—and treating—everybody as a bad egg.

Essentials

You'll need a good understanding of collection procedures—what you can and cannot legally do—including knowledge of the Federal Fair Debt Collection Practices Act and applicable laws in your state. If you're going after health-care dollars, a good grounding in health insurance policies and billing procedures is a must. You should also have an obsessive personality when it comes to tracking down debtors, good communication skills to work with people instead of against them to resolve payment issues, and a healthy dose of self-esteem so you don't take those daily tirades personally.

Tools Of The Trade

Most states will require you to be licensed and bonded, so be sure to check with your secretary of state or the American Collectors Association. You'll also need a computer, a laser printer, a fax machine, the usual office software, special collections software, and a telephone headset so you don't get a cauliflower ear from hours on the phone.

Money Talk

Collect start-up costs of about $2,350—you may want to add in up to another $500 for professional-organization and networking dues. Average commissions for a collection agency range between 15 percent and 35 percent of the amount collected. Annual gross revenues vary greatly, depending on the size and technology of the agency; as a thumbnail you can figure on $30,000 to $60,000.

Pounding The Pavement

Your clients can be businesses of all types, but good ones to start with are retail establishments stuck with bounced checks and doctors, clinics and other health-care providers landed with unpaid bills. If you plan to specialize in deadbeat dads and moms, you can offer your services to state and county agencies or to parents themselves. According to a recent U.S. General Accounting Office report, state and county agencies in 37 states were contracting with or planning to contract with private collectors to secure past-due child support payments.

Land your clients by calling and directly soliciting their business—with the service you're offering, you should attract their attention quickly. Doctors, as everybody who's ever tried knows, can be almost impossible to reach by phone, so ask to talk to the office manager.

Place ads in your local Yellow Pages. Network among professional, civic and small-business groups, and give seminars or workshops.

What's Next

If you don't have a background in debt collection, sign on with a working agency for a while to learn the ropes. Then get licensed and certified and get going!

Organizations

- *American Child Support Collectors Association*, (800) 694-KIDS
- *American Collectors Association*, ACA Center, 4040 W. 70th St., Minneapolis, MN 55435-4199, (612) 926-6547, www.collector. com
- *National Child Support Enforcement Association*, 444 N. Capital St., #414, Washington, DC 20001, (202) 624-8180, www.ncsca.org

Weekend Warrior

BOOKKEEPER

Every business needs a bookkeeper to pay the bills, send out invoices, reconcile bank statements, and handle all those record-keeping tasks that send most of us running the other way. If you're a whiz with figures and you like the satisfaction of putting things in order, you can earn a tidy sum and help small-business owners as a part-time bookkeeper. You'll need to be aware of current tax rules and regulations, and you'll want a computer, printer and accounting software—with a laptop, you can even travel to clients' offices. Send brochures to local SOHOs and place ads in your local newspaper. **Start-up costs: $2,150. Expected annual gross revenues:** Up to $25,000.

Books

- *The Complete Book of Collection Letters, Telephone Scripts, and Faxes/Book and Disc*, by Cecil J. Bond, McGraw-Hill
- *Credit and Collections (Barron's Business Library)*, by James John Jurinski, Barrons Educational Series
- *Credit and Collection: Letters Ready to Go!*, by Edward Joseph Halloran, NTC Business Books

Business Opportunities

- *National Debt Recovery*, 20165 N. 67th Ave., #212, Glendale, AZ 85308, (602) 280-9930

Franchises

- *ACCTCORP International*, 7414 NE Hazel Dell Ave., #209, Vancouver, WA 98665-9937, (800) 844-4024, www.acctcorp.com

PARALEGAL SERVICE

The Inside Scoop

If you've always wanted to be a lawyer—your favorite TV show is "Law & Order" and you've read every John Grisham novel twice—then this could be the business for you.

As a paralegal, you can't give legal advice or defend anybody in a murder trial, but you can complete simple documents and forms for individuals and attorneys, then take those papers down to the courthouse and file them. You'll help lawyers with small practices by taking over the work that would be done by legions of assistants in a large law firm, and you'll lend aid to individuals with matters like evictions and simple divorces so they don't have to pay those high attorneys' fees.

The advantages to this business are that you get the charge of life in the law lane without the slavish hours you'd find in a corporate firm, and you have the satisfaction of helping your clients through the maze of the legal system.

The disadvantages are that completing routine documents day after day can sometimes get boring and that you'll frequently be faced with some sort of deadline or other looming crisis.

Essentials

You'll need a strong background in all matters paralegal; good communication skills; and excellent grammatical, punctuation and spelling abilities—no judge is going to be impressed by a mistake-riddled document. (Neither will your clients.)

In addition, you should have terrific organizational skills and be a good time manager so you can pump out those documents in plenty of time for court dates and filings.

Tools Of The Trade

In some states, you'll need a paralegal certificate or liability insurance—check with your local business licensing agency or department of corporations to find out. You'll need a computer with a laser printer, a fax machine, the usual suite software and special software for completing routine documents like wills, evictions and divorces.

Money Talk

Advise yourself of start-up costs of $2,000 to $3,000. A good paralegal can make $45,000 to $65,000 per year and up, depending on how hard you work and how much work there is in your area. You'll charge your clients $40 to $65 an hour, depending on the going rates in your area.

Pounding The Pavement

Your clients can be individuals and attorneys with small firms in need of assistance. Your best bet for getting business from legal eagles is to send sales letters and brochures, then follow up with phone calls. Join local legal associations and network in professional and civic groups.

To attract private clients, place ads in the Yellow Pages and local newspapers and get yourself written up in your local newspaper.

What's Next

If you don't have a legal background, go out and get it. Take courses or work for a law firm until you know the ropes.

Organizations

● *American Association for Paralegal Education*, 2965 Flowers Rd. S., #105, Atlanta, GA 30341, (770) 452-9877, www.afpe.org
● *National Paralegal Association*, Box 406, Solebury, PA 18963, (215) 297-8333, www.nationalparalegal.org

Books

● *The Independent Paralegal's Handbook: How to Provide Legal*

Services Without Becoming a Lawyer, by Ralph E. Warner, Nolo Press

- *Paralegal: An Insider's Guide to One of Today's Fastest-Growing Careers*, by Barbara Bernardo, Petersons Guides
- *The Paralegal's Desk Reference*, by Steve Albrecht and John W. Witt, MacMillan General Reference

TAX PREPARATION SERVICE

The Inside Scoop

Possibly the two least favorite activities in American life are undergoing a root canal and filling out yearly income tax statements. And with good reason—tax preparation can be time-consuming, detail-oriented, confusing, and, for most people, frightening. Tax laws change frequently, the IRS has a tyrannical reputation, and most of us balk at arithmetic anyway. Put all that together and Form 1040 is a waking nightmare.

But if you've got a head for figures, you like solving puzzles of the financial kind, and you can keep up with changing tax laws, this could be the business for you. You can work with individuals to fill out their yearly tax forms à la H & R Block, specialize in small-business tax preparation, or represent clients who've fallen under the IRS' beady eye and are being targeted for hefty liens or penalties.

The advantages to this business are that you can work at home, you get to learn an awful lot about everybody's personal and company business (although morally, ethically and legally, you must keep it to yourself), it's recession-proof because people will always need to pay their taxes, and it can be very profitable.

The disadvantages are that it can sometimes be dry and dull, it's not a glamourous occupation, it can tend to be seasonal, and the IRS can hold you legally responsible for fraudulent tax information if your client claims it was doctored by you.

Essentials

As a tax preparation expert, you should have a solid working knowledge of tax laws for your target market—individuals, estates, partnerships, or other types of small or large businesses. (Our tax system is too broad for you to know everything.) You'll need a good eye for good ol' math and the people skills to help your clients make the best of a usually nerve-draining situation. You should also have the experience and instincts to judge whether the information your clients give you is A-OK or doesn't quite ring true.

Tools Of The Trade

You don't have to have any sort of license or certification, but you may want to get certified as an EA (enrolled agent) by the IRS. This involves training followed by a rigorous two-day exam, the completion of which is a bonus as far as your credentials are concerned. It also allows you to go before the IRS in place of your client during an audit. (Only enrolled agents, CPAs and attorneys are granted this privilege, which means you can charge more than an uncertified tax preparer.) Whether or not you go for the EA designation, you'll need a computer with a laser printer, a fax machine, a copier, the usual office software, as well as tax preparation software like Intuit's ProSeries. You'll also need reference materials, including the U.S. Master Tax Guide (available from the U.S. Commerce Clearinghouse at 800-248-3248), and regular updates to all this stuff. You can get a diskette containing IRS forms for $20, plus lots of freebies, all for the asking. Be sure to check with your insurance agent about errors-and-omissions insurance as well.

Money Talk

Pencil in start-up costs of about $5,000, plus up to another $500 for professional organization and networking dues. A good tax preparation service can pull in $75,000 to $140,000 per year. Charge your clients $80 to $100 for a routine Form 1040 and $25 to $150 per hour for heavier duty filings, depending on how much is involved and on the going rates in your area.

Pounding The Pavement

Your clients can be individuals or businesses. Get yourself the business by placing ads in your local Yellow Pages and newspapers,

A STAR IS BORN

A Taxing Business

Karen Fessler's 23-year career as a tax preparer began with the birth of her first daughter. "I had just had a baby," the Oklahoma City resident recalls, "and I was looking for something to do. I saw an ad for an H&R Block tax course, and I thought, 'If nothing else, I could at least learn to do my own.'"

She learned a lot more than that. Fessler worked for H&R Block for nine years, a tenure that encompassed a move from Oklahoma to California, where she managed offices in three towns. But when the franchisee bowed out of the business, Fessler decided to go solo with a homebased business—a change that wasn't the least bit taxing.

"I never did any advertising," Fessler says. "I never needed to. I got all my clients through word-of-mouth." In fact, her former H&R Block customers called her at home—and now that she's back in Oklahoma, she still gets home calls from a steady base of clients, some of whom insisted on staying with her despite the interstate transfer.

Between her day job in a local CPA firm and her private clients, Fessler prepares 200 returns per year. She charges by the form (based on its complexity), by the hour or both. The reason? "You would be quite surprised," she says, "how many people—and corporations—bring in a paper bag full of receipts." Her charge for bag-sorting: $50 per hour, although she points out that in larger, more sophisticated areas like California and New York, that rate would be more like $75 to $100 per hour.

Another surprise—if you think tax preparation is dull: not. "Everybody's situation is different from others," Fessler says. "You don't get bored. And you meet a lot of very interesting people."

Fessler got started for only $250 but advises that today you'll have to spend considerably more, mainly for your computer and software. Her other advice for the newbie? "Have a lot of patience."

networking with professional and small-business organizations in your area, and with CPAs and attorneys who can refer their clients to you. Direct-mail your brochures to local businesses or to individuals who have just moved to your area.

What's Next

If you don't have a tax preparation background, take courses and then work for a tax prep firm for a while. Then get busy filing tax forms!

Organizations

- *National Association of Enrolled Agents*, 200 Orchard Ridge Dr., #302, Gaithersburg, MD 20878, (301) 212-9608, www.naea.org
- *National Association of Tax Practitioners*, 720 Association Dr., Appleton, WI 54914, (800) 558-3402, (800) 242-3430 (in Wisconsin)

Books

- *Bookkeeping and Tax Preparation: Start and Build a Prosperous Bookkeeping, Tax and Financial Services Business*, by Gordon P. Lewis, Acton Circle Publishing Co.

Cyber Assistance

- *The Tax Channel* (www.naea.org): Great site, courtesy of the National Association of Enrolled Agents—offers downloadable forms, taxpayer news, tax links, educational information and more
- *The Digital Daily* (www.irs.ustreas.gov): Yes, the IRS can actually be friendly! This entertaining site, which bills itself as the fastest, easiest tax publication on the planet, is packed with tips, forms, electronic filing information and lots more. A must-surf.

Franchises

- *Liberty Tax Service*, 2610 Potters Rd., Virginia Beach, VA 23452, (800) 790-3863, www.libertytax.com
- *People's Income Tax*, 1601 Willow Lawn Dr., #309, Richmond, VA 23230, (800) 984-1040

UTILITY/PHONE BILL AUDITOR

The Inside Scoop

You know how much money you spend every year on utility and phone bills, and it probably seems astronomical. For businesses that use large amounts of utilities, fees can be truly outrageous, especially when you realize that companies routinely pay thousands—even millions—of dollars for incorrectly billed phone, water, gas and electric services. Why are the bills wrong? Meters get read improperly, amounts miscalculated, or the wrong data entered. And because most accounts payable people have neither the time nor the understanding to interpret the jumble of taxes and charges at the bottom of each bill, all this money gets unnecessarily paid out over and over again.

But if you're a detail-oriented person who likes getting to the bottom of financial matters, you can save the day—and the dollars—as a utility and phone bill auditor. You'll not only check for billing errors but also analyze clients' usage patterns and pinpoint areas for savings, and recommend discounts and alternative services that can save money.

The advantages to this business are that you can start part time with low costs, you won't have much competition, and it's recession-proof. It's also a good sell to potential clients because they don't pay you anything unless you find refundable errors or ways to save money—your fee is a portion of the refund or savings they get from your expertise.

The disadvantages are that you only get paid when you find refunds or savings, and since it can take up to 90 days for a utility to pay back funds, your cash flow can be grim. Also, in some states, like New York, utilities are structured so that you can't find much of anything in the way of refunds.

Essentials

You'll need a clear understanding of how phone and utility service billings work—from tariffs to taxes to customer, energy and fuel charges. And since you'll make at least part of your money by recommending discounts or alternative companies, you should have up-to-the-second knowledge of the various suppliers available in your area and their rates and discounts or other perks.

Utility/phone bill auditing is extremely detail-oriented work—you must be able to focus on minutiae and pick up on even minor errors (they add up to big ones). And you should have the financial creativity to design and recommend money-saving alternatives for your clients.

Tools Of The Trade

About all you need to get started is a computer with a laser printer, the usual office software and a good calculator.

Money Talk

Audit yourself into start-up costs of $2,150—you can add up to another $500 for professional organization and networking dues. You can expect to earn $50,000 to $200,000 per year. Your clients will pay you a percentage of the refunds you find or discounts you steer them toward. Charge 50 percent for refunds and up to 50 percent of any savings your clients will realize over one or two years (which means you'll get paid for up to two years after you've put in the work).

Pounding The Pavement

Your clients can be businesses of all sizes and descriptions, but your best bet will be to aim for high energy consumers like hospitals, hotels, restaurants, schools and other institutions, dry cleaners, coin laundries, and 24-hour supermarkets.

Direct-mail sales letters and brochures to these companies, then follow up with phone calls. You can also send brochures to business consultants, accountants and others who can refer you to their clients.

Network among professional and civic organizations and write articles for local publications.

What's Next

If you don't have experience with utility/phone bill auditing, you'll need to get it. You can take courses from companies like the ones listed below, or train yourself by studying the bills of everyone you know who'll let you take a gander at theirs, then calling the utility services and asking lots of questions. You'll also need to make an in-depth study of the programs offered by every phone company and utility service out there in your area.

Books

● *Slashing Utility Costs Handbook*, by John M. Studebaker, Fairmont Press

Business Opportunities

● *Public Utility Consultants*, 9712 Fair Oaks Blvd., Ste. C, Fair Oaks, CA 95628, (800) 833-2998
● *Utility & Tax Reduction Consultants*, 805 W. Jefferson St., Ste. A, Shorewood, IL 60563, (888) 321-7872

ChaPter sixteen

PERFECT PROMOTIONS

Y ou're a people person, one of those extroverted types who's never met a stranger. You're not shy. You can convince anybody to try anything (otherwise known as sales) and you love the challenge and psychology of getting people to go for new products, ideas or services. If so, then this is definitely the category for you.

The Inside Scoop

A career as an ad agency executive has a certain cachet—the combination of three-martini expense-account client lunches (which don't always exist anymore) and cut-throat competition has fueled everybody from poor old "Bewitched" Darrin Stevens to "thirtysomething" Michael Steadman. If you love turning a clever phrase and marrying it with smart graphics, the thrill of the chase for the elusive client, all combined with savvy marketing, then this is the business for you.

Like many other industries in our baby boomer-driven economy, the field of advertising is experiencing a major downsize. Where clients used to turn to the Madison Avenue-type majors on "the Coasts," they're now looking to smaller, friendlier, more specialized agencies in smaller cities—why not make one of them yours?

A one-person ad agency is a lot more fun than the giant conglomerate size. You get to wear all the hats from copywriter to graphic designer to media buyer. (If your skills don't run to writing or designing, you can outsource and give another small-business person the business.) But keep in mind that your clients will rely on you to know it all. You'll not only create those winning ads but place them in the proper media spots and negotiate good rates.

The advantages to this business are that it's creative and keeps you on your mental toes. The disadvantages are that you'll usually be rushing to meet deadlines, you'll occasionally have to juggle your own artistic sensibilities with your clients' desires, and just as for Darrin Stevens, the competition can be fierce.

Essentials

While a background in the field is not a must, you'll find the going far easier if you have experience at an ad agency, public relations firm, or even in the sales or production department of a magazine or newspaper. If you don't have any sort of advertising background, consider specializing in a field where you do know the ropes—say writing ads for boat-sales brokers and boating publications if you're a boating fanatic.

Tools Of The Trade

You'll need a high-end computer with a Zip or Jaz drive, the usual office software, desktop-publishing software, a laser printer, a top-quality color printer, a scanner and a fax machine.

Money Talk

Pencil in start-up costs of $3,350. Annual gross revenues for SOHO ad agencies range from $35,000 to $75,000. You'll charge your clients $75 to $150 per hour. Some agencies charge by the project or take a monthly retainer—if you choose one of these options, be careful that you don't end up short-changing yourself.

Pounding The Pavement

You're not likely to wind up with the Nabisco or Kodak accounts, but once you eliminate corporate monoliths, your clients can be just about any business or organization you choose to go after. It's wise to start off with a field you know. If you've been in the business already, you might go with the same types of clients. If your prior experience is on the minimalist side, try specializing in your own interest zone, like boating or gardening. Or try going after a certain business type like restaurants or boutiques.

How will you nab these special businesses? Network in your community. Place ads in publications catering to your chosen field of interest. Send direct-mail pieces featuring your creative talents to the companies you're targeting.

What's Next

If you're unfamiliar with desktop-publishing programs and you don't plan to outsource your graphic design work, get on a first-name basis with your software. There's nothing worse than a deadline breathing down your neck while you're struggling to master techniques. While you're on your learning curve, put together a few sample ad campaigns to show to prospective clients.

Organizations

● *American Advertising Federation*, 1101 Vermont Ave. NW, #500, Washington, DC 20005, (800) 999-2231, www.aaf.org

● *The Advertising Mail Marketing Association*, 1901 N. Fort Meyer Dr., #401, Arlington, VA 22209-1609, (703) 524-0096, www. amma.org

● *The Direct Marketing Association*, 1120 Ave. of the Americas, New York, NY 10036, (212) 768-7277, www.the-dma.org

Books

● *How to Start and Run Your Own Advertising Agency,* Allan Krieff, McGraw-Hill

Publications

● *Advertising Age*, 740 Rush St., Chicago, IL 60611-2590 (editorial address), (888) 288-5900 (subscriptions), www.adage.com

● *Adweek*, 1515 Broadway, New York, NY 10036, (800) 722-6658 (subscriptions)

● *Catalog Age*, Cowles Business Media, 11 River Bend Dr. S., Box 4949, Stamford, CT 06907-0949, (203) 358-9900 (editorial), (800) 775-3777 (subscriptions), www.CatalogAgemag.com

DIRECT-MAIL COUPON SERVICE

The Inside Scoop

Direct mail isn't just for catalogs crammed with trendy gifts and satin lingerie. It's also a terrific way to advertise local businesses, especially when you couple it with coupons people can use to clip and save. If you like sales—and the idea of helping community businesspeople make money while helping consumers save it—then this is the business for you.

With a direct-mail coupon service, you'll sell businesses on placing coupon ads in your publications, then mail them out to local residents. Everybody benefits, including you! With the new plethora of small businesses these days, direct-mail couponing is positioned for success. Entrepreneurs can advertise in a medium where results can be measured quickly and easily—the more coupons customers bring in, the better the campaign. And coupons generate more sales than other types of ads. People respond to ads where they have to take action, even if it's something as simple as clipping along a dotted line.

The advantages to this business are legion for the extrovert. You get to talk to all kinds of people in all sorts of fields, and you do it all day long. You can feel good about helping people improve their businesses and their revenues while at the same time aiding the consumer with savings. Since you'll visit customers at their business locations, you can be homebased.

The disadvantages—if you're a homebody—are that you'll be out and about all day. You'll have to make a lot of sales calls, so if you're not a people person, you should look at a different industry.

MAILING LIST SERVICE

A mailing list can be one of a business's most important advertising and marketing tools, but it can also take a lot of time to create and maintain. If you've got a computer, a printer, database software and a set of nimble fingers, you can spur companies to direct-mail success with a mailing list service. You'll develop and update lists for clients from condo associations to dentists, retail stores to retiree clubs, then mail out their materials as often as they choose. You'll need to keep up with postal regulations and purchase a postage meter and a standard-mail permit. Then go out and get clients through your own direct-mail campaign. **Start-up costs:** Under $3,000. **Expected annual gross revenues:** Up to $25,000.

Essentials

To succeed in this business, you should have a sales background—or at least a sales personality. It also helps to have a background working with the printing, graphics and mailing industries. You'll outsource all of this work, but you'll need to know the basics to get the best prices and timeliest turnout.

Tools Of The Trade

You'll need a computer and inkjet or laser printer and the usual office software so you can invoice customers, and a fax machine so they can send last-minute changes to their ads, and you'll need a vehicle for zipping around town on your rounds. Since you'll be out-of-pocket a lot, you should also consider a cellular phone or pager so customers can reach you easily.

Money Talk

You can clip out start-up costs of $2,400. Expect annual gross sales revenues in the range of $20,000 to $40,000 if you work the business less than 40 hours a week, and $50,000 to $100,000 and beyond if you devote yourself to it on a full-time basis. Charge your customers 3.5 to 4.5 cents per home on your mailing list or $350 to $450 per 10,000 homes.

Pounding The Pavement

Your customers will be community businesses. Those with mass appeal like restaurants, auto service shops and general interest retail stores will benefit best from your services, but you can also target walk-in clinics, general dentists, hair stylists, carpet-cleaning services, child-care services—get creative and make up your own list!

How will you sell these people on your company? In the best tradition of the sales representative, by walking into their places of business and introducing yourself and your service.

What's Next

If you're not already familiar with printing, graphics and mailing services, start shopping around. Acquaint yourself with what's out there, what types of service various companies offer, and what their prices are. Learn the lingo. Talk to direct-mail entrepreneurs in other communities to find out how they've made their businesses work. Make up a sample publication to show your first prospects.

Organizations

● *The Advertising Mail Marketing Association*, 1901 N. Fort Meyer Dr., #401, Arlington, VA 22209-1609, (703) 524-0096, www. amma.org

● *The Direct Marketing Association*, 1120 Ave. of the Americas, New York, NY 10036, (212) 768-7277, www.the-dma.org

Franchises

● *Super Coups*, 180 Bodwell St., Avon, MA 02322, (800) 626-2620, www.soupercoups.com

● *Val-Pak Direct Marketing Systems Inc.*, 8605 Largo Lakes Dr., Largo, FL 33773, (800) 237-6266, www.valpak.com

● *Yellow Jacket Direct Mail*, 23101 Moulton Pkwy., #110, Laguna Hills, CA 92653, (949) 951-9500, www.yellow-jacket.com

IN-STORE DEMONSTRATOR

The Inside Scoop

Sometimes it seems like you can eat an entire meal—for free—by wandering the aisles of your local supermarket or discount warehouse, sampling goodies served up by in-store demonstrators. You can get your glasses cleaned, learn how to chop food with a fancy gadget, and walk out smelling like a rose after being sprayed with expensive perfume, all courtesy of the in-store demonstrator. If you've got a flair for demonstrations (not the bra-burning kind), people skills and the gift of organization, then an in-store demonstration service might be the business for you.

You'll contract with food brokers and other suppliers and manufacturers to show off their products via your own on-call, personally trained demonstrators. People are more likely to purchase grocery products after tasting them, and customers of other types of goods can also be enticed by something they can see in action, feel, hear or smell, all of which makes the demonstration business valuable to brokers and manufacturers as well as store owners.

You can start small and grow big—some demonstration companies manage as many as 2,000 to 20,000 demonstrators in several states. You'll probably start off by doing the demos yourself and hire others as your company grows.

The advantages to this business are that you're always on the go so there's no time to get bored, you can work from home, and your start-up costs are minimal.

The disadvantages are that there's lots of paperwork involved in keeping track of everybody and everything, hours can be long, and customers are slow to pay, often taking 60 to 90 days to send you reimbursement for your services.

Essentials

Many owners of in-store demo businesses have a background in the grocery industry. This is helpful but not an absolute must. The must-haves are strong organizational skills to keep track of your demonstrators, their assignments and the materials they'll need to bring to each job; and top-notch administrative skills for paying your people and making sure you get paid. People skills are another must—you'll be dealing with lots of personalities, from store managers to food brokers to your own demonstrators. You'll also need a flair for demonstrating products and for teaching others how to do the same.

Tools Of The Trade

You'll eventually need a computer with a laser printer and a fax machine, but to start with, you don't really need anything but a phone and a car to get to your demo sites. You can hire your staff as independent contractors or as employees, depending on the laws in your state. This can be a sticky area as far as the IRS is concerned, so be sure to check with an accountant when you reach the hiring stage. Since demonstrators supply their own equipment, you'll need an electric frying pan or griddle for serving those hot tidbits, a card table on which to operate, and a wastebasket for used paper napkins and toothpicks.

Money Talk

Start-up costs for this business are very low, as little as $150. As a one-person demonstrator starting out, you can expect to earn annual gross revenues of about $18,000 and up, but the sky's potentially the limit. The real money in this business comes when you grow enough to hire independent contractors—many demo companies take on work throughout a region or even across several states. You'll charge your customers $90 per day for a one-person, one-store demo.

Pounding The Pavement

Your best clients will be supermarkets and warehouse superstores like Costco and Sam's Club, but you can also sell your services to department stores. Offer free demos to supermarket managers. Once they see how well you do, they can connect you with food distributors and manufacturers or hire you themselves—some stores offer demos of their own recipe ideas. You can also contact distributors and manufacturers on your own—if you've got access to a computer or a typewriter, make up a letter describing your services and requesting an appointment, then follow up with a phone call. And don't forget companies other than grocers—lots of products lend themselves to demonstrations.

What's Next

Wander supermarket aisles to see what types of products are being demonstrated and how. Work for another company as a demonstrator for a few weeks or months to see how the competition plays it. Then plan and rehearse your own demo. Remember to offer product information and salesmanship along with the free food—this will go a long way toward convincing distributors and managers to use your services.

Organizations

- *Field Marketing Services Association*, 8566 Laureldale Dr., Laurel, MD 20724, (800) 338-6232, www.fmsanet.com

Publications

- *The Communicator*, Field Marketing Services Association, 8566 Laureldale Dr., Laurel, MD 20724, (800) 338-6232
- *Promo Magazine*, Primedia Intertec, 11 River Bend Dr. S., P.O. Box 4225, Stamford, CT 06907, (800) 775-3777, www.promomagazine. com

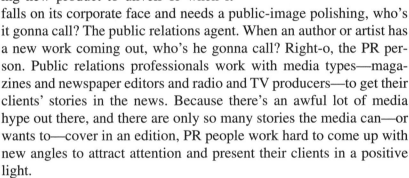

PUBLIC RELATIONS AGENCY

The Inside Scoop

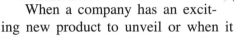

When a company has an exciting new product to unveil or when it falls on its corporate face and needs a public-image polishing, who's it gonna call? The public relations agent. When an author or artist has a new work coming out, who's he gonna call? Right-o, the PR person. Public relations professionals work with media types—magazines and newspaper editors and radio and TV producers—to get their clients' stories in the news. Because there's an awful lot of media hype out there, and there are only so many stories the media can—or wants to—cover in an edition, PR people work hard to come up with new angles to attract attention and present their clients in a positive light.

Public relations agencies also provide their clients with materials like press kits, annual reports, speeches and brochures—all the tools that go toward making that company, celebrity or celebrity-hopeful look good.

If you like exercising your creative abilities, making those mental stretches, and staying on top of trends and issues while blowing your clients' horns, then this is the business for you.

Like advertising agencies, SOHO public relations firms are experiencing a heyday. The downsizing of corporate America has left lots of elbow room for the smaller entrepreneur. Why not you?

The public relations agency's advantages are that you get to use that creativity to the max, you're always on your mental toes, and you deal with a variety of interesting people all day. And you can work from your home.

One disadvantage is that you're always on your toes, rushing from one PR campaign deadline to the next with no breather in between. If you're not a high-stamina type, you might want to consider a different field. Another disadvantage is that competition can be fierce. You'll have to work hard to build a clientele, and it generally takes about two years to start generating a visible income.

Essentials

A degree or certificate in public relations is a plus but not an absolute necessity. You'll need top-notch written and verbal skills—you'll have to write catchy, pertinent press releases and stories for magazines and newspapers as well as be able to convince editors and producers to use your material instead of somebody else's. Follow-up is everything. If you're a procrastinator, you'll need to either mend your ways in a hurry or find a different career.

You should be familiar with the types of stories various publications and TV programs (from the local news to those late-night talk shows) are looking for and the deadlines they work under, and you'll need the confidence to deal with all these stressed-out types on their own terms.

Tools Of The Trade

You'll need a computer system with the usual office software, a laser printer, a color printer, a scanner and a fax machine.

Money Talk

Plan on start-up costs of about $2,700—add in up to another $500 for professional organization and networking dues. After your business gets off the ground and running, you can expect annual earnings of $40,000 to $75,000. Charge your clients $40 to $75 per hour or $200 to $1,500 per day. Rates vary throughout the country, so be sure to check out what your local competition charges—you don't want to price yourself out of the ballpark.

Pounding The Pavement

Your clients can be just about any business, professional individual or celebrity you care to go after—including nonprofit organizations and government entities. As a newbie, you might want to specialize in certain types of businesses or professions, say doctors, writers, bioengineering firms or trendy software companies. And of course, companies in the industries you already know are always promising prospects.

The best way to nab new clients is by networking and through personal contacts. Call in favors from everybody you know in any related fields. Start your own public relations campaign by direct-mailing brochures to prospects. Volunteer yourself as a guest on a

A STAR IS BORN

Doing It Write

Pat Sabiston's client list reads like a local Who's Who. Her Panama City, Florida-based public relations and marketing agency, The Write Place, boasts two chambers of commerce, a medical center, the community college, the school system, the library, the United Way, the local Republican party, an attorney, a bank, a plastic surgeon and a plethora of area corporations. In business for 14 years, Sabiston, 51, has yet to solicit clients. "They come to me," she says simply.

How does she do it? By frequenting the meetings of professional and civic organizations. "You must network every chance you get," she advises would-be public relations people. "And don't just attend. Work them." Don't hesitate to go for pro-bono work, she says—so long as you're choosy about who you give it to. There are lots of key people on the boards of these organizations, Sabiston explains, and helping them helps you as well.

A North Carolina native, Sabiston began her public relations career as the sales manager of an all-female publishing house, then segued into a variety of marketing-oriented jobs as she traveled the country with her then-husband, an oft-transferred FBI man. Along the way, she's written for magazines and newspapers and been an on-air personality for radio and television. When she wanted to learn more about public relations, she joined PR societies and soaked up the training. Her start-up costs? $2,500.

Sabiston works out of a home office, using the family library as a conference room for infrequent client meetings. "The majority of my clients don't come to my office," she explains. "They don't care. They want the product."

local radio chat show. (Make sure you've got material to discuss and stories to tell.)

What's Next

Make up sample press kits, press releases and campaign ideas for your portfolio. Offer your services to charitable organizations in exchange for publicity.

Organizations

- *International Association of Business Communicators*, 1 Hallidie Plaza, #600, San Francisco, CA 94102, www.iabc.com
- *Public Relations Society of America*, 33 Irving Place, New York, NY 10003-2376, (800) WE-R-PRSA, www.prsa.org

Publications

- *Public Relations Tactics*, Public Relations Society of America, 33 Irving Place, New York, NY 10003-2376, (800) WE-R-PRSA, www.prsa.org

SEMINAR PROMOTER

The Inside Scoop

If you've ever fancied your-
self an impresario like Florence Ziegfield or Don King (without the
bottle-brush hair, of course), you delight in the showmanship of
arranging events, and you like the energy and inspiration of a fine
seminar, then this is the business for you.

As a seminar promoter, you'll locate talent—speakers with something interesting and exciting to impart—then line up attendees and make
all the arrangements to provide your guests with a memorable experience.
People who enjoy your first seminar will come back for more.

In addition to the fees you earn from the seminar itself, you can make
additional tidy sums by selling audiotapes or videotapes of each program.

Essentials

You'll need the nose to sniff out terrific speakers, people who can
amuse, inspire and teach others and infuse the program with a healthy
positive energy. You'll also need sales and marketing skills and the
ability to plan and organize events. Previous experience in event-
planning jobs is a big help but not an absolute necessity. If you've
produced community theater shows or charity fund-raisers, you've
got what it takes. You'll also need good writing skills to devise
intriguing brochures and sales materials.

Tools Of The Trade

You'll need a computer with a laser printer, a color printer, a
scanner, the usual office software, database software to maintain

mailing lists of attendees, and a desktop publishing program for designing brochures and fliers.

Money Talk

Promote yourself with start-up costs of $2,650. Once you get established, you can expect annual gross revenues of $30,000 to $50,000. You'll take a 25 percent to 40 percent commission from each seminar—your speakers should earn $125 to $500 per engagement.

Pounding The Pavement

Your customers will be the people who attend your seminars. The best way to attract them is to come up with a niche, a range of topics both unique and trendy in your area, and fill it. Another good way to start is by hosting seminars in a field or hobby you already know—if you're into astrology and other metaphysical arts, for instance, you'll know just what others in your interest group will want to learn.

Start a direct-mail campaign. Send brochures describing your seminars to lists of prospects. You can purchase these from a list broker, or you may already have access to mailing lists of people in interested organizations or associations. Place ads in local publications.

What's Next

Decide on your niche market. Line up speakers. Get acquainted with hotels and other meeting facilities in your area; find out what they offer and what their prices are. Talk to audio and video specialists about taping your programs and dubbing copies for sale.

Organizations

- *International Society of Meeting Planners*, 1224 N. Nokomis NE, Alexandria, MN 56308, (320) 763-4919, www.iami.org/ismp.html
- *International Special Events Society*, 9202 N. Meridian St., #200, Indianapolis, IN 46260-1810, (800) 688-ISES, www.ises.com

Books

- *Entrepreneur's Business Start-Up Guide #1071, Seminar Promotion Business*, Entrepreneur Media Inc., 2392 Morse Ave., Irvine, CA 92614, (800) 421-2300, www.smallbizbooks.com

Publications

- *Professional Speaker*, National Speakers Association, 1500 S. Priest Dr., Tempe, AZ 85281, (602) 968-2552, www.nsaspeaker.org
- *Successful Meetings*, 355 Park Ave. S., New York, NY 10010-1789, (212) 592-6403, http://successmtgs.com

Cyber Assistance

- *National Speakers Association* (www.nsaspeaker.org): Geared more toward speakers than promoters but has great links to all sorts of information. Check it out.

Chapter seventeen

THE PERSONAL TOUCH

You're a natural nurturer, organizer and planner, the one everybody calls on for help with all the day-to-day tasks of life—recommending the perfect pediatrician or geriatrics specialist, helping out with the new baby and finding tickets to that sold-out concert. You think nothing of rolling up your sleeves to help friends and family move house, clean house or find a house. If so, you're in the right place at the right time. With so many people in the workplace today, purveyors of personal services are primed for successful business and tidy earnings.

PACKING/ UNPACKING SERVICE

The Inside Scoop

We live in a mobile society. The average American moves about once every two years—but nobody likes the nitty-gritty of it. You've got to scrounge up all those boxes, save newspapers for wrapping breakables, then physically pack up every item in your home from stacks of CDs down to that half-container of oatmeal that's been sitting in the back of the pantry for the last six months. And when you get to the other end, the whole process has to be reverse-engineered, including the hours spent buried in pots and pans, linens, clothing, knickknacks and scrunched newspapers. Even worse, in today's two-income families, nobody has the time to do all this work.

But if you've got a penchant for boxing things up and you're organized and efficient, you can ease the process with a packing/unpacking service. You can supply packing materials as well as muscle and, if you're doing the packing, you'll neatly and carefully label everything so your customers can easily locate items at the other end of the line.

The advantages to this business are that you can start on a shoestring, part time if you like, you're always on the move yourself, and you get a peek at lots of different residences and lifestyles.

The disadvantages are that even for a pro, packing and unpacking can sometimes get boring, and you'll occasionally have to deal with cranky people. Some may feel you can't take proper care of their delicate objects and hover over you while others may take out their anger over the move—if it's a divorce, undesired transfer or other unhappy situation—on you.

Essentials

For this business, you'll need to be organized, efficient and fairly detail-oriented. You should have the people skills to deal with customers in a stressful situation (what move isn't stressful?) and enough experience to know how to safely pack items that can potentially spill, ooze or break.

Tools Of The Trade

This is truly a shoestring start-up. All you really need is yourself. If you like—and it's a nice touch—you can also provide packing boxes and materials, but if you do, be sure to figure these costs into your price.

Money Talk

Pack up your troubles with start-up costs of under $500. You can expect annual gross revenues of $30,000 to $45,000, depending on how aggressively you market yourself and how hard you want to work. You'll charge your customers $20 to $30 an hour or a flat rate, by the job—be sure you estimate carefully so you don't end up working for packing peanuts.

Pounding The Pavement

Your clients will be homeowners, apartment renters and businesses who are moving in or out. Post fliers at apartment and condominium complexes, office complex leasing offices, laundromats, supermarkets, and ask moving truck rental firms like U-Haul and professional moving companies to refer you—be sure to give them supplies of your business cards. You might consider paying them a small commission or finder's fee for referrals. Introduce yourself to real estate, rental and insurance agents and give them your cards as well.

What's Next

You may want to get bonded or carry insurance. Check into this. Then get networking and get packing and unpacking!

Organizations

- *American Moving and Storage Association*, c/o John Brewer, 1611 Duke St., Alexandria, VA 22314, (703) 683-7410, www.amconf. org

Books

- *Century 21 Guide to a Stress-Free Move*, by Judy Ramsey, Dearborn Trade
- *The Complete Idiot's Guide to Smart Moving*, by Dan Ramsey, MacMillan General Reference

PERSONAL CONCIERGE

The Inside Scoop

It used to be that you'd only find a concierge in a really fine hotel. He'd be the person sitting at a discreet desk in the lobby—the one you'd turn to for help getting tickets to that great Broadway show, finding a florist to deliver peonies in December, a pet-sitter for your prize pooch, or a shop specializing in antique Roman coins. But it's no longer necessary to be a guest in a swanky hotel to get that kind of treatment. The concierge concept of impeccable personal service for any request that's legal has filtered down to the rest of us.

This is a growing field: According to a recent report by the U.S. Bureau of Labor Statistics, there are nearly 16 million two-income families in this country. And when everybody's out in the workplace, no one's left at home to take care of all those little things that take up so much of a day—things like finding a dinosaur birthday cake for a kid's party, tracking down a service to reweave slacks, running the car to the shop, standing in line at the post office, or making hotel and dinner reservations for visiting guests.

If you like being on the go and in the know, doing something different every day, then this could be the business for you. You can specialize in helping corporate clients and denizens of office complexes, or you can concentrate on the homeowner who's not at home. Or if you live in an area like Los Angeles, Chicago or New York, where there's lots of entertainment, you might specialize in obtaining event tickets.

The advantages to this business are that your days will always bring something new and different, and you get the satisfaction of helping people's lives run more smoothly and easily.

The disadvantage is that this can be one of those businesses where you can only be so many places at once. Occasionally you'll run into a situation where somebody wants something sooner than you can easily deliver.

Essentials

You'll need a strong organizational sense, loads of get-up-and-go, and you'll have to be a master or mistress of multitasking. You should have good time-management skills and a detective's ability to track down even the most oddball requests.

You should have a good source of contacts and resources in a variety of industries and occupations and the people skills to build new ones on a daily basis. And last but definitely not least, you need to be obsessive in fulfilling your clients' requests. If you have to tell someone you couldn't find what they wanted, you lose them.

Tools Of The Trade

To get going, you'll need a computer with an inkjet printer, the usual software, a fax machine, Internet access, and your little black book of contacts and sources. You may also want to invest in an electronic data service so customers can pay by phone.

Money Talk

Pencil in start-up costs of about $2,500. You can expect annual gross revenues of $40,000 to $60,000 and up, depending on what services you offer and what sorts of clients you target. Personal concierge services generally charge clients a variety of membership fees—for instance, an individual or family membership with a certain number of requests allowed per month, a corporate membership for companies to give their employees (again with a specified number of requests per month), and a one-time membership for one-time services. Annual memberships can go for $1,500 for an individual to much higher for corporations, depending on the size of the company and how many requests each employee will be allowed. In addition, concierges often receive referral fees from vendors like event planners or florists to whom they send business. And don't forget that whatever you purchase for your clients gets billed to them.

Pounding The Pavement

Your clients can be private parties and businesses—anybody who needs an extra head, pair of arms and legs to accomplish the

A STAR IS BORN

Five-Star Service

Cynthia Adkins is in the business of fulfilling wishes. As the owner of San Diego, California-based Concierge@Large, she tackles the wants and needs of 40 personal clients and literally thousands of corporate clients—magically obtaining everything from tickets to a sold-out art exhibit to a used golf-green mower.

Adkins, a former flight attendant, had seven and a half years of experience as a hotel concierge under her belt when she left the industry to start a family. But when a year went by and she was still getting calls from all over requesting assistance with concierge-type projects, she decided she could go into business on her own.

Adkins started with less than $2,000—the proceeds of her tax return—but explains that the major investment is not so much in dollars as in time developing a database of contacts. And that she already had.

Concierge@Large was an immediate success. Adkins, 40, gets most of her clients from referrals and her company Web site. She does speaking engagements for service organizations like the Kiwanis Club but otherwise doesn't advertise.

Homebased, she fields an average of 100 to 150 service calls a week. Though she's now hiring an assistant, who will also be homebased, Adkins has handled all the work herself. How? By prioritizing, contracting out work to others when three things need to be done at once (which doesn't happen often) and calling on colleagues across the country for assignments in their home towns.

To be a successful concierge, Adkins advises, you have to be extremely resourceful. You don't need to know all the answers, but you do need to know how to find them.

Adkins loves the business—so much so that she's in the planning stages for a Concierge@Large franchise operation. And why not? It's fun, she says, it embodies an element of glamour, and when people call on you—to arrange a night on the town or a pair of tickets to a special event, for example—they're in a good mood.

tasks they haven't got time for. Direct-mail your brochures to people in targeted neighborhoods, those with enough discretionary income to afford your services. Send brochures to the human resources departments and executives' desks of large corporations and hand-deliver them to small companies located in office complexes and parks.

Place ads in local publications and be sure to send press releases or write articles about your service—it's still novel enough that it's likely to get publicity.

What's Next

Have your brochures and business cards made up and get out there and get busy!

Organizations

● *National Concierge Association*, P.O. Box 2860, Chicago, IL 60690-2860, www.lpconcierge.com

The Inside Scoop

If you're a neat-a-holic—your cooking spices are all organized alphabetically, your clothes are hung according to color in your closet, and your kitchen doesn't have a junk drawer—then this could be the business for you.

As a personal organizer, you'll bust clutter in your clients' homes, neatly arranging kitchens, closets, file drawers, garages and attics, and teaching them to keep things tidy for easier, less-stressful lives. Most personal organizers take on tasks in the corporate world as well, straightening out executive messes—you can wear this hat if you like or stick to home work.

The advantages to this business are that you can start part time on a shoestring, it's creative and gives you the chance to peek into lots of people's lives, and if you're a natural neatnik you get the satisfaction of helping others become one, too.

The only disadvantages are that if you do your job properly, your clients won't need you back, so you'll always be on the lookout for new business, and that this career is not recession-proof. Most people will consider your work as something of a luxury, so if the economy gets tight, so might new jobs for you.

Essentials

You'll need a healthy dose of organizational ability, which you must be able to apply to other people's homes and situations. You'll also need to be an organization-oriented shopper, with a keen knowledge of what home furnishings and accessories are in the marketplace so you can make recommendations. You should have good people skills because you'll be working with clients in their most intimate surroundings. You'll need to make suggestions and deal with junk that might best be tossed in a tactful manner.

Tools Of The Trade

All you really need to get started is that creatively organized brain and a planning book, although as you grow you'll want to invest in a computer, a printer, a fax machine and all the usual software.

Money Talk

Get yourself organized with start-up costs of less than $500. Once you get established, you can expect annual revenues of $40,000 to $60,000, although this can vary according to how corporate your clients are and how major your metropolitan area is. Charge your clients $40 to $50 per hour, depending on the size of the task and the going rates in your area. You can also charge a flat or per-diem fee for a particular job, say weeding through a kitchen and linen closet or redoing a filing system.

Pounding The Pavement

Your clients can be homeowners and apartment dwellers who are tired of living with clutter and losing time looking for things that should be under their noses. Your best bets for attracting clients are placing ads in your local paper and writing articles for local publications. Give talks to women's groups, place ads offering discounts in coupon mailers, and donate a free makeover to a local charity in exchange for publicity.

What's Next

Join professional organizer associations—you'll get referrals from them and plenty of business start-up support.

Organizations

● *National Association of Professional Organizers*, 1033 La Posada, #220, Austin, TX 78752, (512) 206-0151, www.napo.net

A STAR IS BORN

Clutter Buster

Stephanie Denton busts clutter for a living. As the owner of Denton & Co., a professional organizing firm in Cincinnati, she's been helping people create order out of chaos since 1994.

Denton, 32, was working in the marketing and business world when the first glimmerings of self-employment as a professional organizer struck. The more she considered the idea, the better she liked it. Just when she'd decided to go for it, an acquaintance asked if she knew anyone willing to take on a financial papers organization project. Denton stepped up to the plate, and her business, she says, has taken off from there.

To attract intial clients, Denton placed classified ads in monthly neighborhood magazines. One of the publications interviewed her and then asked her to write a column, a task she cheerfully performed for a few years. Six years later, she doesn't need to advertise—she gets plenty of business from word-of-mouth and public relations, including articles in national magazines like *Family Circle* and a recent TV interview.

Denton's clients represent every rung on the disarray ladder. Some call on her to make sense of stacks of junk, while others, fairly well-organized already, want advice on making better use of their time. Others look for confirmation that their own organizing projects are on the right track. Corporate CEO clients find that it's more cost-effective to have a professional come in and organize a project than to do it themselves. And some personal clients use her services on an ongoing basis, tackling first the home office, for example, then the kitchen, garage or a child's room.

Start-up costs for Denton's homebased business were minimal—letterhead, business cards and a separate phone line for a grand total of $250 to $350. She's quick to point out, though, that a professional organizer should also have a computer: You can't help clients with bookkeeping software like Quicken and QuickBooks if you're not familiar with the programs. Plus, with a computer, you can perform product research on the Internet, do computerized scheduling, and send and receive e-mail.

Denton's advice to start-ups planning a professional organizer business? "Organizing skills are only 50 percent, if that," she says. "The business half is just as important, if not more so. Managing clients, handling sales, marketing, accounting, legal issues—you have to like running a business."

Books

- *Everything's Organized*, by Lisa Kanarek, Career Press
- *Organized to Be the Best! New Timesaving Ways to Simplify and Improve How You Work*, by Susan Silver, Adams Hall Publishing
- *Organizing for the Creative Person*, by Dorothy Lehmkuhl and Dolores Lamping, Crown Publishing

The Inside Scoop

Every year Americans suffer billions of dollars in losses due to theft, fire and natural disaster, yet most people have no record of their possessions. When damages occur from theft or natural disaster and the insurance company asks for descriptions, serial numbers and other details, victims are at yet another loss.

But if you have a camera and are willing to travel around town, you can save the day with a photo inventory service. You'll take pictures of clients' possessions and mark them with serial numbers and the purchase price or replacement value so that if a burglary occurs your clients are prepared.

The advantages to this business are that you can start part time on a shoestring, you meet lots of people, and you provide both a valuable service and your clients with peace of mind.

The disadvantages are that this is not creative photography—you may occasionally feel bored taking photos of inanimate objects—and you may have to work weekends or evenings to make life more convenient for your clients (which is what makes this a good part-time business). As another disadvantage, people can be skittish about inviting you into their homes to view their valuables—you'll have to be bonded and insured and market aggressively to overcome this situation.

Essentials

Although you don't have to be an Ansel Adams, you do need to know the basics of good photography. You'll also need to know the sorts of details insurance companies are interested in—when you snap a photo of that computer, for instance, you'll want to make sure the model number is visible.

Tools Of The Trade

The biggest tool of your trade will be your camera. You can go with whatever model you already have on hand, but you may want to invest in a digital camera, a computer, photo software, and a high-quality color printer. Digital models can store hundreds of pictures at a time, which saves on film costs and time spent changing and labeling rolls—and there's no developing involved. Or you may choose to go with a video camera. You should also have a notebook to record the details to go with your pictures and, of course, a supply of pens and pencils.

Money Talk

Picture yourself in business with start-up costs of under $2,500—you may want to add in up to another $250 for networking dues. Once you get established, you can expect annual gross revenues of $30,000 to $60,000, depending on your locale and how aggressively you market. Charge your customers by the image, using prices that work for your area and your clientele—as a thumbnail you can start with $5 per photo.

Pounding The Pavement

Your clients will be individuals and businesses of all types. An excellent way to solicit trade is by establishing relationships with insurance agents who can refer you to their customers—be sure to leave plenty of business cards for agents to hand out. Introduce yourself to the detectives in charges of property thefts in your police or sheriff's departments and give them your cards as well.

You can also send out brochures in direct-mail campaigns—a good time to do this is when a rash of burglaries makes the morning papers. And don't forget networking and giving talks to professional and civic organizations.

What's Next

Research insurance company requirements and reimbursement policies. Make a photo inventory of your own home and use a few of your shots in a portfolio for potential clients.

Success For Less

Organizations

● *American Insurance Association*, 1130 Connecticut Ave. NW, #1000, Washington, DC 20036, (202) 828-7100

● *Professional Photographers of America*, 229 Peachtree St. NE, #2200, Atlanta, GA 30303, (800) 786-6277, www.ppa-world.org

Business Opportunities

● *Easy Method Property Documentation*, P.O. Box 3715, Evergreen, CO 80437-3715, (888) 774-6867

REFERRAL SERVICE

The Inside Scoop

If you're the one everybody in your circle calls for help when they're trying to find a good doctor, attorney, plumber or cleaning service, and if you love being on the phone, then a referral service could be the business for you.

You can specialize in one area or several, depending on your preferences and the size of your town. You might run an attorney referral service, matching callers to specialists in family, real estate or criminal law; a physicians' service matching up potential patients with pediatricians, cardiologists and other health-care specialists; or a homeowners' network, referring consumers to plumbers, painters, and cleaning and lawn care services. Keep in mind that most areas have attorney and physician referral services through local bar associations and hospitals—if you want to compete with these, you'll have to come up with a special niche that will bring consumers to you.

You can also specialize in travel and tours, entertainment, apartment rentals, baby-sitters, real estate agents, bridal services—just about any service that people need help with. And more: How about roommates or pets? You can also run your referral service online instead of on the phone—or do both. The choice is yours.

The advantages to this business are that you get to spend all day on the phone and you get to talk to lots of interesting people. The disadvantage is that you're tied to that phone—during business hours, you've got to be on-call all the time.

Essentials

It's a good idea to have some background or experience in the type of referrals you'll specialize in—if you've worked in the medical field, for instance, you might want to concentrate on physician referrals. You'll thoroughly screen the businesses on your list, finding out how they work and what they do best, then checking references so you know you're referring consumers to only the best, which means you'll need good communication and people skills.

You should also truly enjoy talking on the phone—if you don't, you'll grow to hate this business in short order—and you must be adept at fielding several calls at a time without losing your cool.

Tools Of The Trade

You'll need a computer and database software capable of handling all the businesses on your list and a two-line phone with a telemarketer-type headset so your ears don't get sore. If you can't afford a computer for starters, you can get going with a good handwritten list and purchase your electronics later. Of course, if you're going with an online service, you'll have to have the computer as well as a good Web site.

Money Talk

Refer yourself start-up costs of $2,600 to $5,000 if you'll go for the whole nine yards, Web site and everything, depending on how complex your site will be and what sort of design fees you negotiate. If you plan on the computer but not an online setup, you can plan on costs of about $1,200. And if you're not going computerized at all, you can get going for under $500. Once you get established, you can expect annual gross revenues of up to $50,000. There are several methods for pricing your services—you can charge local businesses an annual fee or a commission per referral, or if you're running a service like roommate referral, you can charge a fee to both mates for a successful match. Your specific fees will depend on comparable rates in your area and what you feel your market will bear—do your homework before you start, but as a guide you can work with annual rates of $1,600 to $3,000 per business or, for businesses like contractors, 10 percent of each referred project. For roommate-type referrals, you might charge 50 percent of the first month's rent or a flat fee.

Pounding The Pavement

Your customers will be both the businesses on your list and consumers who call in to get referrals, so you'll conduct your marketing campaign in two stages. First, investigate the businesspeople you'd like on your list. If they check out well, send them a sales letter or contact them by phone and explain that you've already given them an "A" and would like to include them in your service. Sell them on the benefits.

When you get a good list of referrals worked up, you'll need to attract consumers' attention so you can give your businesses their money's worth. The best way to go about this is to place prominent ads in the Yellow Pages under each category where people might look—if you're doing homeowner referrals, for instance, you'll want to place ads under lawn care, cleaning services, plumbing and the like. You can also place service ads in the classified sections of your local paper and post fliers where your target consumers will see them. If you're referring baby-sitters, put them up at kid-oriented areas like karate and dance academies, day-care centers, public libraries and parks. And don't forget churches and supermarkets for any type of referral service.

What's Next

If you don't already have a firm grasp on who's who in your specialty around town, get in touch with the Better Business Bureau or chamber of commerce and ask for tips.

ChaPter eighteen

PET PARADE

So you're a pet person—you never met a four-legged or finned creature you didn't like, and there's never been one that didn't adore you. Like Dr. Doolittle, you can talk to the animals and they talk to you (although probably not in English). If you're a card-carrying honorary member of the canine set or a fish fancier extraordinaire, there's a business in this category that's perfect for you.

The Inside Scoop

If you love aquariums—the colorful tropical fish darting from side to side, gently waving water plants, and those funky little bubble-activated deep-sea divers—then an aquarium maintenance service is the business for you.

You'll clean and maintain the tanks, feed and care for the fish on a routine basis, make additions and replacements as necessary and administer any special medications. You can also set up and stock aquariums for clients who don't already have them up and running, perform tasks like changing filtration systems, replacing plumbing and moving aquariums. And you can set up, stock and maintain ponds as well—water gardens complete with fish are the hottest new trend in residential landscaping.

The advantages to this business are that you can start with a minimal investment, part time if you like, and you get all the fun of working with fish every day. If you're a fish person, this a wonderful business, but if you're not a true hobbyist, you won't be happy.

The disadvantage is that you'll occasionally have to deal with owners ignoring your advice and with the consequences—smelly, slimy tanks and ponds that can try your nose and your patience.

Essentials

Fish, especially those that live in saltwater tanks, can be very difficult to care for. You must have knowledge and experience in dealing with these delicate creatures in addition to a genuine love for them. You'll need to have a real concern for your finny charges' lives and for maintaining them at their optimum.

Tools Of The Trade

You don't need a lot to get started—some resource books and equipment like siphons, nets, algae pads, buckets, planting sticks and tongs, and plastic tarps and towels. You'll purchase fish food, salt-water test kits and any necessary medications but pass the costs along to your clients. You'll also set up aquariums for clients, so you'll need to establish relationships with fish stores or wholesalers who can give you good deals, or else stock your own home tanks from which you can draw.

Money Talk

Get in the swim with start-up costs of less than $200. Once you get established you can expect to earn annual gross revenues of $31,250 to $62,500 and up, depending on how hard you want to work and what the going prices are in your area. You can charge your clients by the month based on the size of the aquarium. Use these figures as a guide: Freshwater tanks, 75 cents to $1 per gallon; saltwater tanks, $1 to $1.25 per gallon; and reef tanks, $2 per gallon. Or you can charge per call, depending on the particular project, with an hourly fee—going prices range from $25 to $75. However you set up your pricing, be sure to consider factors like tank size, filtration, environment, frequency of the contract, and your drive time.

Pounding The Pavement

Your clients can be businesses that find fish to be relaxing for their customers—doctors, dentists and restaurants are all good candidates, but you'll also do work for various other businesses. You'll also find that some of your clients will be private parties who love fish but don't have the time, desire or expertise to care for their finny friends. And of course, you'll have business and residential customers with ponds and water gardens.

Establish relationships with fish-store and pet-store owners and ask them to refer their customers to you. You can offer them a finder's fee for each successful referral. (Don't forget to leave plenty of your business cards for them to hand out.) Place ads in the pet section of your local newspaper. Send brochures to interior designers who specialize in commercial establishments—they can refer you to their clients. And if you plan to go the pond route, get in with garden and nursery retailers, and landscape architects and contractors, who can give you referrals.

What's Next

A polo or good-quality T-shirt with your company name emblazoned on it is good advertising and contributes to your professionalism. Get several made up. Then go fishing for customers!

Books

- *Aquarium Fish Survival Manual: A Comprehensive Guide to Keeping Freshwater and Marine Fish*, by Brain Ward, Barrons Educational Series
- *A Fishkeeper's Guide to Aquarium Plants: A Superbly Illustrated Guide to Growing Healthy Aquarium Plants, Featuring Over 60 Species*, by Barry James, Tetra Press
- *How to Have a Successful Aquarium: The TFH Book of Aquarium Science, Fishes, Water Plants, Water Technology*, by Stephan Dryer, TFH Publications

Cyber Assistance

- *Aquarium & Fish Stuff at The Link Farm* (http://linkfarm. junglenet.com/fish): Is this fishy or what? More fish-oriented links than you can shake a fin at. A definite must-surf.

- *Fish Link Central* (www.fishlinkcentral.com): OK, maybe this one's the best. Fish discussion groups, fish chat room, fish software (not recommended for in-tank use), fish links, fish games, fish postcards. You name it, it's got it!

- *WetNet!* (www.brightsight.com/WetNet): Tank volume and salinity calculators, water recipes, tank chemistry and analysis, forums, chemical reference sheet, plus lots more. Another must-surf!

DOG OBEDIENCE TRAINER

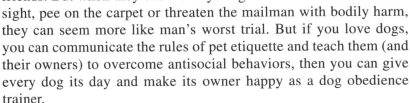

The Inside Scoop

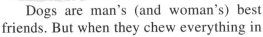

Dogs are man's (and woman's) best friends. But when they chew everything in sight, pee on the carpet or threaten the mailman with bodily harm, they can seem more like man's worst trial. But if you love dogs, you can communicate the rules of pet etiquette and teach them (and their owners) to overcome antisocial behaviors, then you can give every dog its day and make its owner happy as a dog obedience trainer.

You can teach general obedience with classes of a dozen or so students, give individual heel-and-toe lessons at your pupils' homes, or specialize in hard-core cases where you're as much a pet psychiatrist as a trainer.

The advantages to this business are that you can start on a shoestring, part time if you like, and if you're a dog lover, you can't do much better than a business where you're surrounded by puppies and pooches every working day.

The disadvantages are that you'll occasionally run into situations where the owner is the real problem and cannot be properly trained, and you'll sometimes encounter over-aggressive dogs who can scare you if you're not up to the task of confronting and then teaching them.

Essentials

The premier qualifications for this business are a genuine love of dogs and the innate ability to communicate with them. You'll also need terrific people skills because you're training not only dogs, but also their owners. You must be able to teach old and new owners new tricks to help their dogs behave, or you won't have accomplished your job.

To go along with all this, you'll need the healthy dose of self-confidence all good teachers of any species possess, and you should have a good working knowledge of dog psychology.

Tools Of The Trade

This is a terrific shoestring start-up operation—all you need are your own skills and experience.

Money Talk

Train yourself into start-up costs of about $150. You can charge your clients anywhere from $50 to $80 per hour and up, depending on the going rates in your area. Annual gross revenues for a full-time dog trainer in a high-income area can be more than $100,000—again, it depends on the competition, what the market will bear, and how good your services are.

Pounding The Pavement

Your clients will be dogs and their owners who want general obedience training like heeling and coming on command, as well as problem personalities who need help with chewing, biting, furniture-watering and other unpleasant activities.

The best way to get business is by establishing relationships with veterinarians, groomers, humane society facilities and pet-store people. Introduce yourself, ask for referrals and leave plenty of cards and brochures for them to hand out to prospective customers. You can also network among local dog breeders, give seminars and workshops at local colleges and community centers, and write articles for local publications.

What's Next

Make sure you can practice what you preach. If you don't have experience, take classes yourself, attend seminars, read everything you can, and practice on your own pooch and those of friends and neighbors. (Your successes will bring word-of-mouth advertising, which is the best kind.)

Dog's Best Friend

If you were a dog and Rocky Boatman said "Heel," you'd do it. Boatman used to be with counter intelligence in the U.S. Army. He's got presence. He's also got almost 30 years of dog-training experience. And he's been the owner of the Arizona Training Academy in Sierra Vista, Arizona, since 1990.

In response to overwhelming requests for assistance, Boatman, who's taught oodles of poodles and other canine types, formed the Academy for the express purpose of training people to train dogs for a living. He and his team of nine (five volunteers and four independent contractors) teach an eight-week course restricted to five students at a time. The hands-on, 14-hour-a-day sessions teach not only in-depth dog training, but also business basics, including marketing and market research. The cost for each course is $5,000, which includes a completely furnished, turnkey studio apartment for the length of the course.

Boatman's start-up costs for the academy ran about $7,500, but a homebased dog-training business, he says, can get up and running for less than $1,000. And he should know. Besides people, Boatman, 43, also trains dogs. He garners lots of repeat business—about a 60 percent retention—by offering a variety of courses: basic, advanced and competition, as well as agility and confidence-building.

A former Army Intelligence Master Instructor and present business instructor at Cochise College, Boatman says his best advertising is word-of-mouth. But he's experimenting with other venues as well. A new Web site, up and running for two months, has already netted over 1,100 hits, three deposits for trainer courses and 20 course requests. And he's just placed an ad in *Dog Fancy* magazine.

Boatman recommends that newbie dog trainers apprentice with a trainer they believe in and learn a variety of techniques. "You have to satisfy the client," he says. "You can't say 'Do it my way or go away'—because they will."

Organizations

- *National Association of Dog Obedience Instructors*, Attn.: Corresponding Secretary, 729 Grapevine Hwy., #369, Hurst, TX 76054, www.kimberly.uidaho.edu/nadoi

Books

- *ASPCA Complete Dog Training Manual*, by Bruce Fogle and Roger A. Caras, DK Publishing
- *Bark Busters: Solve Your Dog's Behavioral Problems*, by Sylvia Wilson, Crossing Press
- *Good Dog, Bad Dog: Dog Training Made Easy*, by Mordecai Siegal and Matthew Margolis, Henry Holt & Co.
- *How to Be Your Dog's Best Friend: A Training Manual for Dog Owners*, by the New Skete Monks, Little Brown & Co.

Publications

- *Dogs USA*, Division of Fancy Publications Inc., P.O. Box 57900, Los Angeles, CA 90057, (213) 385-2222
- *Dog World Magazine*, 500 N. Dearborn, #1100, Chicago, IL 60610, (312) 396-0600

The Inside Scoop

People love their pets, but neither Puss, Rover nor their owners loves the bathing and grooming process. That adorable dog or cat can transform itself into a soggy terror, fighting as if it were being tortured and exhausting itself and its beleaguered owner before the weekly bath or monthly flea dip is over.

But if you love pets and you have that special touch that makes them putty in your hands, you can make everybody happy (and much drier) with a mobile pet-grooming service. You'll roll to clients' homes in your specially outfitted van, then take Boots and Fido aboard and work your miracles. The pet industry is big—according the American Veterinary Medical Association, more than 58 million U.S. households are home to dogs and/or cats.

The advantages to this business are that you can start part time, your earning potential is excellent, and you get to work with animals every day you choose.

The disadvantages are that you'll be on your feet all day except when driving between jobs and that if your clients are not in a relatively small area, you'll spend as much time driving as grooming, and that can cut into your earnings.

Essentials

You'll need plenty of experience in pet-grooming, including the proper ways to clip and brush various breeds and a knowledge of animal behavior. You should also know something about human behavior and be able to handle a fair share of kibbutzing. When owners take their four-footed friends to a traditional groomer, they generally have to leave until the job's done, but when you pull up in the driveway, they'll want to watch you work.

Tools Of The Trade

You'll need a van (or an old but serviceable motor home if you already have one) set up for pet grooming with a tub, grooming table, generator or outdoor cords long enough to give you access to an outside power supply and, of course, all your grooming tools and supplies.

Money Talk

Groom yourself with start-up costs of $10,000 to $15,000, depending on whether you already have wheels and how much conversion you'll need to do. You can expect annual gross revenues of $30,000 to $50,000 and up. You'll charge your clients $30 to $50 per clip or bath.

Pounding The Pavement

Since your clients will be dog and cat owners, you'll want to make the rounds of pet shops and veterinary offices with your brochures and business cards. Introduce yourself, leave your materials and ask for

Weekend Warrior

PET-SITTER

What could be a better business for a pet-lover than playing with Pooch or Puss? That's what a pet-sitter does for out-of-town or work-all-day owners, feeding, watering and horsing around with his four-footed clients, providing love and attention along with essential nutrients. Some pet-sitters also handle medical needs, administering insulin injections or providing in-home after-surgery care. Remember that you'll be on duty during holidays when people tend to leave town and you'll need wheels to take you to clients' homes. To get started, distribute fliers to veterinary clinics and pet stores and ask them to refer customers to you. **Start-up costs:** $150. **Expected annual gross revenues:** Up to $10,000.

referrals. Place an ad under "pets" in the classified section of your local paper and in the pet-grooming section of your local Yellow Pages.

What's Next

Shop around for a good used van, then have your company name and phone number painted on the sides. It's OK for your vehicle to be a senior citizen, but make sure it's clean, freshly painted and well-cared for. No one's going to trust you to do a good grooming job on their Fluffy if your "shop" isn't well groomed.

Organizations

- *American Grooming Shop Association*, 4575 Galley Rd., #400A, Colorado Springs, CO 80915, (719) 570-7788
- *American Pet Association*, P.O. Box 725065, Atlanta, GA 31139, (800) APA-PETS, www.apapets.com
- *International Professional Groomers*, 1108 W. Devon, Elk Grove Village, IL 60007, (800) 258-4765

Books

- *All-Breed Dog Grooming/All 160 Breed Dog Grooming*, by Isabelle Francais and Richard Davis, TFH Publications
- *From Problems to Profits: The Madson Management System for Pet Grooming Businesses*, by Madeline Bright Ogle, Madson Group Inc.
- *The Stone Guide to Dog Grooming for All Breeds*, by Ben and Pearl Stone, Howell Book House

Publications

- *Dog Fancy*, Division of Fancy Publications Inc., P.O. Box 57900, Los Angeles, CA 90057, (213) 385-2222
- *Groom & Board*, H.H. Backer & Associates, 200 S. Michigan Ave., #840, Chicago, IL 60604, (312) 663-4040
- *Groomer to Groomer*, Barkleigh Productions Inc., 6 State Rd., #113, Mechanicsburg, PA 17055, (717) 691-3388

Cyber Assistance

- *Pet Groomer.com* (www.petgroomer.com): Directory of everything for the groomer—associations, education, services, software and more. A must-surf!

ChaPter nineteen

SHOP 'TIL YOU DROP

You're a shopping fiend. You love finding just the right merchandise for the right occasion or that perfect something you didn't even realize you were looking for, the ambience of a storefront filled with intriguing pieces, and the pleasant burble of other contented shoppers. If this is you—if you dream of life in the retail lane, then this is your category.

CART/KIOSK RETAILER

The Inside Scoop

Not every retailer has a storefront on Main Street or a shop at the mall—one of the hottest trends in moving merchandise is merchandise that moves, or at least has the capability of being moved, on a cart or in a kiosk. Where these micro-minishops were once the sole purview of crotchety characters pushing a peddler's barrow, carts and kiosks today are upscale—and highly lucrative—ventures.

The difference between a cart and a kiosk is that a kiosk is larger, enclosed and has space for you to sit while you work. You can purchase your own cart or kiosk and have it custom-built for your merchandise, or you can rent one from a mall. And you can sell just about anything—from sunglasses to sunflowers, hot dogs to dog figurines, perfumes, personalized coffee mugs, T-shirts, sweatshirts, chocolate chip cookies and cooked-to-order health foods.

You can operate your shop at a wide variety of locations—in a mall, at sporting and entertainment events, at flea markets, on busy downtown streets, at tourist promenades, or where workers convene for meals or snacks.

The advantages to this business are that it's much less expensive to get into than a traditional retail location, you can start part time if you like, the earning potential is excellent, and if business gets slow at one location you can pick up and move to another.

The disadvantages are that—unlike most of the businesses in this book—this is not a homebased opportunity (unless you stick your cart in your front yard), hours can be extremely long, and unless you're working a special event or tourist area, you've got to keep regular hours to build a base of repeat customers.

Essentials

You'll need the stamina to stick to your post for long hours (especially if you'll be outdoors), a good working knowledge of retail operations and a flair for attention-grabbing displays.

You should also have an extroverted personality because a large part of cart and kiosk sales is interacting with passersby—while you don't want to trip them as they go by, you do need to make eye contact and offer a smile and perhaps an invitation to examine your wares or sample your treats.

Tools Of The Trade

You'll need a resale license so you can purchase your products wholesale, and if you'll be serving food, you'll need a permit from your local Health Department. And if your cart or kiosk will follow behind your vehicle like a trailer, you'll need a license for it. If you'll set up shop in a mall or office building, you'll need to get permission from the mall or building manager. On a street corner, park or event site, you'll need an OK from city, county or event authorities.

Your minishop should be equipped with a cash register and adequate display or preparation space (if you're making food) for your products, plus any grills, refrigerators, freezers, steamers or ovens you'll require. You should also stock a stool to give your feet a rest; sales tickets and tags; and boxes, bags and papers for wrapping up merchandise.

Money Talk

Plan on start-up costs of $5,000 to $20,000, depending on whether you purchase a cart or kiosk and what products you'll be selling. You can expect annual gross sales of up to $100,000 and more—but this is a variable based on what you're selling, where you're selling it, and how hard you want to work. Your prices, too, will vary with your merchandise—a hot dog goes for a lot less than a gold bracelet.

Pounding The Pavement

Who your customers are will depend on your products and location, and the best way to earn their business is by stocking a clean, trendy, eye-catching cart or kiosk; looking clean, enthusiastic and cheerful yourself; and doing the market research to place yourself in the best possible location.

Think about where you'll find people who'll want your goods, then case the site at different times over a two-week period to get a feel for traffic flow and customer demographics.

What's Next

Decide what you want to sell and where, whether you'll buy or rent a cart, and if you'll need it specially outfitted. Then start shopping for a custom make or a rental and make arrangements for your location.

Organizations

● *International Council of Shopping Centers (ICSC)*, 665 Fifth Ave., New York, NY 10022, (212) 421-8181, www.icsc.org. ICSC hosts an annual Temporary Tenant Short-Term Specialty Retailing Conference—call for details.

Weekend Warrior

FLEA MARKET ENTREPRENEUR

If you've got an eye for cast-offs that can become somebody's treasures and you love combing garage and estate sales, then you'll have a ball as a flea market entrepreneur. You can specialize in a particular collectible—anything from old record albums to Depression-era pottery to antique tools—or you can go eclectic with a wide assortment of pre-owned goodies. Or you can forego the collectible trade and buy new close-out merchandise from wholesalers to sell at major discounts. To get started, you'll need to obtain a resale license, then start shopping for flea markets with a base of free-spending customers and reserve your space. **Start-up costs:** $2,000. **Expected annual gross revenues:** Up to $25,000.

- *National Retail Federation*, 325 Seventh St. NW, #1000, Washington, DC 20004, (800) 673-4692, www.nrf.com

Books

- *Directory of Major Malls*, Directory of Major Malls Inc., P.O. Box 837, Nyack, NY 10960, (800) 898-6255
- *Specialty Shop Retailing: How to Run Your Own Store: Innovative Ideas for Retail Success*, by Carol L. Shroeder, John Wiley & Sons
- *Retail in Detail: How to Start and Manage a Small Retail Business*, by Ronald L. Bond, Psi Research/Oasis Press

Publications

- *Shopping Center Digest*, P.O. Box 837, Nyack, NY 10960, (800) 898-6255

Business Opportunities

- *All Star Carts and Vehicles*, 1565-D Fifth Industrial Ct., Bayshore, NY 11706, (800) 831-3166
- *Carriage Works*, 707 S. Fifth, Klamath Falls, OR 97601, (541) 882-0700

KIDS/CLOTHING CONSIGNMENT SHOP

The Inside Scoop

Recycling is in these days—and not just for tin cans and newspapers—but for clothes as well. Where once upon a time no one would ever admit that they'd purchased a previously owned dress or pair of slacks, today recycled clothing—especially designer duds—is trendy and definitely worth bragging about. The resale field is hot these days, with over 15,000 shops across the country and an industry association growth rate of 15 percent per year.

And not just for adults, but for kids, too! Children are a delight—but they're also expensive. You've barely paid off the credit card bills for those cute little rompers and they're already outgrown. And you need another whole set of credit cards (and the cash to back them up) for toys that cost far more than it seems they should.

But if you've got an eye for fashion, design and quality, and great buys make your heart soar, then a consignment clothing shop or kids' consignment shop could be the business for you. If you go the children's route, you can specialize in toys or clothing, or both, stocking everything from red wagons to Barbies and Barneys, teddy bears to video games, toddlers' overalls to party dresses for the kindergarten set. For adults, you can do strictly designer duds, strictly women's fashions, or men's and women's glad rags.

You'll take clean, well-cared-for garments or toys and display and merchandise them for their owners, splitting the profits when you make a sale. Clothing consignors sell mostly women's garments—along with accessories like costume jewelry, belts and handbags—but men's clothing is becoming increasingly popular as a resale item as well.

Because you're taking the items on consignment, you don't pay anything for your inventory until it's sold, which makes this business ideal for the start-up entrepreneur. You price garments and other goodies, then have the owner pick them up if they don't sell within a given period of time.

The advantages to this business are that it's creative, your start-up costs are small compared to most retail operations, you get the satisfaction of helping your customers get great buys for little money, and if you love the rag trade, you'll be in consignment heaven.

The disadvantages are that—unlike most of the businesses in this book—this is not a homebased opportunity, and unless or until you employ help, you'll be tied to the store every hour that you're open.

Essentials

The key to a successful consignment shop is an atmosphere that's clean, fresh and fashionable—that musty Salvation Army scent is a definite no-no—so you'll need a flair for display and merchandising. You should also have a good eye for current fashions and quality and the ability to properly price your merchandise so that shoppers get the discount they expect and you and your consignees make a profit.

To complement all this, you'll need excellent people skills. You'll be dealing with customers of all ages, sizes and styles, and also with would-be consignees, who may bring in items unsuitable for your shop—you'll need to be able to deflect them tactfully.

Tools Of The Trade

You'll need a shop and the display furnishings to put in it—glass cases for jewelry, clothes racks, hangers and tables or shelves. You'll also need sales tickets and tags, shopping bags and a cash register. A computer with an inkjet printer and retail operation software will be a big help but aren't necessary for starters if you can't afford them.

Money Talk

For a retail operation, a consignment clothing shop is a wonderful shoestring start-up—pencil in costs of $4,000 to $6,000. (This figure does not include leasing your storefront because that price will vary considerably depending on location and size.) Average gross

A STAR IS BORN

Secondhand Mary Jane

Mary Jane Nesbitt's consignment clothing shop in upscale Los Gatos, California, is called Nine Lives. Nesbitt herself has lived at least three—the first as an employee in the legal department of a commercial real estate brokerage where she became increasingly unhappy. The switch from employee to entrepreneur came about on a walk through town with her husband, David Butcher.

"I was unhappy and frustrated," Nesbitt recalls. "We had talked about the possibility of my opening a consignment shop for maybe six months. We got to this end of town, and my husband pointed across the park and said, 'Look, that space is for rent. This is it. You're doing it.'"

And she did. She started the business with $17,000 from her retirement plan, which went for initial lease costs, racks, hangers, shelves, bags, printing, lighting and other necessities of her new business. David, a Webmaster for a large networking company, wrote the shop's custom financial and inventory management software.

Nesbitt is particularly proud of one facet of the software program, the Personal Shopping Assistant, which allows shoppers to request specific items online; for example, a navy blue Anne Klein blazer in a size 5. When a matching garment is logged into inventory, the customer is automatically notified by e-mail. Average number of Personal Shopping Assistant e-mails per day? About 100. Consignors—85 percent of whom come back and number close to 2,000—can check on how much of their clothing has sold at any time via the Nine Lives Web site. The site, Nesbitt says, lends her shop an identity that is much more sophisticated than the average consignment operation—an identity so strong that she no longer does any advertising.

And what of Nesbitt's third life? It's as a part-time lady of leisure. After six years of shopkeeping, she's granted herself two days off a week. She says simply, "I've come full circle."

Nesbitt's advice for the newbie is to take pains to ensure that your shop exudes quality and style, and that includes learning to turn down consignments that don't fill the bill. "The most important thing you can learn," she counsels, " is how to say 'no' quickly and diplomatically."

sales for a consignment shop are about $200,000. The best way to price your merchandise is to mark it at about one-third of the original retail value—but you can adjust that price up or down according to the item's desirability. And don't forget: Part of the fun of consignment for shoppers is that you mark down merchandise about 20 percent for every three weeks it sits in your store. (This is an excellent technique, as it keeps shoppers coming back!)

Pounding The Pavement

Your customers will be people interested in the type of merchandise you've got for sale—basically the same people who shop at regular retail outlets. The trick is to attract their attention and sell them on the benefits of shopping with you.

Besides routine advertising methods like local radio and newspaper ads, you can host fashion shows for local women's groups and hand out fliers in front of your shop. If you're located near a business district, you can also deliver your fliers to offices in the area—women love to shop at lunch time, and you'll whet their appetites for your merchandise as well as a sandwich. And don't forget ads—perhaps with get-acquainted coupons—in your local *Pennysaver*-type publication.

What's Next

Start shopping for a storefront. Share your new business plans with friends and family and begin soliciting merchandise.

Organizations

- *National Association of Resale and Thrift Shops*, P.O. Box 80707, St. Clair Shores, MI 48080, www.narts.org
- *National Retail Federation*, 325 Seventh St. NW, #1000, Washington, DC 20004, (800) 673-4692, www.nrf.com

Books

- *Entrepreneur's Business Start-Up Guide #1229, Consignment Clothing Store*, Entrepreneur Media Inc., 2392 Morse Ave., Irvine, CA 92614, (800) 421-2300, www.smallbizbooks.com
- *Too Good To Be Threw: The Complete Operations Manual for Consignment Shops*, by Kate Holmes, 4736 Meadowview Blvd., Sarasota, FL 34233, (941) 924-4142, www.tgtbt.com

Publications

- *Too Good To Be Threw, The Resale Industry Newsletter*, 4736 Meadowview Blvd., Sarasota, FL 34233, (941) 924-4142, www.tgtbt.com

Cyber Assistance

- *Too Good To Be Threw* (www.tgtbt.com): A must-surf site, packed with tips, hints, resale-shop-owner sharing, and even an Ask Auntie Kate advice column. Check it out!

CONSIGNMENT FURNITURE SHOP

The Inside Scoop

The nice thing about furniture and home furnishings is that they don't get old—they become antiques or collectibles. And while antique stores specialize in only the priciest goods, a furniture consignment shop can stock everything from a 100-year-old highboy to a 10-year young sofa. Just as in clothing, the trend these days is toward recycling, finding delightful ways to make everything old seem new (or just beloved) again. And while just a few years ago, no one would admit that they'd purchased someone else's sofa, today even the trendiest decorators are happily espousing the joys of used furniture.

Furniture is one of the fastest-growing segments of the resale industry, with more and more nonfurniture consignment stores either adding furniture to their inventories or opening a second, furnishings-only location. So if you love interior design, you've got the nose for sniffing out both antiques and good quality, then a consignment furniture shop could be the business for you.

You'll take clean, well-loved furniture and accessories, and display and merchandise them for their owners, splitting the profits when you make a sale. You can take on more than sofas and tables—like any good home furnishings or antiques shop, you'll also stock prints, paintings and decorative items from silver salvers to funky '50s ashtrays. You'll also spend a fair amount of time going out to people's homes to appraise furniture pieces, then taking them back to your shop.

Because you're taking the items on consignment, you don't pay anything for your inventory until it's sold, which makes this business ideal for the start-up entrepreneur. Some consignment shops mark items at a set price, then have the owners pick them up if they don't sell within a given period of time. Others mark down merchandise 10 percent for every month it remains unsold.

The advantages to this business are that it's creative, your start-up costs are small compared to most retail operations, you get the satisfaction of helping your customers get great buys for little money, and you never know what fascinating piece is going to walk through your door at any moment.

The disadvantages are that—unlike most of the businesses in this book—this is not a homebased opportunity, and unless you've got help, you'll be tied to the store every hour that you're open.

Essentials

The key to a successful consignment shop is an atmosphere that's clean, fresh and stylish—the Goodwill cast-off scene is a turn-off—so you'll need a talent for display and merchandising. You should also have a good eye for quality as well as current fashion. (That orange-and-green brocade sofa that was so cool in 1975 may be a hard sell today.) You'll want to know something about antiques and collectibles so you can tell a period piece from a reproduction. And you'll need the savvy to properly price your merchandise so that shoppers get the discount they expect and you and your consignors make a profit.

To complement all this, you'll need the people skills to tactfully deal with the occasional hopeful consignee who thinks you're a great alternative to the thrift shop for his less-than-attractive cast-offs.

And last but definitely not least, you'll need the muscle—or the on-call assistance—to load heavy furniture onto your truck from consignees' homes and then from the truck into your shop, then back out to customers' vehicles.

Tools Of The Trade

You'll need a shop and not a whole lot else as far as display furnishings—a few glass cases for small collectibles should do it because you'll have plenty of tables and dressers on which to display larger items. You'll also need sales tickets and tags, a supply of shopping bags and tissue paper for wrapping collectibles, and a cash register. A computer with an inkjet printer and retail operation software will be a big help but aren't necessary for starters if you can't afford these things. Stock up on antiques and collectibles reference books; you'll also need a reliable pickup truck for collecting furniture from consignees' homes and a few furniture dollies and carts.

In some states, it's illegal to sell used mattresses, so be sure to check with local authorities before doing so.

Money Talk

For a retail operation, a consignment furniture shop is a great shoestring start-up—pencil in costs of $4,000 to $6,000. (This figure does not include leasing your storefront because that price will vary considerably depending on location and size.) Average gross sales for a consignment furniture store are about $200,000. The best way to price your merchandise is to mark it at about one-third of the original retail value—but you can adjust that price up or down according to the item's desirability. And don't forget: Part of the fun of consignment for shoppers is that you mark down merchandise about 20 percent for every three weeks it sits in your store. (This is an excellent technique as it keeps shoppers coming back!)

Pounding The Pavement

Your customers will be the same sorts of people who shop at antiques stores and other home furnishings outlets. The trick is to attract their attention and sell them on the benefits of shopping with you.

Besides routine advertising methods like local radio and newspaper ads, you can host furniture and collectibles shows or talks for local women's groups, give seminars or workshops on furniture design, antiques and collectibles for colleges and community centers, and hand out fliers in front of your shop. Shopper ads in your local *Pennysaver*-type publication are also a terrific advertising tool.

What's Next

Start shopping for a storefront. Share your new business plans with friends and family and begin soliciting merchandise.

Organizations

- *Home Furnishings International Association*, 110 World Trade Center, Box 420807, Dallas, TX 75342, (800) 942-4663, www.hfia.com
- *National Association of Resale and Thrift Shops*, P.O. Box 80707, St. Clair Shores, MI 48080, www.narts.org
- *National Retail Federation*, 325 Seventh St. NW, #1000, Washington, DC 20004, (800) 673-4692, www.nrf.com

Books

- *Too Good to be Threw: The Complete Operations Manual for Consignment Shops*, by Kate Holmes, 4736 Meadowview Blvd., Sarasota, FL 34233, (941) 924-4142, www.tgtbt.com

Publications

- *Too Good to be Threw, The Resale Industry Newsletter*, 4736 Meadowview Blvd., Sarasota, FL 34233, (941) 924-4142, www.tgtbt.com

Cyber Assistance

- *Too Good to be Threw* (www.tgtbt.com): A must-surf site, packed with tips, hints, resale-shop-owner sharing, and even an Ask Auntie Kate advice column. Check it out!

Franchises

- *Teri's Consign & Design Furnishings*, 1826 W. Broadway Rd., #3, Mesa, AZ 85202, (800) 455-0400

The Inside Scoop

Network marketing is one of the hottest retail industries out there. Based on the hair-commercial principle of "you tell two friends and they'll tell two friends," it functions on the idea that you sell products to people who in turn sell to other people who sell to other people . . . and so on. Network marketing programs feature a minimal upfront investment—usually a few hundred dollars or less for the purchase of a product sample kit—which gives you the opportunity to sell the product line directly to family, friends and other contacts. Most network programs also ask that you recruit other sales reps—those same family members, friends and acquaintances. These sales rep recruits constitute your "downline," and their sales generate income for you. Then whoever they recruit becomes part of their downline as well as yours, generating income for them as well as for you. So the more people you bring on board, the better your income potential.

If you're a sales-savvy type who can convince others of the beauty of this plan and keep them selling sales memberships (as well as products), you can earn a substantial amount of money. And you've got lots of network marketing plans to choose from. The most popular sell health supplements and beauty aids, but you can go with everything from long-distance phone services to fine art prints. And since there are now more than 20 million people in the industry, it seems to be one with staying power.

The advantages to this business are that start-up costs are minimal, hours are flexible, you can start part time, and you can work from home. If you like sales and aren't bashful about signing up others, you can just about write your own ticket.

The disadvantage is that this business is not as easy as it sounds. Network marketing parent companies will lead you to believe that you can make millions—and you can. But not without working at it. Lots of people think they'd like to be involved in network marketing, but once you sign them aboard, they fizzle out fast. Since your earnings are based more on what your distributors below you on the ladder make than on how many vitamins or whatever you sell, this can make things tough. And although the business may seem easy at first as you sign up friends and relatives, you soon run out of "easy" prospects, and the real sales work begins.

Essentials

About the only thing you need in this business is a sense of salesmanship. If you've got a background in sales, you're ahead of the game, but if you've never sold so much as a Girl Scout cookie, you can still succeed. Just make sure you believe in the products and the company you're working with. Honest enthusiasm goes a long way toward convincing others to buy.

Tools Of The Trade

You don't need any special tools or equipment, except for a phone to keep in touch with your distributors, parent company and prospects, and a car to go out and sign people up and attend the weekly pep-talk meetings that are a feature of this business.

Money Talk

Your start-up costs will be minimal. You'll have to pay a fee to the parent company—these usually run in the range of $20 to $300, although you'll find some that require no funds at all— and you may need to purchase sample products (at special wholesale prices) to show to prospects. Along with this, the company will probably provide you with a sales kit and selling tips. You can expect annual sales of $12,000 to $120,000, although some people sell far more and most dabblers far less. (About 3 percent of the industry sells more than $50,000 a year, says the Network Marketing Association.) What you charge your customers for products or services depends entirely on the prices the parent company sets.

Pounding The Pavement

Your customers will be anybody and everybody you know or meet. Most network marketers start off soliciting friends and family. If there are others working for the same company in your area, they may have organized weekly meetings at which salespeople and prospects gather to cheer each other on and sign up new members. If so, make it a point to attend with your own prospects. It's harder for people to decline your invitation to join in a room full of other enthusiastic newbies.

In this business, it's important to keep your distributors selling. Don't sell them a membership and ignore them, or they're liable to drop down their link in the chain. Talk to them often about how they're doing. Go with them on sales calls to offer moral support and enthusiasm and help sign up prospects.

Many network marketers sell via the party plan—as Maxwell Smart would say, "the old Tupperware trick." It's easy and it's fun. Have a host or hostess invite friends to sample your products. You sell products, sign people up, and the party-giver gets a free gift or a discount on her purchases.

What's Next

Shop around for a company to join. Examine their histories, talk to others who are selling for the firm, and find out how long they've been with it and what their sales are. Look at the products or services offered and decide if you'll be happy selling them on a daily basis. Network marketing can get sticky when people are compensated primarily for recruiting others rather than for selling products. A network system where most of the revenues come from recruiting can be considered an illegal pyramid scheme, so be sure you investigate carefully before you plunk your money down. You should also make sure the company offers a buy-back clause in which it buys back your initial inventory if you decide the program's not for you.

Organizations

● *Multi-Level Marketing International Association*, 119 Stanford Ct., Irvine, CA 92612, (949) 854-0484, www.mlmia.com

Books

● *Entrepreneur's Business Start-Up Guide #1222, Networking*

Marketing Business, Entrepreneur Media Inc., 2392 Morse Ave., Irvine, CA 92614, (800) 421-2300, www.smallbizbooks.com

- *How to Build a Multi-Level Money Machine: The Science of Network Marketing*, by Randy Gage, Gage Research Development Institute
- *Street-Smart Network Marketing: A No-Nonsense Guide for Creating the Most Richly Rewarding Lifestyle You Can Possibly Imagine*, by Robert Butwin and Russ Devan, Prima Publishing
- *Your First Year in Network Marketing: Overcome Your Fears, Experience Success and Achieve Your Dreams!* by Mark Yarnell, Rene Reid Yarnell and Richard Poe, Prima Publishing

Business Opportunities

- *The Carlyle Collection*, 6749-B Top Gun St., San Diego, CA 92121, (888) 706-4800, www.carlylecollection.com
- *Discovery Toys Inc.*, 6400 Brisa St., Livermore, CA 94550, (800) 426-4777, www.discoverytoysinc.com
- *Earth Angels*, 735-G N. Park St., Castle Rock, CO 80104, (888) 395-0136, www.earth-angels.com

SPECIALTY CATALOGS

The Inside Scoop

With the exception of bills and letters from the IRS, everybody loves to get something in the mail—a package makes it feel like Christmas, and a catalog filled with potential packages is like window-shopping without having to leave home. Specialty mail order catalogs are one of the hottest businesses going these days. With so many two-income and single-parent families around, nobody has much time to shop. And people today are more interested in spending their scant leisure hours on quality time at home with family and friends than on exhausting expeditions to the mall. So catalogs are the obvious alternative. And they're fun!

If you've got a flair for marketing and advertising, an eye for product and design, and shopping in your blood, then specialty catalogs could be the business for you. The key to success is the word "specialty"—you'll need to choose a niche market, one that you know well and that has a built-in customer base. If you or your kids are into horses, for instance, you might sell horse-care and grooming products and gifts. You'll know what products horse-minded people will want and what sort of customers to target—those in equestrian associations and organizations, for starters.

The advantages to this business are that you can start part time if you like, it's creative and often challenging, and it gives you a wonderful opportunity to shop (you've got to purchase products for the catalog).

The disadvantages are that your only sources for attracting customers are direct-mail and magazine advertising, and these can be expensive. And if you're not careful to purvey quality products, you can run into difficulties with returned merchandise.

Essentials

You should have a background and experience in whatever specialty you decide to sell. You can go with anything from contractors' hardware to chocolates to maternity wear, but the more you know about your products and the people who'll buy them, the better you'll do.

You should also have a well-developed sense of marketing and advertising, because that's how you'll get your customers; and last but definitely not least, you need to be a savvy number-cruncher—mail order is at least 50 percent about calculating how many products you'll need to sell at what retail prices, advertising and mailing costs to make a profit.

Tools Of The Trade

You'll need a computer with a laser printer, a fax machine, the usual suite software, a good desktop-publishing program and electronic data terminal software so you can process credit cards. A postage meter and scale is a must, and you'll need a phone because—despite the mail-order moniker—most people like to order by phone. As your business grows, you'll need to contract with a call center to handle the volume for you, but for starters you can field calls yourself.

Money Talk

This is not a budget start-up—pencil in $10,000 to $12,000, most of which will go for printing and mailing your catalog. Annual gross revenues for specialty catalogs range from $40,000 to well over $100,000, depending on how long the business has been in operation and how much you've invested in building the business. (It generally takes two to five years for a catalog to become profitable.) How you price your products will depend on what those products are, but mail order entrepreneurs generally mark up merchandise 300 percent to 400 percent to cover the costs of advertising, mailing and product manufacture or purchase.

Pounding The Pavement

Your customers will be anybody who's interested in (and can afford) your products. You'll reach them through your catalog, which can be simple and fairly inexpensive as you start out. It's entirely possible to grow a fancy, 28-or-more-page full-color catalog from a one-page black-and-white flier, provided that you understand your market, employ clever techniques and sell the right products at the right price.

To effectively mail your catalog (or brochure or flier), you need mailing lists of people who have a proven interest in your specialty. A good list broker can help you choose the right lists, or if you've got enough contacts of your own, you can develop your own list. You can also advertise in magazines that cater to your niche market, sell to the people who answer your ad and then develop a mailing list from those customers.

What's Next

Specialty catalogs can be a lot of fun, but you have to know what you're doing. If you don't have experience in the field, read everything you can get your hands on and do your market research. Then start planning your catalog!

Organizations

- *The Advertising Mail Marketing Association*, 1901 N. Fort Meyer Dr., #401, Arlington, VA 22209-1609, (703) 524-0096, www.amma.org
- *The Direct Marketing Association*, 1120 Ave. of the Americas, New York, NY 10036, (212) 768-7277, www.the-dma.org
- *Mail Advertising Service Association International*, 1421 Prince St., Alexandria, VA 22314-2806, (800) 333-6272, www.masa.org
- *National Mail Order Association*, 2807 Polk St. NE, Minneapolis, MN 55418-2954, (612) 788-1673, www.nmoa.org

Books

- *Building a Mail Order Business*, by William A. Cohen, Ph.D., John Wiley & Sons
- *Entrepreneur's Business Start-Up Guide #1015, Mail Order*, Entrepreneur Media Inc., 2392 Morse Ave., Irvine, CA 92614, (800) 421-2300, www.smallbizbooks.com
- *Home-Based Mail Order, A Success Guide for Entrepreneurs*, by William J. Bond, Liberty Hall Press
- *How to Start a Mail Order Business*, by Mike Powers, Avon Books

A STAR IS BORN

Romancing The Catalog

What do romance novels and specialty catalogs have in common? Mary Martin, co-owner with daughter-in-law Michelle of Love & Lace, a St. Louis-based specialty catalog with a romantic theme. Martin had penned and published a half-dozen historical romances when an auto accident sidelined her career. Undeterred, Mary and Michelle, who's also a writer and a graphic artist, brainstormed what else they could do that would fulfill their artistic needs while bringing in an income.

"It was an effort of combining everything we love," Mary explains. "Michelle could contribute her graphic arts abilities, and I could do the writing. We both love decorating, and of course romance was the primary theme. So we decided to offer romantic gifts and home décor that convey the spirit and style of romance. It's reflected in everything we offer."

Mary and Michelle spent a year just in planning the business. "We knew nothing," Mary says candidly. "I had been in wholesaling years before, but it was totally different from what we're doing now. I did some interior design, which I always loved, but I really had no idea how to work with purchasing wholesale goods from vendors."

Three years later, the partners are pros at dealing with mail order vendors and suppliers and have segued their paper catalog-driven operation to a Web-centered one (www.love&lacegifts. com). The online catalog—put up and maintained by Mary's son—has outshone its paper predecessor.

But don't imagine that paper is a thing of the past. The partners are now in the planning stages of a small black-and-white catalog aimed at corporate buyers.

Their start-up costs—everything, Michelle reports, from software, scanner, digital camera, Internet service provider for the Web site, merchant I.D. for accepting credit cards, to a toll-free number and a few other assorted miscellanies—ran about $8,000. (They already had their first computer.)

Mary's words of wisdom for newbie catalogers? "Don't plan a big campaign," she cautions. "Start off small. And barter with everyone you can—for advertising, photography and printing."

● *How to Start and Operate a Mail-Order Business*, by Julian L. Simon, McGraw-Hill

Publications

● *Catalog Age*, Cowles Business Media, 11 River Bend Dr. S., Box 4949, Stamford, CT 06907-0949, (203) 358-9900 (editorial), (800) 775-3777 (subscriptions), www.CatalogAgemag.com

● *The Catalog Marketer*, Maxwell Sroge Co. Inc., 522 Forest Ave., Evanston, IL 60202, (847) 866-1890

● *Direct*, Cowles Business Media, 11 River Bend Dr. S., Box 4949, Stamford, CT 06907-0949, (203) 358-9900 (editorial), (800) 775-3777 (subscriptions)

● *Direct Marketing*, 224 Seventh St., Garden City, NY 11530, (800) 229-6700

● *Target Marketing*, 401 N. Broad St., Philadelphia, PA 19108, (800) 627-2689, www.targetonline.com

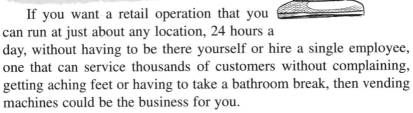

The Inside Scoop

If you want a retail operation that you can run at just about any location, 24 hours a day, without having to be there yourself or hire a single employee, one that can service thousands of customers without complaining, getting aching feet or having to take a bathroom break, then vending machines could be the business for you.

It used to be that coin-operated machines stocked only a limited number of items—gumballs, gluey sandwiches, sodas and those cheese-and-peanut butter crackers that stick to your teeth in orange globs. Now those same machines can take not only coins, but also paper money and credit cards, and pump out an astonishing variety of products. Via vending machine, you can sell everything from artwork to Internet access, imported cigars to CDs, popcorn, pantyhose, perfume, temporary tattoos, golf-club cleaning, and of course gumballs—and a whole lot more. This is big business—*Vending Times* counted more than $31 billion in sales during one recent year.

You'll set up your machines wherever you determine the market for their products is best—at airports, college campuses, movie theaters, arcades, skate rinks, supermarkets, restaurants, offices, warehouses, factories, tourist venues and even at seemingly snooty locations like Bloomingdale's. Some locations like large corporations will allow your machines on-site for free because of the convenience to their employees, but most "hosts" will require a small percentage of your sales as rent.

The advantages to this business are that you can start part time with minimal costs and you don't need to put in much time—a visit to each machine once a day to once a month (depending on how much it takes) is usually sufficient.

The disadvantages are that while most modern machines are fairly maintenance-free, you'll occasionally have problems with an ailing "employee." (Most machine suppliers offer ready support, but you'll need to check this out thoroughly.) And since you're not on-site to keep an eye on things, you may run into theft or vandalism problems. (You can compensate for this at least in part by placing machines where on-site employees at your host location can keep an eye on them.)

Essentials

All you really need is a good working knowledge of what types of vending machines are available and the reputations of their suppliers or manufacturers. You should also have enough mechanical aptitude to fix ailing machines without help or to be talked through a repair operation by a supplier's techie.

Tools Of The Trade

You'll need a few fix-it tools like screwdrivers and pliers and a car to take you on your rounds—and, of course, your machines. That's it!

Money Talk

Start-up costs for this business depend on what sorts of machines you want to buy and how many. You can purchase a gumball machine for as low as $64 or a fancy-shmancy foods dispenser for $5,500. Annual gross revenues also vary wildly, depending on what machines you have, how many you have, and where you place them. Your best bet on determining sales is to do your homework—talk to the National Automatic Vending Association, read up and shop wisely.

Once you've got your machines, you'll need to stock them, and again, prices will vary with your products. As a guide, however, you can figure that the cost to stock one sandwich machine is $100, one gumball machine $5, and one soda machine $7 per case (and each machine takes about 12 cases). Where do you find the goodies to put in your machines? At your local warehouse club, discount superstore, or through wholesalers you can find in the Yellow Pages under "Vending Machine Services." You can also try the Hanna Co. in

Lenexa, Kansas, at (800) 397-8363 for a terrific selection of both machines and products.

Pounding The Pavement

Who your customers are will depend on the products in your machines and their locations—you're not going to sell many cigars at kid-oriented restaurants like Chuck E. Cheese's, and you won't sell a lot of gumballs at a gentleman's club.

As with a cart or kiosk business, think about where you'll find people who'll want your goods, then case the site at different times over a two-week period to get a feel for traffic flow and customer demographics.

What's Next

Scope out the many possibilities for vending machines, scout out locations, then approach hosts about placing your machines on-site.

Organizations

● *National Automatic Merchandising Association*, 20 N. Wacker Dr., #350, Chicago, IL 60606, (312) 346-0370, www.vending.org

Books

● *Entrepreneur's Business Start-Up Guide #1375, Coin-Operated Vending*, Entrepreneur Media Inc., 2392 Morse Ave., Irvine, CA 92614, (800) 421-2300, www.smallbizbooks.com

● *Vending Success Secrets: How Anyone Can Grow Rich in America's Best Cash Business*, by Bill Way, Freedom Tech Press

Publications

● *Vending Times*, 1375 Broadway, 6th Fl., New York, NY 10018, (212) 302-4700, www.vending.org

Franchises

● *Hot N' Fast*, 3820 Premier Ave., Memphis, TN 38118, (901) 368-3333

● *Kameleon International Inc.*, 16018 SW Parker Rd., Ste. A, Lake Oswego, OR 97035, (503) 635-9880

Chapter twenty

SOAP BRIGADE

If you like making the world a cleaner, brighter place—you love bubbles and suds, squirt bottles of cleaners, polishes and germ busters, and you get a charge out of banishing dirt—and you're a Felix Unger without the neuroses, then this is the category for you.

CARPET/ UPHOLSTERY CLEANING

The Inside Scoop

Here's how it happens—the kids get a little carried away with the Koolaid, Dad tracks in dirt from the garden, and the dog doesn't quite make it to the backyard for his morning romp. And all of a sudden, the battle of the dirt transforms that pretty beige carpet into one ugly mud puddle. Those rentable carpet shampooers down at the supermarket don't really do a professional job and the in-laws are coming to visit in a week. And now that you look, your sofas have somebody's chocolate fingerprints on them plus a nice film of smoke from the time you burned the burgers under the kitchen broiler.

If you like putting the spring back in a carpet's fibers and making dingy upholstered furniture clean and bright, you can save the day—and clean up profits in the process—with a carpet and upholstery cleaning service.

The disadvantages are that you'll need a fair amount of muscle for wrestling equipment in and out of your vehicle and keeping it under control while you work, and while this is a steady, fairly recession-proof industry, it's not usually viewed as a prestigious career.

Essentials

All you need to get started is some experience with carpet- and upholstery-cleaning machines and the basic skills to operate them safely and effectively, plus the marketing know-how to make your own spot in the field.

Tools Of The Trade

As a carpet/upholstery cleaner, you'll need a good steam, rotary or dry-cleaning system, a commercial-grade vacuum cleaner, and of course, lots of shampoos, stain removers and stain guards, along with a sturdy vehicle to cart it all around in. You can also invest in a polo or good-quality T-shirt with your company name on it to lend a professional image.

Money Talk

Assuming you already have a van or other suitable transportation, you can plan on start-up costs of $1,000 to $5,000, depending on whether you purchase your equipment or lease it as a less expensive option. Annual gross revenues for a carpet/upholstery service range from $30,000 to $60,000. Charge your customers $35 to $50 per room or by the square foot. You can also bump up your revenues by adding on services like carpet and upholstery stain protection.

Pounding The Pavement

Your customers can come from both residential and commercial sectors. Apartment and rental property owners and managers make good target markets because people are always moving in and out, and even the tidiest tenant leaves carpeting in need of cleaning. You can also target real estate agents who may have vacant or lived-in properties that need a good shampoo to put their best feet forward.

Visit these businesspeople and leave your card or brochure, call and introduce yourself and your services, or initiate a direct-mail campaign. Advertise to residences through coupon mailers, offering specials like a discount for one room if you do two or more.

What's Next

Decide which cleaning method you'll use, then check into renting, leasing or purchasing your equipment. Give your vehicle a shampoo and polish so it sparkles like your customers' carpets will, and have your business name and phone number painted on the sides.

Organizations

- *Association of Specialists in Cleaning and Restoration*, 8229 Cloverleaf Dr., #460, Millersville, MD 21108, (800) 272-7012, www.ascr.org

Business Opportunities

- *Cleanpro*, 3400-425 First St. SW, Calgary, AB, T2P 3L8, CAN, (888) 888-7771

Franchises

- *Heaven's Best*, P.O. Box 607, Rexburg, ID 83440, (800) 359-2095
- *Steam Brothers Inc.*, 933-1/2 Basin Ave., Bismark, ND 58504, (800) 767-5064

COMMERCIAL CLEANING

The Inside Scoop

If you've ever walked into an office or shop where sunlight barely penetrated the film of dirt on the windows, dust lay thick on every surface, or—the worst—the restroom looked like an auto mechanics' pit after a hard, greasy day, then you know how important cleanliness is to business. You probably wanted to turn around and walk right back out again. A dirty establishment is a sure way to lose customers. But who in an office or store has the time—or the inclination—to get in there with the cleanser and scrubby sponge? The answer is nobody.

But if you like making the world sparkle and you're not afraid of elbow or any other kind of grease, then you can lather up a good living with a commercial cleaning service. You can take the usual route to squeaky-cleanness with familiar products, or you can go green and use only environmentally healthy products.

The advantages to this business are that you can start on a shoestring and, provided you're not one of those rare cleaning-challenged people who leave things more streaked after a good mop-up than before, you don't need any special skills, background or experience. Another plus is that this is an ideal part-time start-up business because offices and stores want you to work after hours, leaving you plenty of time to maintain your present job until you get established.

The disadvantages are that you'll have to work evenings when most folks are home watching television with their feet up, you'll work hard—this is not the kind of business for people who don't like to get down and dirty (and then clean)—and although commercial cleaning can be physically and financially rewarding, it's not a glamorous industry.

Essentials

To shine at commercial cleaning, all you need is a steady supply of good old-fashioned elbow grease coupled with a knowledge of cleaning products and how to use them—especially if you're going green. (Janitorial supply houses are good sources for both materials and advice.)

Tools Of The Trade

Your tools will include a good commercial-grade vacuum cleaner (for shoestring start-ups you can use your home model, but it probably won't hold up for long), a floor buffer, rubber gloves, a mop, a bucket, sponges and rags, a squeegee, a supply of garbage bags, and your cleaning products. You'll need a reliable vehicle to cart everything around in, and you should be bonded because companies will entrust the keys to their kingdoms to you.

Money Talk

This can be a real shoestring start-up—you can get started for as little as $400. Annual gross revenues for a one-person commercial cleaning business range from $15,000 to $30,000. As you grow, you may want to take on employees, and while this will cost you some, you can increase your business exponentially. Charge your clients $20 to $30 per hour or by the job, depending on the size of the task and on going rates in your area.

Pounding The Pavement

Your clients can be small businesses—everything from doctors' offices to insurance agencies to companies in strip centers and office parks—as well as retail shops. Large corporations are not your best bet because you'll need several crews to cover the whole place every night or so, but with smaller firms, you can contract to do one or more a night over the course of a week.

Visit prospective clients and give them your fliers and business cards or start a direct-mail campaign, perhaps offering an introducto-

GARAGE & ATTIC CLEANING/ HAULING SERVICE

Nobody likes to spend a weekend cleaning out the garage, attic or garden shed—it's dirty and time-consuming, and when it's done, there's still hauling off all that discarded junk. But if you don't mind putting in the physical labor, a cleaning and hauling service can be a lot of fun. You can usually find a few treasures among the trash, which most people are delighted to give away, and you can add to your income by recycling bottles, newspapers and metal cast-offs. You'll need a pick-up truck or other vehicle capable of carrying everything from cast-iron sinks to old timbers. Start off by advertising in your local newspaper. **Start-up costs:** $500, assuming you already have wheels. **Expected annual gross revenues:** $10,000 to $20,000.

ry discount. If you're cleaning green, be sure to stress the benefits of your service and products over your competitors'.

Dress for success with a polo or good-quality T-shirt imprinted with your company name, and be sure your vehicle sparkles, too—potential customers won't be impressed if you pull up in a dusty rattletrap.

What's Next

Investigate local janitorial supply companies to find out who stocks which products and at what prices, then establish relationships with the best ones. Get yourself bonded and get cleaning!

Organizations

- *Building Owners and Managers Association International*, 1201 New York Ave. NW, #300, Washington, DC 20005, (800) 426-6292, www.boma.org

Books

- *Cleaning Up for a Living: Everything You Need to Know to Become a Successful Building Service Contractor*, by Don A. Aslett, Betterway Publications
- *Entrepreneur's Business Start-Up Guide #1034, Janitorial Service,*

Entrepreneur Media Inc., 2392 Morse Ave., Irvine, CA 92614, (800) 421-2300, www.smallbizbooks.com

- *Inside the Janitorial Business: How to Start from Scratch and Succeed in Commercial Cleaning*, by Frederick R. Massey, MBM Books

Business Opportunities

- *Professional Cleaning Associates*, 1902 Central Dr., Bedford, TX 76021, (800) 796-4680

Franchises

- *Coverall Cleaning Concepts*, 3111 Camino Del Rio N., #950, San Diego, CA 92108, (800) 537-3371, www.coverall.com
- *iCLEAN*, 1 Park Plaza, #600, Irvine, CA 92614, (877) 898-9500, www.iclean.com
- *Jani-King*, 16885 Dallas Pkwy., Addison, TX 75001, (800) 552-5264, www.janiking.com

MAID SERVICE

The Inside Scoop

Not that long ago, in the days when our grandparents or even parents were young, every middle-income family had a maid. She kept the house clean, washed the dishes and clothes, and cooked the meals. She's since been replaced by the vacuum cleaner, dishwasher, washer, dryer and microwave oven—but not entirely. None of these technological marvels can apply elbow grease like a real person and keep our homes clean. And in today's two-income and single-parent families, we don't have the time or the energy to do it ourselves.

But if you get a charge out of making things sparkle, you love the unmistakable scent of a freshly cleaned house and the glow of accomplishment from a good day's work, then you can shine with a maid or housecleaning service.

You'll clean homes, apartments and condominiums, either with the usual supplies or with environmentally healthy products, working alone or with a partner. As you grow, you can take on employees, your "maids," and take the catbird seat as a supervisor instead of a scrubber.

You'll treat your clients to routine weekly cleaning services, in which you'll perform pre-arranged tasks like dusting, bathroom cleaning and floor mopping. And you can earn lots of extra income by offering add-on services like oiling kitchen cabinets, stripping and waxing floors, and cleaning and contact-papering pantries and linen closets.

The advantages to this business are that you can start on a shoestring—part time if you like—with no formal skills or experience, and build up a lucrative business.

The disadvantages are that this is a labor-intensive job—you've got to be willing to get in there and scrub—and unless you want to hire employees, you can only grow so far.

Essentials

You'll need the physical stamina to scrub homes 'til they sparkle and the skills to make surfaces shine. People can be picky about how their houses are handled, so if you're a lick-and-a-promise type around your own home, you'll either have to upgrade your standards or choose another business.

A STAR IS BORN

Cleaning Up

Linda Camp has been cleaning up in Panama City Beach, Florida, for two years and loving it. A former motel manager, Camp, 46, realized the demand for housecleaning assistance in her resort community. Besides the usual residential cleaning jobs, the area is rife with beach condos that rent by the week and need servicing between guests. So Camp took the soap bucket plunge, distributing fliers advertising her services all over the prime beach area. Since then, she's done no advertising—all her clients come through word-of-mouth referrals. Her start-up costs were an absolute minimum, consisting of cleaning supplies she brought from home.

The mother of two, Camp maintains a steady base of about 10 clients, half residential and half beach rentals. During the bustling spring and summer seasons, Camp works six or seven days a week, earning $100 to $120 per day—off season, the pace drops to a three- or four-day workweek. She charges most clients an hourly fee of $10 but sometimes rates rental unit cleaning on a flat-fee basis because she provides necessities like toilet tissue and garbage bags as part of the service. And she's careful to keep all her clients within a small geographic area so she doesn't lose time driving across town.

Camp's advice for the newbie looking to get into the business? "You have to be honest and dependable," she says. "Then get ready to roll up your sleeves and get at it."

Tools Of The Trade

It's best if you come armed with your own cleaning supplies (and a must if you're going environmentally green), but if you want to start on an absolute shoestring you can have your clients provide their own. If you arrive prepared, you'll need a caddy of cleaning products, rubber gloves, a mop, a bucket, a squeegee, sponges, rags and paper towels, a broom and dustpan, and a vacuum cleaner. Again, for minimal start-ups, you can use what you've got at home and buy replacements as you bring in revenues.

You'll also need a reliable vehicle to take you and your tools on your rounds, and since you'll be home alone in homes while clients are at work, you'll want to be bonded and insured.

Money Talk

Clean up with a shoestring start-up—as little as $150. Expect annual gross revenues of $15,000 to $30,000, and you can up your earnings by offering special one-time services that pay more. Charge your clients by the hour or by the job, based on going rates in your area and how much work you'll be tackling—as a thumbnail you can use $10 to $20 per hour or $35 to $75 per job.

Pounding The Pavement

Your clients will be home and apartment owners who don't have the time or the inclination to keep their residences gleaming. The best way to attract their business is by advertising in local newspapers or throwaways like the *Pennysaver* or *Thrifty Nickel* and by word-of-mouth among satisfied customers.

What's Next

Decide whether you want to start by doing-it-all-yourself or by hiring maids to send out on jobs. (Keep in mind that when someone calls in sick or quits, which can happen frequently, you're the replacement.) Get bonded and insured, and get going!

Books

- *The Cleaning Encyclopedia*, by Don Aslett, Dell Books
- *Entrepreneur's Business Start-Up Guide #1160, Maid Service*, Entrepreneur Media Inc., 2392 Morse Ave., Irvine, CA 92614, (800) 421-2300, www.smallbizbooks.com
- *Talking Dirt: America's Speed Cleaning Expert Answers the 157 Most Asked Cleaning Questions*, by Jeff Campbell and The Clean Team Staff, DTP

Franchises

- *Cottage Care*, 6323 W. 110th St., Overland Park, KS 66211, (800) 469-6303, www.cottagecare.com
- *Merry Maids*, 860 Ridge Lake Blvd., Memphis, TN 38120, (800) 637-7962, www.merrymaids.com
- *Molly Maid*, 1340 Eisenhower Pl., Ann Arbor, MI 48108, (800) 665-5962, www.mollymaid.com

The Inside Scoop

Almost everybody's got at least one set of miniblinds in their homes or offices—and everybody who has them also has a major problem with the dust and grime that sticks to blind surfaces and defies soap and water. You wash one side and dirt drips to the other. Tackle that side and you wind up with globby streaks on your first side.

But you can conquer dirt and prove that grime doesn't pay with a miniblind cleaning service. You'll roll to customers' homes with your ultrasonic cleaning system on board and give each miniblind a maxi shine.

The advantages to this business are that you're always on the go so there's no time to get bored in one place and there's plenty of room for growth.

The disadvantages are that—compared to some other businesses in this Interest Category—your start-up costs are on the high side, and you may have to do some energetic advertising.

Essentials

You'll need experience or training in ultrasonic miniblind cleaning, which you usually receive when you purchase your machine, and the marketing skills to reach customers who may not be aware that systems like yours exist.

Tools Of The Trade

Your major piece of equipment, of course, is the ultrasonic machine, but you'll also need the cleaning solutions that go with it and a reliable utility vehicle like a van to transport it and you around town.

Money Talk

Assuming you already have the van, pencil in start-up costs of about $11,000 to $20,000, most of which will go for your machine. You can expect annual gross revenues of $30,000 to $100,000, depending on how hard you want to work and how aggressively you market. You'll charge your customers $8 to $15 per miniblind.

Pounding The Pavement

Your customers can be both residential and commercial. Tackle them by placing ads, perhaps with a discount for the first set of blinds, in coupon mailers or with a direct-mail campaign. You can visit small businesses directly, leaving your flier and business card, and place ads in the Yellow Pages and your local newspaper.

What's Next

Turn your vehicle into a mobile advertisement by giving it a fresh paint job if necessary, shining it until it gleams, and then having your business name and phone number emblazoned on the sides.

Business Opportunities

- *All American Mobile Mini-Blind Cleaning Systems*, 23052 Alicia Pkwy., Ste. H-202, Mission Viejo, CA 92692, (949) 459-8931
- *Super Sonic Shine-a-Blind*, 5920 St. Clair Hwy., P.O. Box 7, St. Clair, MI 48079, (800) 446-0411, www.shineablind.com

Franchises

- *Slats Blind Cleaning*, 105 Pioneer, Ste. A, Santa Cruz, CA 95060, (800) 667-5287

MOBILE AUTO DETAILER

The Inside Scoop

America is a commuter country. Everybody has a car, and most people consider theirs an extension of their family or indeed of their own personality. According to the U.S. Bureau of Economic Analysis, there were more than 15 million new vehicle sales in one recent year—and that's not mentioning the untold numbers of already owned cars, trucks and assorted sport-utility vehicles rolling down the roads. The problem is that in our hectic, workaholic society, nobody has the time—or the inclination—to keep ol' Bess looking her best.

But if you love cars and keeping them beautiful, you can provide the solution as an auto detailer. You'll travel to clients' homes or offices to wash, wax and pamper the family wheels. Besides the usual bath and wax, you'll shampoo carpets, clean upholstery, polish chrome and shine shoes (er, tires).

The advantages to this business are that you can start on a shoestring, part time if you like, you're out in the fresh air all day, and you get the glow of accomplishment that comes from putting in a good day's physical labor.

The disadvantage is that you're at the mercy of the weather—you'll be on the job whether it's 110 in the shade or 40 in the sun, and if it rains or snows, you can't work at all, which wreaks havoc with your cash flow. (You can compensate at least in part by taking on at-home clients with garages during inclement weather or by having customers bring cars to your garage, if you have one.)

Essentials

You'll need some experience with washing, waxing and detailing vehicles. You must know which products are safe for which finishes and which give the best results. You'll also need the physical stamina to work outdoors all day doing fairly intensive labor and the drive to keep at it even when it's hot and sticky.

Tools Of The Trade

Assuming you already have a vehicle, this is a real shoestring start-up. All you need is a wet/dry vacuum; minicarpet shampooer; buffer/polisher; brushes; rags; soap; window cleaner; wax; leather, upholstery and tire cleaners; a bucket; a hose; and a truck or van to cart them around in, plus access to an electric outlet and an outdoor water spigot. Since you'll be dealing with people's automotive babies, you may want to carry liability insurance—check with your agent for prices and terms.

Money Talk

Assuming you already have the vehicle, you can lather up start-up costs of less than $500. Expect annual gross revenues of $30,000 to $75,000, depending on what types of cars you're detailing—basic models that you can't do a lot for, or expensive jobbies with lots of leather, chrome and other goodies to pamper. You'll charge your clients $20 to $50 per hour or by the job—take the kind of car, owner and economic area into consideration.

Pounding The Pavement

Your clients can be anybody who has a vehicle and the discretionary income to pay for your services. Place fliers on car windshields in office complex parking lots and distribute them inside the offices, too. Introducing yourself to denizens of small companies and the human resources staff of large corporations can go a long way toward gaining business, especially if you invest in a polo or good-quality T-shirt with your company name on it.

Solicit business from car dealers by selling them "free" coupons they can give to people who buy their vehicles. Go after homeowner and homebased businesses by placing your fliers under doormats or as door hangers, or by running ads in direct-mail coupon books.

What's Next

Make sure your own vehicle sparkles—it doesn't need to be new, but it should have a good paint job and look clean and shiny. Obviously, no one's going to trust you with their car if yours is a mobile disaster area. Your vehicle can be a terrific source of on-the-road advertising, so have your company name and phone number painted on the sides or get a vinyl/magnetic-backed sign.

Organizations

- *Car Care Council*, 42 Park Dr., Port Clinton, OH 43452, www. carcarecouncil.org

Books

- *Automotive Detailing: A Complete Car Care Guide for Auto Enthusiasts and Detailing Professionals*, by Don Taylor, H.P. Books
- *Entrepreneur's Business Start-Up Guide #1146, Automobile Detailing*, Entrepreneur Media Inc., 2392 Morse Ave., Irvine, CA 92614, (800) 421-2300, www.smallbizbooks.com

Business Opportunities

- *National Detail Systems*, 1534 N. Moorpark Rd., #351, Thousand Oaks, CA 91360, (800) 356-9485

POOL-CLEANING SERVICE

The Inside Scoop

Swimming pools can be a haven on a hot day, a source of pride for homeowners, and a necessity for apartment and condominium complexes and hotels and motels. But keeping them pristine is not a job for the uninitiated or those with no time, and a pool that's ignored for even a week can quickly become a setting for The Creature From the Black Lagoon. Besides being unsightly, a dirty pool can be costly. Business owners whose pools don't meet local health department standards can be fined or have their watering holes closed down, which can cost not only money, but also customers.

But if you like working outdoors with the sun on your back and the sound of water at your feet, then you can banish the pool pH blues with a pool-cleaning service. You'll make weekly rounds, checking and adjusting chemical levels, maintaining pumps, skimmers, filters and other equipment, and doing routine cleaning. In addition to pools, you can service spas and hot tubs, too.

The advantages to this business are that you can start part time if you like with a minimal investment; you get to work outdoors; and pool cleaners, like that other outdoor water-oriented worker, the lifeguard, have a sort of mystique in our social consciousness.

The disadvantages are that you're at the mercy of Mother Nature—you've got to be on the job on broiling days as well as chilly ones, and when the weather's inclement, your cash flow goes awry. And while pool-cleaning may be socially cool, it's also hot, hard work.

Essentials

You'll need a good working knowledge of pool-cleaning techniques and supplies, from pH levels to chlorine tablets and beyond.

You'll also need the physical strength to manipulate poles and skimmers through the drag created by water all day and the motivation to work quickly and efficiently.

Tools Of The Trade

In some states, you need to be certified to clean pools used by the public—be sure to check with your local health department. You'll need poles, hoses, skimmers, chemicals and test kits, and a pickup truck or trailer to carry them around in. And don't forget your sunscreen and a hat!

Money Talk

Assuming you already have the truck or a trailer, you can dip into start-up costs of about $500. You can expect to earn annual gross revenues of $50,000 and up, depending on how hard you want to work and the going rates in your area. Charge your customers $75 to $150 per service.

Pounding The Pavement

Your clients will most likely be homeowners and owners of apartment and condominium complexes and hotels and motels, but you can also target schools and health clubs.

The best way to sell to businesses is to introduce yourself to the manager (or maintenance manager if it's a large facility) and leave your business card and flier. If you don't get an immediate offer—which you probably won't—check back or call to remind them that you're available.

For homeowners, purchase a mailing list of pool owners in your area or check with your county tax assessor's office—it may have a list of pool owners on file. Then send a brochure or flier—you can offer an introductory discount or a free pool checkup.

Establish relationships with pool supply stores and pool builders in your area, leave a batch of your business cards and ask them to refer you to their customers.

What's Next

If you don't have pool-cleaning experience, go out and get it by working for an up-and-running service for a stretch. Invest in inexpensive uniforms in the form of a polo or good-quality T-shirt with your company name on them, and have your company name, logo and phone number painted on your vehicle.

Organizations

- *National Swimming Pool Foundation*, 10803 Gulfdale, #300, San Antonio, TX 78216, (210) 525-1227

Books

- *The Complete Swimming Pool Reference*, by Tom Griffiths, Mosby-Year Book
- *The Pool Maintenance Manual*, by Terry Tamminen, McGraw-Hill
- *What Color Is Your Swimming Pool? The Guide to Trouble-Free Pool Maintenance*, by John M. O'Keefe, Storey Books

Franchises

- *PFS Pool Franchise Service*, 2149 O'Toole Ave., Ste. I, San Jose, CA 95131, (800) 399-4070, www.pfspool.com

Chapter twenty-one

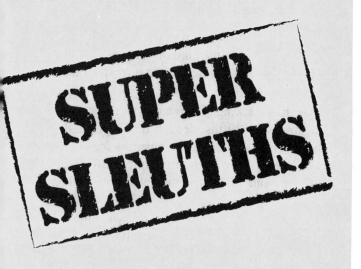

SUPER SLEUTHS

There's more than one way to be a sleuth. Besides the fabled private detective, there are information investigators, delvers into family secrets called genealogists and mystery shoppers. If you love snooping into secrets of all kinds, you've got boundless curiosity and a passion for digging to the bottom of any mystery, then you can be a modern-day Miss Marple or Philip Marlowe—this could be the category for you.

GENEALOGICAL RESEARCHER

The Inside Scoop

Almost everybody likes to know their roots, where they came from and what personality traits may be at the base of their own characters. It gives you a sense of tradition, a firm tie to the past as well as the present, and a chance to adopt the land of your forebears. And you never know if that family history search might turn up a link to distant royalty!

If you love nothing better than tracking historical mysteries, tracing the sometimes tangled threads of births, deaths, marriages and emigration to foreign shores, then this could be the business for you. As a genealogical researcher, you'll delve deep into family histories, sketch family trees and inform your clients of the secrets of their pasts.

The advantages to this business are that you can start with a minimum investment, part time if you like, and if you like historical research, you'll have a ball spending your time digging into the past.

The disadvantages are that while you can earn a respectable income, you're not likely to get rich, and, like all research businesses, the search part can sometimes become frustrating when lead after lead fails to pan out.

Essentials

You'll need experience in genealogical research, an obsession with getting to the root of your clients' roots, and an organized, detail-oriented personality.

Tools Of The Trade

You'll need a computer with an inkjet or laser printer, the usual office software, genealogy software and Internet access—you'll find scads of sources on the Web.

Money Talk

Find your roots with start-up costs of $2,250. You can expect annual gross revenues of $15,000 to $40,000. You'll charge your customers $25 to $135 per month. (Searches generally take four to six months, depending on whether they're foreign or domestic.) You can bring in extra income by doing quick charts for $15 to $25 for people who already have ancestral information and by giving workshops and seminars.

Pounding The Pavement

Your clients will be people who want to discover their family histories. Attract their business by advertising in local newspapers and national or regional history-oriented publications. Write articles and give seminars or workshops at local colleges and for civic or special-interest groups like Civil War re-enactors and historical societies.

What's Next

Familiarize yourself with genealogical research sources like state bureaus of vital statistics, the National Archives and Records Administration in Washington, DC, and the Mormon's Family History Library in Salt Lake City, which—surprisingly—is not just for and about Mormons.

Organizations

- *Association of Professional Genealogists*, P.O. Box 40393, Denver, CO 80204-0393, www.apgen.org

Books

- *Becoming an Accredited Genealogist: Plus 100 Tips to Ensure Your Success*, by Karen Clifford, Ancestry Inc.

- *Netting Your Ancestor: Genealogical Research on the Internet*, by Cyndi Howells, Genealogical Publishing

Cyber Assistance

- *Cyndi's List of Genealogy Sites on the Internet* (www.cyndislist. com): Boasts more than 41,200 links, categorized and cross-referenced, in over 100 categories. A must-surf!

- *SierraHome Family Tree* (www.sierra.com/sierrahome/familytree/ gencorner): Hosted by the Sierra Home software people—contains ideas, suggestions, fun stuff and links to lots of genealogical sites

INFORMATION CONSULTANT

The Inside Scoop

It's been said that knowledge is power—this is perhaps more true today than at any time in history. And the amount of knowledge—information—available is staggering. For companies planning new products and patents or scoping out the competition, and for many other types of businesses, the trick is in figuring out how to access the information they need.

If you love research—the excitement of sifting through a maze of books, magazines, journals and other esoteric sources for bits of information—you can ride to the rescue as an information consultant.

You can seek out material for all sorts of clients—attorneys preparing cases; advertising, public relations and market research firms preparing campaigns; financial wizards; medical researchers; environmental engineers; or management consultants. Despite this wealth of potential customers, however, you should plan on specializing in a particular field. This way, you'll be familiar with the usual "suspects" or avenues of research, so you'll be able to complete assignments faster. And since this can be a difficult business to market, by sticking to one industry, you increase your word-of-mouth advertising capacity.

The advantages to this business are that you can start part time if you like, you're always learning something new, the industry has lots of room for growth, and if you love digging through information for the sheer joy of discovery, you'll be in information nirvana every working day.

The disadvantages are that not everybody understands what an information consultant does—you may face an uphill marketing battle until word-of-mouth advertising about your skills does its magic.

And if your assignment is particularly obscure, you may have difficulties finding material on time and within your budget.

Essentials

You'll need the dogged persistence of all top-notch investigators and the skills and experience to take you down the proper research avenues, plus the creativity and intuition to lead you in new directions when the usual methods fail. In addition, it helps to have a background in the field you choose to specialize in (especially if it's something multisyllabic like biogenetic physiology), but this is not an absolute requirement.

Tools Of The Trade

You'll need a computer with a laser or inkjet printer, a fax machine and the usual office software. And since you'll do most of your research online, you must have a good Internet service provider and accounts with a variety of subscription research sites like Lexis/Nexis and E-Journal. Plan on having a separate, or dedicated, line for your Internet access—otherwise clients won't be able to reach you.

Money Talk

Get informed with start-up costs of just under $2,400, unless you've already got all this stuff, in which case you can pencil in $500 for advertising. In either case, you may want to add another $1,000 for professional organization dues. Expect to earn annual gross revenues of $35,000 to $100,000. You'll charge your clients $25 to $100 an hour.

Pounding The Pavement

Who your clients are will depend on what field you specialize in. Once you decide, the best ways to reach them are by networking in professional groups and organizations and spreading the word among present and former colleagues. Write articles for and place ads in professional or trade journals. Give seminars and talks to industry groups. Establish relationships with other information consultants who can pass overflow or out-of-their-field work on to you.

What's Next

Be your own first client. Decide what field you'll specialize in, then research professional or trade associations and organizations, and same- and other-industry information consultants.

Organizations

- *Association of Independent Information Professionals*, 10290 Monroe St., #208, Dallas, TX 75229-5718, (609) 730-8759, www.aiip.org

Books

- *Entrepreneur's Business Start-Up Guide #1237, Information Broker*, Entrepreneur Media Inc., 2392 Morse Ave., Irvine, CA 92614, (800) 421-2300, www.smallbizbooks.com
- *The Information Broker's Handbook*, by Sue Rugge, Computing McGraw-Hill
- *The Online Deskbook: Online Magazine's Essential Desk Reference for Online and Internet Researchers*, by Mary Ellen Bates, Independent Publishing Group

Cyber Assistance

- As an information broker, the entire World Wide Web is at your fingertips—cyber assistance in spades. Get surfing!

MYSTERY SHOPPER

The Inside Scoop

If you've ever dreamed of being a spy, here's your chance. As a mystery shopper, you won't slink around in a trench coat, leave secret messages under statues in the park, or be outfitted with any of James Bond's arsenal of gadgets (or guns). But you will infiltrate "enemy" territory, filing reports on what you find.

Mystery shoppers work for businesses like retail stores and restaurants. Disguised as ordinary nondescript patrons, they shop or dine, then report to owners or managers on customer service issues and food quality. As a mystery shopper (also called a secret shopper or anonymous evaluator), you can also do undercover surveillance on suspected (or unsuspected) employee theft by observing things like whether bartenders put all their take in the till or retail employees are lifting goods. You can report on the quality of care at hospitals, the treatment you receive from collection agency representatives, or the effects of corporate customer training programs.

Mystery shopping is a big benefit to businesses, both in the customer service arena and in averting employee thefts. Most unhappy customers don't complain—they simply take their business elsewhere, and so do the friends and family they tell about their dissatisfaction. And $2 of every $3 lost to retail theft is attributable to employees rather than customers.

The advantages to this business are that you can start on a shoestring, part time if you like, it can be creative, and you get to be out and about all day.

The disadvantages are that, like surveillance work, it can get tedious at times, and while eating out every day for pay sounds like fun, it, too, can get tiring.

Essentials

It goes without saying that you need excellent observational skills—if you're someone who's easily distracted, you'll have a hard time counting the number of movie theater patrons to make sure the take matches the customer count or keeping your eye on that suspicious bartender all evening.

You should also be able to provide an accurate and detailed written or oral report that cites examples without resorting to trivia. For written reports, you'll need good grammar, punctuation and spelling skills as well.

And last but not least, you need the good detective or spy's ability to look nondescript so you can return to the same location several times and not be noticed or remembered.

Tools Of The Trade

In some states, a mystery shopper is viewed as a private investigator and you'll need to be licensed. If yours isn't one of them, all you need is your trained eye and a reliable vehicle or public transportation to take you on assignments. A computer with a laser or inkjet printer and word-processing software will be a plus for providing written reports but isn't necessary if your clients will accept oral reports.

Money Talk

This is a shoestring start-up—you can get up and running for as little as $150, or if you want to go computerized, $2,150. Annual gross revenues for a mystery shopper range from $17,500 for a one-person operator in a smaller area to $100,000 for a company with multiple independent contractor/shoppers in one or more large metropolitan areas. You'll charge $25 to $200 per evaluation, depending on what your area will bear and the caliber of the investigation. You can also take your clients' services or products in exchange for payment.

Pounding The Pavement

Your clients can be almost any type of business, although large chains and smaller firms with absentee owners make good starting

A STAR IS BORN

Mystery Man

Wayne Moberly used to be a Ford dealer. With 26 years in the car business, he knew the power of customer service—so much so that he often hired people to come onto the lot and evaluate how they were treated by the sales staff. "Everything always seems fine when the manager or owner is around," says Moberly, owner of Business Research Group, a Springfield, Missouri-based mystery shopping service. It's when management's not around that problems occur.

So how did a car dealer become a secret shopper? Moberly had sold his dealership when a magazine article on mystery shopping—the very concept he'd been using for years—caught his attention. He purchased a book on the subject, became hooked on the value of the mystery-shopping industry, and started his company. That was in 1996, with start-up costs of about $2,000.

Moberly now fields 75 to 80 independent contractors and counts as his clients everybody from the local McDonald's restaurants to a 129-store, 10-state chain of brake and muffler centers.

The secrets of the secret shopper? Moberly started off by mailing out 50 sales pieces, out of which he got two calls—and two clients. From there, word-of-mouth fueled his business. He does no advertising, although he still sends out sales pieces to specially targeted potential clients. (With a base primarily made up of apartment complexes, banks and restaurants, he's aiming now for the hotel and casino trade.)

When a company contracts with Moberly, he sits down with its owners and managers and tailors an evaluation for their operation. Then he sends his shoppers out on seek-and-report missions. But, he advises would-be mystery shoppers, take care to look for the good as well as the bad. Your aim is to give a true report, not a slam.

points. So do hotels, which stake their reputations on excellent customer service. The best way to sell to these potential clients is through a direct-mail campaign of sales letters and brochures. Be sure to follow up with a phone call.

What's Next

Call your state's department of business regulation to find out if you'll need an investigator's license.

Organizations

- *National Retail Federation*, 325 Seventh St. NW, #1000, Washington, DC 20004, (800) 673-4692, www.nrf.com

Books

- *Starting Your Secret Shopping Business*, by Judith G. Rappold, Business Resource Publications. This book comes with a hefty price tag ($600), but is considered *the* manual for mystery shoppers.

Business Opportunities

- *Bottom Line Management Inc.*, 1150 Lake Hearn Dr. NE, #200-B, Atlanta, GA 30342-1506, (404) 847-0103. Specializes in mystery shopping as well as business brokerage and debt negotiation
- *Invisible Audit*, P.O. Box 272, Southbridge, MA 01550, (508) 764-8400

The Inside Scoop

If you've always wanted to be a private eye—your favorite TV shows are "Magnum, P.I." and "Rockford Files" and you've read every Kinsey Milhone and Spencer novel ever written—then this is the business for you.

As a private investigator, you'll delve into the secrets of people's lives and solve mysteries, but you'll spend far more time on the phone and at your computer than any fictional private eye ever does, and odds are you'll never be involved in high-speed chases or shootouts with baddies. Instead, you'll perform background checks on prospective employees, tenants, business partners and marriage mates; do skip traces (detective talk for missing-persons searches) on parents who owe child support or people who've left town owing money, investigate insurance claims, and nose out evidence for lawsuits.

You can specialize in any of these activities, or in finding lost loves, children abducted by noncustodial parents, or corporate fraud. If you're a computer whiz, you can specialize in hacker crimes and advise on company online security.

The advantages to this business are that it's creative, challenging, glamorous if not conventionally exciting, and reuniting people with loved ones or finding criminals who can be brought to justice can be very rewarding.

The disadvantages are that the hours can be extremely long and unpredictable—you can't quit in the middle of a stakeout because it's time for your favorite TV show or a movie date—and your work can sometimes take tedium to new heights. (Stakeouts can be very dull, and so can searching through every public file on record.)

Success For Less

Essentials

Like the best private and police detectives, you'll need dogged self-motivation—you can't give up the chase when searching public records or dialing phone numbers gets boring. And like those other detectives, you'll require high levels of creativity and intuition to guide you to new and innovative ways of obtaining information when normal channels fail.

You should also have A-plus people skills, the ability to sift truth from prevarication, and a healthy dose of self-confidence—you'll deal with all sorts of characters, and not all of them will want to talk to you or tell you the real story.

Tools Of The Trade

In most states, you'll need a private investigator's license, which requires you to have experience in a similar field—law enforcement in the public or military sector, collections, claims adjusting, sometimes investigative journalism, or of course a background in a private investigative agency.

To set up your office and get going, you'll need a computer with a laser or inkjet printer, the usual office software, Internet access, and a fax machine. You should also have a camera or a video camera, a tape recorder, and a pocket organizer or notebook for keeping track of expenses, which you'll bill to your clients.

Money Talk

Investigate start-up expenses of about $3,000—you can add up to another $1,000 for professional organization and networking dues. Once you get established, you can expect annual gross revenues of $37,500 to $100,000 and up. You'll charge your clients $25 to $125 per hour based on comparable rates in your area and your level of expertise.

Pounding The Pavement

Your clients can be attorneys who handle criminal or civil cases, insurance companies, apartment complexes, corporations and private parties with a variety of mysteries to solve.

Solicit all of these entities, except individuals, by sending your sales letter and brochure in a direct-mail campaign, then following up with phone calls. The best way to reach individuals is through an ad in the Yellow Pages.

You can also develop clients by networking among professional and civic groups and giving talks or seminars.

What's Next

Find out if you need a license in your area—even if your state doesn't require one, your local city or county may require you to register with the police department. If you don't have experience that can lead to a license, sign on with a private investigative agency to learn the ropes. Get licensed and get investigating!

Organizations

- *Council of International Investigators*, 2150 N. 107th St., #205, Seattle, WA 98133-9009, (888) 759-8884, www.cii2.org
- *International Security and Detective Alliance*, P.O. Box 6303, Corpus Christi, TX 78466-6303, (512) 888-6164

Books

- *Private Investigation: How to be Successful!*, by Bill Copeland, Absolutely Zero Loss Inc.
- *Private Investigation Training Manual*, by William Patterson, Paladin Press

Cha**p**ter twenty-two

WORD WISE

So you're the writer in your circle—you may or may not have penned the Great American Novel, but you can turn out a mean letter, a fascinating e-mail missive, and you send the quirkiest, most interesting postcards of anybody you know. If you love to write, you're entranced with the art and science of words, and books are your passion, then this is definitely the category for you.

BOOK INDEXER

The Inside Scoop

When you dip into a nonfiction book, hunting for a particular piece of information, your first stop is the index at the back. There's everything neatly organized, alphabetically by subject matter with the exact page or pages on which to find that nugget of data.

Who puts together that index, tidily chronicling each page of text? If you love books and snippets of fact, you're detail-oriented and a stickler for accuracy, it could be you as owner of a book indexing service.

The advantages to this business are that you can start on the proverbial shoestring, your overhead is minimal, and you get to learn all sorts of interesting things from books on a wide variety of topics.

The disadvantages are that you'll usually be working on a tight deadline and, although you can earn a respectable living, you're unlikely to become rich at it.

Essentials

As a book indexer, you'll need to be a highly organized, detail-oriented personality—this is another business where nitpicking is a virtue. You should enjoy books and the written word and be able to put in long hours hunched over a manuscript without suffering the fidgets.

Tools Of The Trade

All you need to get started are a computer with a laser or inkjet printer, the usual office software, and a comfortable work space with good lighting.

A STAR IS BORN

The Index Of Success

Take one retired research chemist—with a Ph.D. from the University of Texas—and one actor, and mix them together. What do you get? ALTA Indexing Service, an El Cerrito, California-based book indexing business, which also happens to be a father-son operation. Aubrey McClellan, 76, is the chemist, and Ted, 39, is the actor.

"I'm not exactly certain why I got into the book indexing business," says Aubrey, who's been at it professionally since 1992, "but I like doing it." It probably had something to do with the fact that after 33 years with Chevron, he found himself retired but definitely not inactive. Realizing he'd already created 40 indexes for books he'd written, Aubrey decided the business might be the way to go. A prominent publishing contact at a party clinched the deal and the chemist-turned-indexer was off and running. Ted came on board to supplement his typically sporadic actor's income.

The McClellans—who already had a computer system—count start-up costs of just over $500 for an indexing program found through the American Society of Indexers. "This is not a very high-tech operation," Aubrey says. But it is a busy one.

The team is now on project number 107, and although most indexes are for books, they've also done CD-ROMs and book chapters. They collaborate at least in part on just about everything but otherwise split up assignments by time—Ted bows out, for example, when he's studying lines—and by subject matter, with Ted handling consumer-oriented publications like cookbooks and Aubrey tackling volumes like *Advanced Techniques in Catalyst Synthesis*.

The McClellans charge their clients by the hour or by the indexable page. Fees vary with book content and can run from $2 to $4 per page or about $25 per hour. Aubrey drummed up business at the outset by joining the American Society of Indexers and the Bay Area Editors Forum, which netted plenty of industry contacts. But joining a professional organization is not enough. "Nobody's going to blow your horn for you," Aubrey advises. "Instead of sitting quietly in the back, become an active member and get noticed."

Money Talk

Index start-up costs of $2,150. Expect to earn annual gross revenues of about $37,500. You'll charge your clients $2 to $4 per page or $25 per hour.

Pounding The Pavement

Your clients will be editors and publishers of nonfiction books. Thanks to FedEx and its competitors, you can live anywhere and work with clients in New York, California or wherever they happen to be based.

The best way to solicit business is to call editors and offer your services, then follow up with a letter and your business card.

What's Next

Join the American Society of Indexers, which gives you a cachet in the biz. Have letterhead and business cards printed up. Then start drumming up business!

Organizations

- *American Society of Indexers*, P.O. Box 39366, Phoenix, AZ 85069-9366, (602) 979-5514, www.ASIndexing.org. Be sure to check out the wonderful Web site, packed with indexer FAQs, and other information and a (naturally) terrifically indexed online guide to indexing the Web. A must-surf.

Books

- *Indexing Books*, Nancy Mulvany, University of Chicago Press
- *Indexing From A to Z*, Hans H. Wellisch, H. W. Wilson Co.

Publications

- *Keywords*, ASI Administrative Support Office, P.O. Box 39366, Phoenix, AZ 85069-9366, (602) 979-5514
- *The Indexer*, Journal of the Society of Indexers, Journal Subscriptions Officer, 16 Coleridge Close, Hitchin, Herts U.K., SG4 0QX, Hitchen 011-04-62-45-2222

COPYWRITER/ PROOFREADER

The Inside Scoop

The written word makes the world go round. It's what businesses, associations and organizations of every description use to entice, inveigle and educate their target audiences, potential customers and existing clients. The problem is that most people view any sort of writing assignment with the sort of dread reserved for high school civics term papers.

But if you're a word wizard—you thrive on the creative challenge that goes with turning out clever, compelling and concise copy on just about any subject—then you can put your talents to work as a copywriter. You'll pen everything from direct-mail pieces to annual reports to product information pamphlets, press releases to grant proposals to radio commercials, mail order catalogs, marketing brochures and more. And if you're an all-star at spelling, punctuation and grammar, you can take on supplemental assignments as a proofreader, checking clients' copy for errors and then correcting them.

The advantages to this business are that you're always working on something different, each project gets wrapped up fairly quickly so there's no time for tedium, and finding new and interesting ways to communicate information about sometimes dull subjects can be creative and challenging.

The disadvantages are that you'll usually be juggling several projects at once, and they'll all involve tight deadlines.

Essentials

As a copywriter and proofreader, you'll need a talent for putting together words in packages that are fresh and appealing. You should also have the ability to absorb new information and concepts and the skills to translate this material into copy that others can easily grasp. You'll need the mental stamina and agility to juggle projects without going into stress overload and of course, top-notch spelling, punctuation and grammar skills.

For proofreading, you'll also need to be detail-oriented—this is one place where nitpicking is a virtue.

Tools Of The Trade

You'll need a computer, a laser printer and a fax machine. You should also have a good word-processing package, desktop-publishing software, and a reference library including a heavy-duty dictionary, thesaurus, encyclopedia and style guides.

Money Talk

Write up start-up expenses of about $2,600. Annual gross revenues for copywriter/proofreaders vary considerably with level of expertise, type of project and geographic region. You can expect to make anywhere from $20,000 to over $100,000 as you gain a foothold in the business. Charge your clients by the hour or the job— as a thumbnail, you can use $10 to $75 per hour or $2,000 to $7,000 for a direct-mail piece or package.

Pounding The Pavement

Your clients can come from all walks of business and nonprofit organizational life. Solicit projects by networking in professional and trade organizations—especially in fields where you already have experience—and by asking for work and/or references from present or former colleagues and employers.

Establish relationships with graphic designers, photographers, public relations agencies, marketing consultants and printers who can refer their clients to you. When you learn of new businesses opening in your neighborhood, chat them up about writing their grand opening and advertising material.

To get proofreading work, call magazine, newsletter and journal editors and offer your services—they're always looking for reliable assistance. If they don't need you immediately, check back every month or two.

What's Next

Develop a portfolio of samples to show clients. You can invent projects, or better yet, take on a few free of charge to gain experience and garner invaluable word-of-mouth advertising.

Organizations

- *Copywriter's Council of America*, Communications Tower, 7 Putter Ln., Box 102, Middle Island, NY 11953-0102, (516) 924-8555
- *Freelance Editorial Association*, P.O. Box 380835, Cambridge, MA 02238-0835, (617) 576-8797, www.tiac.net/users/freelanc

Books

- *The Copywriter's Handbook: A Step-by-Step Guide to Writing Copy That Sells*, by Robert W. Bly, Henry Hold
- *Go Ahead, Proof It!*, by K.D. Sullivan, Barrons Educational Series
- *Persuading on Paper: The Complete Guide to Writing Copy That Pulls in Business*, by Marcia Yudkin, Plume

The Inside Scoop

If you've always wanted to pen articles for magazines or news-papers—writing all those fascinating pieces people clip out and stick on their refrigerators or send to Mom back in Minnesota—then this is the business for you.

As a freelance writer, you can specialize in a particular industry or area of interest, or you can play the field, writing about anything that catches your fancy. There are thousands of magazines devoted to more specialities than you can imagine—everything from *American Window Cleaner* and *Party and Paper Retailer* to old standbys like *Cosmopolitan, Ladies Home Journal* and *Popular Mechanics.* You can also write for corporate publications aimed at employees or cus-tomers and for the bounty of e-zines (electronic magazines) that pro-liferate on the Internet.

A terrific way to start is by writing about subjects in which you're already an expert. Many scientists, for instance, have turned science writers. If you're a sales and marketing whiz, you can write how-to articles for business publications; if you're a dog breeder, you can write about raising Labrador retrievers; and if you're a stay-at-home parent, you can write parenting articles.

The advantages to this business are that you get to exercise your creative talents on a continuous basis, you can immerse yourself in whatever subjects interest you, dictate your own hours, and the job title carries a certain amount of glamour, especially if you're writing investigative material. As an added bonus, one of your articles may be picked up by syndicated services that will pay you a fee for every newspaper that carries your story.

The disadvantages are that it takes time to build a relationship with editors so your articles don't end up in the circular file, and the postman will deliver a sizable number of rejection letters. Also, smaller publications—the ones that are most likely to accept material from newbies—don't pay much, so until you can develop a clientele of big-name publications, your income can be on the low side.

Essentials

First and foremost, you'll need the creativity to pen interesting materials, but you'll also need the technical skills to put your ideas and information into the proper format, including top-notch spelling, punctuation and grammar talents. You'll also need an eye for the kinds of stories readers (and therefore editors) of your target publications will be interested in—you can write a stellar piece on the mating habits of cockroaches, but if you're pitching it to *Woman's Day* magazine, you may well as pitch it in the wastebasket. You should also have a flair for marketing your products, presenting them professionally but with enough pizzazz to make them sparkle among the scads of other hopefuls that weary, overworked editors receive on a regular basis.

Tools Of The Trade

You'll need a computer, a laser printer, a fax machine, and the usual office software. In addition, you'll want plenty of reference books, including a dictionary, encyclopedia, thesaurus and style guides.

Money Talk

Pencil in start-up costs of about $2,600. Once you become established, you can expect annual gross revenues of $25,000 to $35,000 and up, depending on the caliber of your clientele. Fees paid by magazine, journal and newspaper publishers vary wildly, anywhere from 5 cents a word to $2,500 per article.

Pounding the Pavement

Your customers will be the editors of your target publications. The best (and until you become established, only) way to garner business is to send query letters that describe your story idea and explain your qualifications for writing the piece. If you've got writing credentials from your present or previous job, be sure to include them. If not, you might say, for instance, that you've traveled extensively in the area you're writing about; you have a dyslexic child and have done dyslexia research; or that you've interviewed in depth the survivors of a natural disaster. The query letter is the first test of your writing abilities, the one that will attract the editor's attention, so make sure it shines.

Once you establish relationships with editors, you can often call them with story ideas, and they'll sometimes call you with requests. But until then, you'll need to send well-developed and enticing queries to a variety of publications—and keep sending them.

What's Next

Study your craft by reading up on how to write an all-star query letter. Bone up on your target markets by reading the publications you want to write for and learning their editorial styles. Most magazines will send writer's guidelines—tip sheets explaining what stories they want, the format they accept, and how much they pay, along with sample issues—if you write or call and ask. You can also find writer's guidelines for thousands of publications in *Writers Market*, published annually by Writer's Digest Books. (It also provides a nice selection of guidelines on its Web site, which we've listed below.)

Now get writing! If you don't have written materials to use as credentials, don't get discouraged by the biggie magazines. Start small with those that pay little but are eager for contributions, and keep sending to the majors.

Organizations

- *American Medical Writers Association*, 9650 Rockville Pike, Bethesda, MD 20814, (301) 493-0003, www.amwa.org
- *American Society of Journalists and Authors*, 1501 Broadway, #302, New York, NY 10036, (212) 997-0947, www.asja.org
- *Editorial Freelancers Association*, 71 W. 23rd St., #1910, New York, NY 10010, (212) 929-5400, www.the-efa.org
- *National Association of Science Writers*, P.O. Box 294, Greenlawn, NY 11740, (516) 757-5664, www.nasw.org

Books

- *Handbook for Freelance Writing*, by Michael Perry, VGM Career Horizons Writing
- *Articles About the World Around You*, by Marcia Yudkin, Writer's Digest Books
- *Writer's Digest Handbook of Making Money Freelance Writing*, by the editors of *Writer's Digest* magazine, Writer's Digest Books

Publications

- *Writer's Digest*, 1507 Dana Ave., Cincinnati, OH 45207, (800) 888-6880, www.writersdigest.com

Cyber Assistance

- *Inkspot: The Writer's Resource* (http://inkspot.com): Articles, discussion groups, chat sessions, and lots of links to just about everything a freelancer could need
- *Writer's Digest* (www.writersdigest.com): Online version of the venerable writer's publication. Offers writer's guidelines, a Hot List of "the coolest places to get published," a "Market of the Day," articles and lots more. A must-surf.

NEWSLETTER PUBLISHER

The Inside Scoop

The newsletter—that short and breezy or snappy and factual journal-ette that arrives in your mailbox every month or four times a year—is one of the hottest marketing vehicles around. It's a terrific way for businesses and professionals from event planners to periodontists to keep themselves in their clients' minds and promote new business. It's also a great way for the word-wise entrepreneur to develop a subscription publication with far less cost than a full-fledged magazine or newspaper would entail.

If you've got a flair for the written word and a talent for turning out new material in a specific field on a regular basis, then you can shine as a newsletter publisher. You can write custom-tailored newsletters for clients to send to their current and potential customers. You can develop a boilerplate newsletter for a particular set of clients such as dentists to send to their patients—you change the masthead and add in a few personalized tidbits for each dentist. Or you can design, write and publish your own newsletter on any area of interest that appeals to you and enough readers to make it pay—everything from cooking to travel to single parenting to local or global business and more.

The advantages to this business are that you can immerse yourself in the subjects that interest you and write about them to a built-in audience (once you've sold your subscriptions). And once you've developed a name as a newsletter publisher/expert, you can go on to publish audiotapes and videotapes, books and special reports, and conduct seminars and workshops.

The disadvantages are that, if you don't choose your interest area carefully enough, you can run out of subject matter and that, like other publishing ventures, it can take time to build up a loyal readership.

Essentials

If you plan to publish your own newsletter, you'll need an insider's knowledge of, and enthusiasm for, your area of interest. If you'll publish newsletters for others, you'll want a working familiarity with the subject matter and the same enthusiasm—your readers won't find dental hygiene interesting if you can't give it a little zing.

You should have a copywriter's talents including top-notch writing, spelling, punctuation and grammar skills. In addition to all of this, you'll need to be a desktop publishing demon with the graphic skills to design a visually appealing and readable composition.

Tools Of The Trade

You'll need a computer, a laser printer, a color printer, a scanner, and a fax machine. You should have top-notch word-processing software, a desktop-publishing package, a few clip-art programs, and a database program for maintaining your mailing list.

Money Talk

Give yourself the news with start-up costs of just under $3,000. If you plan to publish your own newsletter, plan on annual gross revenues of $25,000 to $40,000. Your subscription price will depend on your interest group—perhaps $15 per year for a general interest newsletter that will garner thousands of subscribers to $69 per year for a newsletter aimed at a small, specialty audience. Some newsletters targeted toward a very select but highly motivated group go for up to $1,000 per year, but this is not the norm.

Pounding The Pavement

Your clients will be the businesses and professionals for whom you develop newsletters or, if you develop your own concept, businesses or individuals who subscribe. If you plan to publish for others, for instance dentists, send direct-mail pieces, perhaps in the form of sample issues, soliciting work. Network among associations for whom you want to write newsletters, and establish relationships with printers who can refer their customers to you.

The best—and by the far the least expensive—way to develop a subscriber base for your own newsletter is to make up a sample issue (one that you can use as your sample for years to come) and a really good press release. Send this press kit to editors at every publication that touches on your specialty. From the ensuing articles, you'll get

A STAR IS BORN

Bringing Up Baby

Lynn Kerrigan knows newsletters. She's been the brains behind a newsletter targeted toward newsletter editors; currently publishes *Food Writer* for the culinary industry; and at one time published three newsletters simultaneously. Kerrigan's current baby, *Food Writer*, was born when the Ardmore, Pennsylvania, resident—hard at work on an earlier publication, *The Culinary Sleuth*—began developing a series of resources for other cuisine-oriented newsletter editors. Her tips on topics like how to obtain free publicity and get subscribers to renew soon led far beyond the friendly little group of 15 editors she started out with.

Two years later, *Food Writer* boasts 350 subscribers, including luminaries like Rodale Press and the American Dietetic Association, as well as a wide assortment of freelance writers and editors. Food entrepreneurs also subscribe for the bevy of marketing tips available in every issue.

"*Food Writer* is still an infant," says Kerrigan—it takes two to three years to see a profit on a newsletter. "It's easy and inexpensive to start and pays for itself, but profits don't come right away."

Kerrigan counts as her start-up costs: printing 500 copies of the first issue at $275, 200 press releases and samples to media at $175, an ad in a culinary trade newsletter at $75, and 200 samples and order forms for potential subscribers at $175. Total cost: $700. "No need to rent a mailing list," she adds, "as my International Culinary Professionals member directory provides all the customers I need."

You can earn a fairly good income, Kerrigan advises, but be prepared to work hard. The best way to succeed is to constantly market your baby through press releases, sample issues, direct-mail campaigns, and networking in your specialty industry or field.

scads of people requesting sample issues, a fair number of whom will become subscribers. Be sure to require a nominal fee—$1 to $3—for your sample as insurance against "looky-loos" who just want to get a freebie in the mail.

What's Next

If you're publishing your own newsletter, do your homework first—conduct market research to verify that you've got a significant audience. If you'll publish for others, determine which field or fields you'll target. Then, for either option, study the competition and decide what works and what you can do better. Develop a sample issue. Then get selling!

Organizations

● *Newsletter Publishers Association*, 1501 Wilson Blvd., #509, Arlington, VA 22209-2403, (800) 356-9302

Books

● *Home-Based Newsletter Publishing: A Success Guide for Entrepreneurs*, by William J. Bond, McGraw-Hill
● *Producing a First-Class Newsletter: A Guide to Planning, Writing, Editing, Designing, Photography, Production and Printing*, by Barbara A. Fanson, Self Counsel Press

The Inside Scoop

One of the rudest awakenings in the writer's world is that, even though you've penned a terrific book, nobody wants to publish it. And not necessarily because they don't like it. It could be that it doesn't fit their marketing plan or fails to fall into an easily categorized niche, is too long or too short, or a square peg in a round hole for any of dozens of other reasons, which can be downright discouraging.

But if you believe in your book and you've got an entrepreneurial edge, you can take your written baby to success as a self-publisher.

Not too long ago, self-publishing was looked down upon as the venue only of people whose work was truly awful. Now, however, self-publishing is not only respectable but "in." Major publishers are concentrating their efforts on mega-blockbusters, leaving the midlist or smaller writers out in the cold, which has led to the advent of the self- and small-press publisher as a solid professional group. And since U.S. book sales totaled well over $21 billion in 1997 alone, there's definitely a market out there for well-written books.

As a self-publisher, you'll not only write your book, but also see it through all the details the publishing house attends to—editing, choosing cover art, working with the graphic artist, getting it printed and, perhaps most important, getting it marketed so that it finds a readership.

The main advantage to this business, of course, is in seeing your book in print. But that's not the only one. As a self-publisher, you've got far greater control over every aspect of the final product, from paper to artwork to the blurb on the back jacket, than you would at the hands of a traditional publishing house. You can go on to publish other works of your own, or publish other writers' materials. You get far more of the revenues—up to 50 percent—than at a traditional publishing house, which pays royalties of 7 percent to 10 percent of sales. As a final advantage, if your book does well, you can segue into related products like audiobooks, videotapes and a wide variety of licensed products. And it's not unheard of for a major publisher to snap up your book once they see that it's a success.

The disadvantages are that self-publishing can be a more expensive start-up than the other businesses in this Interest Category, and if your book isn't well-written and appealing to its target audience, it may not sell despite your best efforts. And it isn't going to sell itself. As a self-publisher, you'll also have to be a stellar marketing and promotions person.

Essentials

Before anything else, you'll need the talent to pen a really good book, whether it be fiction, nonfiction or a children's picture book. You should have plenty of marketing smarts, a working knowledge of publishing contracts, terms and conditions from distribution rights to what constitutes intellectual property, and the ability to pull together the varied elements of a pre-production manuscript into a professional final product.

Tools Of The Trade

You'll need a computer, a laser printer and a fax machine, the usual office software, and desktop-publishing software. In addition, you'll want the usual tools of the writer's trade: plenty of reference books, such as a dictionary, an encyclopedia, a thesaurus and style guides.

Money Talk

You can figure your basic office start-up costs at about $2,500. Aside from that, the cost of producing one book has been estimated at $16,000—conservative for a product that looks professional enough to sell. Self-publishers' book prices are based on production and where the books will be sold (retail, catalog or the back of somebody's service center). If you go the retail route, you can arrive at a book price by estimating your production cost times eight to 10. A first print run of typically 2,000 copies won't usually pay for itself—it takes two to four runs to make a profit. Keep in mind that publishers have to give wholesalers and distributors a discount of 55 percent to 60 percent, and unless direct sales are generated, the real book price is the discounted one. A range of annual gross revenues for a self-publisher, according to the National Association of Independent Publishers (NAIP), is being in the hole to six figures, depending on the book's title, promotion and acceptance—very much, says the NAIP, like going to Las Vegas.

Pounding The Pavement

Your customers will be the readers who buy your books, but in publishing it's not quite that simple. Unless you sell through mail order, you'll have to go through intermediaries like bookstores, which makes them your first line of attack in the sales and marketing process. The organizations listed below can be great sources of information for sales and marketing.

Large chain bookstores rely on a complex distribution system for their stock, which means that even if the manager loves your book, he can't sell it. Bottom line—you'll have to capture the distributors' interests or sell to smaller, independent book stores. You should also aim for alternative sales sources—for instance, if your book deals with gardening, try selling it to garden centers and nurseries whose customers already have an interest in your subject.

What's Next

Research the publishing business. You can outsource everything from editing to graphic design to publicizing your book, but you'll have to know who you're dealing with and how each sector of the industry works. Get a variety of bids, especially from printers.

Organizations

- *National Association of Independent Publishers*, P.O. Box 430, Highland City, FL 33846-0430, (941) 648-4420
- *Publishers Marketing Association*, 627 Aviation Wy., Manhattan Beach, CA 90266, (310) 372-2732, www.pma-online.org
- *Small Publishers Association*, P.O. Box 1306, Buena Vista, CO 81211, (719) 395-4790, www.spanet.org. The SPAN Web site is chock-full of helpful goodies and definitely deserves a surf.

Books

- *Book Promotion for the Shameless: 101 Marketing Tips That Really Work (3.5 disk)*, by Lorna Tedder, Spilled Candy Publications

- *The Complete Guide to Self-Publishing: Everything You Need to Know to Write, Publish, Promote and Sell Your Own Book*, by Tom Ross, Writer's Digest Books

- *Self-Publishing Manual: How to Write, Print and Sell Your Own Book*, by Dan Poynter, Para Publishing

Cyber Assistance

- *Association of American Publishers* (www.publishers.org): Statistics, conferences, publications and more

- *PMA Newsletter Online* (www.pma-online.org/news.html): Feature stories, articles archive, classified ads—check it out!

The Interior Design Business Handbook, 183

The Interior Designer's Marketing Workbook, 183

Interior design license, 181

Interior Landscaper, 138-140

  All About Houseplants, 140

  American Horticultural Society, 140

  Associated Landscape Contractors of America, 140

  Foliage Design Systems (franchisor), 140

  National Gardening Association, 140

  The Garden Gate (Web site), 140

  The House Plant Encyclopedia, 140

  The House Plant Expert , 140

  The Sun Room (Web site), 140

Internet Training, 68-70

  A Trainer's Guide to the World Wide Web and Intranets, 70

  Computer Technology Industry Association, 70

  Inside Technology Training (magazine), 70

  Internet magazine (Web site), 70

  ITrain-International Association of Information Technology Trainers, 70

  Searching Smart on the World Wide Web, 70

  The McGraw-Hill Internet Training Manual, 70

J

Jewelry & Accessories Design, 49-51

  National Craft Association, 51

  The Art and Craft of Jewelry, 51

  The Bead Fairies Page (Web site), 51

  The Book of Beads, 51

  The Encyclopedia of Jewelry Making Techniques, 51

K

Kid's/Clothing Consignment Shop, 340-344

  Entrepreneur's business start-up guide Consignment Clothing Store, #1229, 343

  National Association of Resale and Thrift Shops, 343

  National Retail Federation, 343

  Too Good to Be Threw, 343

  Too Good to Be Threw (Web site), 344

  Too Good to Be Threw: The Resale Industry Newsletter, 344

Kids' Taxi Service, 229-231

Automobile Association of America (Web site), 231

Drive to Survive , 231

L

Lawn Care, 141-144

  Cyberlawn (Web site), 144

  Entrepreneur's business start-up guide Lawn Care Business, #1198, 144

  Lawn Care & Gardening , 144

  Nutri-Lawn (franchisor), 144

  Professional Lawn Care Association, 144

  Spring-Green Lawn Care Corp. (franchisor), 144

  The Lawn Institute (Web site), 144

Liability insurance, 13, 174, 376

Licenses

  business, 19-21, 35

  computer repair, 59, 60

  contractor, 167

  cosmetology, 257, 260

  county, 22

  debt collector, 273

  freight broker, 104

  interior designer, 181

  liquor, 21, 43, 235

  massage, 263

  private investigator, 389, 392-394

  resale, 21, 43, 235, 337

Liquor license, 21, 43, 235

Loans

SBA, 16

M

Magazine publisher. *See* E-zine Publisher

Maid Service, 369-372

  Cottage Care (franchisor), 372

  Entrepreneur's business start-up guide Maid Service, #1160, 372

  Merry Maids (franchisor), 372

  Molly Maid (franchisor), 372

  Talking Dirt , 372

  The Cleaning Encyclopedia, 372

Mailing lists, 12

Makeup Artist, 260-261

  Color Me Beautiful's Looking Your Best, 261

  DK Living: Classic Makeup & Beauty, 261

  National Cosmetology Association, 261

  The Art of Makeup, 261

Marketing, 3-12

Massage license, 263

Medical Claims Billing, 150-154

"Wouldn't it be great...

if you could look into the future and see how all your decisions will affect your bottom line? "

...*well now you can!*

Great for Start-ups too!

It's easy with Entrepreneur Magazine's *What If?* This step-by-step program takes the guesswork out of making small business financial decisions. It gives you the power to quickly create financial forecasts so you can see if your new business ideas or strategies will be successful.

Just starting out? *What If?* will help you lay the financial groundwork for your new business and create projections you can use to generate capital.

Already own a business? *What If?* can show you how such strategies as hiring additional employees or expanding your product line will affect your bottom-line. Then you can use that information to make better informed decisions.

Best of all, you don't need to be a financial wizard to use *What If?* In fact, with its intuitive interface and context-sensitive help, you don't need any financial expertise at all.

Get the vital financial information you need to ensure the success of your business. Fill out the coupon below or call 1-800-421-2300 and order Entrepreneur Magazine's *What If?* today!

...in just minutes, you can easily create and print sales and expense forecasts, P&L statements, balance sheets, cash plans and more.

What If? System requirements: 100% IBM-compatible, Pentium or higher PC running Microsoft Windows® 95/98/NT4, 16MB RAM, 20MB free hard disk space, VGA or higher resolution monitor (800 x 600 recommended), CD-ROM drive.

Help ensure your success with this easy-to-understand guide.

> **" ...all true entrepreneurs won't want to put this book down."**
> **LILLIAN VERNON**
> **Chairman and CEO**
> **Lillian Vernon Corporation**

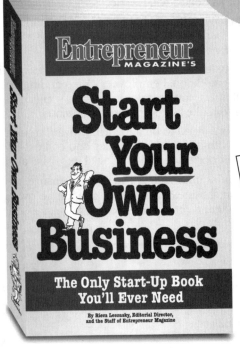

You'll find our special tip boxes loaded with helpful hints on everything from working smarter to saving money.

The easy-to-follow, illustrated format features plenty of forms, work sheets and checklists you can actually use in your business.

Whether you're just thinking of starting a business, have taken the first few steps, or already have your own business, this comprehensive, easy-to-understand guide can help ensure your success.

Written in a friendly, down-to-earth style, *Start Your Own Business* makes it easy to understand even the most complex business issues so you can reach your goals and enjoy the rewards of owning your own business.

Inside you'll find:

- Our easy-to-navigate format loaded with work sheets, tip boxes features, charts, graphs and illustrations.
- Practical, proven, hands-on techniques so you can get started right away.
- Expert guidance from the nation's leading small-business authority, backed by over 20 years of business experience.
- And much more!

Powerhouse Marketing Tactics for Making Big Profits

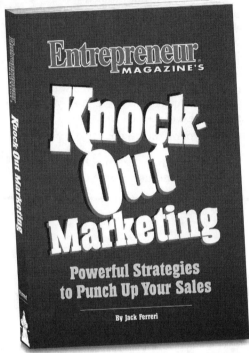

Entrepreneur MAGAZINE'S

Knock-Out Marketing

Powerful Strategies to Punch Up Your Sales

By Jack Ferreri

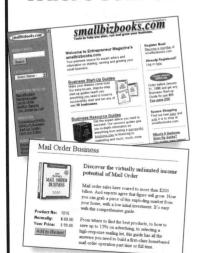

MILLION DOLLAR SECRETS

free issue!

Exercise your right to make it **big**.
Get into the small business authority—
now at **80% off** the newsstand price!

Yes! Start my one year subscription and
bill me for just $9.99. I get a full year of Entrepreneu
and save 80% off the newsstand rate. If I choose no
to subscribe, the free issue is mine to keep.

Name ☐ Mr. ☐ Mrs. _____
(please print)

Address _____

City_____ State _____ Zip _____

☐ BILL ME ☐ PAYMENT ENCLOSED

Guaranteed. Or your money back. Every subscription to Entrepreneur comes with a 100% satisfaction guarantee: your money back whenever you like, for whatever reason, on all unmailed issues! Offer good in U.S. and possessions only. Please allow 4–6 weeks for mailing first issue. Canadian and foreign: $39.97. U.S. funds only.

5G

Mail this coupon to **Entrepreneur** MAGAZINE. P.O. Box 50368, Boulder, CO 80321-0368

OPPORTUNITY KNOCKS!!!

save 72%!

free issue!

Please enter my subscription to Business
Start-Ups for one year. I will receive 12 issues for
only $9.99. That's a savings of 72% off the news-
stand price. The free issue is mine to keep, even if
I choose not to subscribe.

Name ☐ Mr. ☐ Mrs. _____
(please print)

Address_____

City_____ State _____ Zip_____

☐ BILL ME

☐ PAYMENT ENCLOSED

Mail this coupon to

Entrepreneur's Business Start-Ups.
P.O. Box 50347
Boulder, CO 80321-0347

Guaranteed. Or your money back. Every subscription to Business Start-Ups comes with a 100% satisfaction guarantee: your money back whenever you like, for whatever reason, on all unmailed issues! Offer good in U.S. and possessions only. Please allow 4–6 weeks for mailing of first issue. Canadian and foreign: $34.97. U.S. funds only.

5HB